Mastering CSS Grid

MW00838025

A comprehensive and practical guide to creating beautiful layouts with CSS Grid

Pascal Thormeier

BIRMINGHAM—MUMBAI

Mastering CSS Grid

Group Product Manager: Rohit Rajkumar

Publishing Product Manager: Bhavya Rao

Content Development Editor: Abhishek Jadhav

Technical Editor: Simran Udasi

Copy Editor: Safis Editing

Project Coordinator: Manthan Patel

Proofreader: Safis Editing

Indexer: Sejal Dsilva

Production Designer: Joshua Misquitta

Marketing Coordinator: Nivedita Pandey

First published: June 2023

Production reference: 2110723

Published by Packt Publishing Ltd.
Livery Place
35 Livery Street
Birmingham
B3 2PB, UK.

ISBN 978-1-80461-484-6

www.packtpub.com

To my parents, Marlies and Michael, my sister, Sandra, and my grandparents Hannelore and Lothar for teaching me to stay curious and that technology and numbers are fun, and for supporting me every step of the way. To all my co-workers at Liip for their vast knowledge and expertise, from which I learned a ton. To my partner, Denise, for supporting me endlessly in all my endeavors and always offering a second brain for many challenges. Without you, this book would not have been possible!

– Pascal Thormeier.

Contributors

About the author

Pascal Thormeier, born in 1990, is a senior software developer at Liip AG, a leading Swiss web agency, and he considers himself at home in both the frontend and backend. Initially programming in PHP as his first language in the early 2000s, Pascal has experience in many technologies, languages, and frameworks, such as Java, Python, NodeJS, and Vue.

After 4 years of part-time studying, Pascal received a bachelor's degree in computer science with a specialization in design and management from the University of Applied Sciences and Arts Northwestern Switzerland in 2020, and he started to write a tech blog on `dev.to` shortly after. He has since published over 75 articles and an online course on Vue.

I want to thank those who supported and challenged me during the writing process, especially my co-workers at Liip and my partner. I love you, Denise!

About the reviewers

Giuseppe Caruso started his career when the most used web framework was an HTML table and spacer.gif was a thing. In response to the misuse of tables, he donned a blue beanie and began to develop websites with web standards. CSS taught him, in a lot of quirks modes, that position is everything.

He is a senior frontend developer, with expertise in building design systems with CSS and semantic and accessible HTML. His background in architecture and design made him passionate about bridging the gap between developers and designers.

He has worked for many kinds of companies, from medium start-ups such as Tado to larger public companies such as Trivago. Currently, he is part of the Digital Incubator team, shaping the future at Vodafone GmbH in lovely Düsseldorf.

I would like to thank Alice for her unwavering support and love throughout the journey we call life. She is my wonderland.

I am grateful to my son, Nicola, who through his own eyes, makes me a better person every day. He constantly surprises me with his courage, his wisdom, and his smile.

Lastly, I would like to thank Patrick for being a friend, a mentor, and a constant source of inspiration. You are my favorite alien.

Michelle Manemann is a seasoned veteran of the publishing industry, having created hundreds of custom websites for her company over the past decade. Her previous experience as a technical reviewer includes *Responsive Web Design with HTML5 and CSS*, published by Packt in 2022.

Upon graduating from Grinnell College, she established a full-fledged web design department. Under her leadership, her team crafts captivating websites for educators across North America. She is dedicated to creating environments – online and in person – that favor inclusion and accessibility for all.

When business hours are over, Michelle is on the move, exploring the natural beauty along her native Mississippi River or traveling the world to uncover new founts of inspiration.

My success is due to the unconditional love of my family, including my parents and brother. I am grateful for their support, which blossomed from loving roots planted by my grandmothers, Mary Kay and Debbie. My gratitude is as endless as their devotion to us all.

Sabya Sachi is a passionate UI developer and has been working in the IT industry for the past 11 years. He graduated in computer science engineering from Rajasthan Technical University, Kota.

He mostly spends his time with CSS, HTML, JavaScript, and other UI frameworks/libraries. He has worked with a few big MNC companies, such as L&T Infotech, Fidelity Investments, Mu Sigma, Empower Retirement, and Omnicom Media Group. He has designed a few responsive websites for his clients.

Exploring the world of CSS is his passion. He has also architected, designed, and migrated web apps, always adhering to normalized CSS layouts, responsive designing, and optimal practices. He has also optimized web app performance on the existing development.

The latest trend in CSS, HTML, and JavaScript keeps him busy all the time.

Table of Contents

3

Building Advanced Grid Layouts   63

Part 2 – Understanding the CSS Grid Periphery

4

Understanding and Creating Responsive and Fluid Grid Layouts   107

Part 3 – Exploring the Wider Ecosystem

7

Polyfilling CSS Grid's Missing Features   195

8

Grids in the Wild – How Frameworks Implement Grids   229

Part 4 – A Quick Reference

9

Quick Reference and Cheat Sheet   269

Preface

Hello, world! With this book, you hold a guide to a CSS feature that the entire frontend development community has longed for since the early days of HTML and CSS – **CSS Grid**. This book covers all of CSS Grid:

- The basics
- The advanced things
- How grids can be used in design
- When not to use grids at all
- CSS Grid's relation to its cousin Flexbox

You will also find an exhaustive cheat sheet and quick reference at the end of the book.

However, before we dive into the details, let me take you on a journey into the early 2000s, when I started to learn to program while still in high school.

Back then, before the invention of smartphones – the first iPhone was released in June 2007 – we didn't have much. CSS 2 was the current version, with CSS 2.1 not being released until 2011. CSS 2 was the version that brought us relative and absolute positioning, but we would not get the first version of Flexbox until 2015, and CSS Grid only in 2018.

According to legend, the original purpose of HTML was to display scientific papers. In any case, scientific papers don't need precise, fancy layouts. Instead, they need typography, such as headings and paragraphs, images, and tables.

However, as soon as the World Wide Web took off, people did come up with fancy layouts, and they used the tools at hand. For example, if configured suitably, you can use a table to build something that resembles a grid layout. And that's what we did – all the time, everywhere.

At some point, people started using floating elements. This feature was initially intended to make text float around images and other objects, but it was more or less instantly used as a layout tool for entire websites.

We defined a grid with the width of the elements and their position in a document. So, for example, a header would have a width of 100% and not be floating, whereas a sidebar with navigation would be considered a left-floating element or, at times, a right-floating one if you wanted your website to be unique.

We slowly start to see a pattern here. In the early days, people used tools in ways they were not intended. There's nothing wrong with that; that's how innovation happens. A quote by the famous webcomic *Saturday Morning Breakfast Cereal* that I love even says that the "*deep abiding goal of any engineer is to take a thing and make it do a thing it wasn't meant to do.*" And that's fine!

There are issues, however. The problems with table layouts and floating elements were manifold. First, they needed a large amount of boilerplate code and sometimes felt like pure magic. To correctly align floating elements, we must also consider all elements around them.

Second, a table is a way of displaying data, not a layout tool. People were not nearly as aware of accessibility as they are today, and we still have room for improvement. When early screen readers encountered a table, they interpreted it as a table. And tables have data, not navigations.

Flexbox solved many positioning problems. There were many tricks to center-align elements both vertically and horizontally. Some are still viable today. Flexbox simplified the task, and the code was much more straightforward. The intent of `display: flex; justify-content: center;` is much more explicit than the one of `margin: 0 auto;`.

But what ultimately happened was that people – again – used Flexbox to create grid layouts almost immediately. Many frameworks offer a `.container` CSS class that applies Flexbox to the element and then works with column classes to achieve a horizontal grid. Vertical grids work with nested flexboxes. So, Flexbox is a layout tool, but we still needed to go one or two steps further for grids.

With the release of CSS Grid, developers finally got what they had improvised since the inception of the World Wide Web – a working grid layout tool. Finally, we could build grids as they had been implemented in many other languages and frameworks for ages. For reference, the oldest occurrence of JavaFX's GridPane I could find on the web is from 2003, almost 15 years before the production-readiness of CSS Grid.

And with this, our little journey through the decades is over. Today, thanks to the deprecation of Microsoft's Internet Explorer 11 in 2022, every significant browser fully supports CSS Grid. As a result, we can use it to finally live up to the fantastic designs UX experts come up with and use grids, instead of thinking about how we can make something behave like a grid.

However, there is one use case for which we still need to go back to nested tables, floating elements, and non-Flexbox, non-CSS Grid layouts – email templates. Of course, there are solutions to that, too, but that's a different story.

Who this book is for

This book is for aspiring (frontend) web developers who want to improve their layout skills and learn the ins and outs of this magnificent tool.

This book may also benefit UX experts with a rudimentary knowledge of frontend development who want to learn an effective tool to create prototypes faster.

What this book covers

Chapter 1, Understanding the Basic Rules and Structures for CSS Grid, covers the fundamentals, such as grid terminology, creating your first grids, arranging grid elements, and grid templates.

Chapter 2, Project Introduction: What We'll Work on and First Tasks, introduces the accompanying project that we will work on throughout the book.

Chapter 3, Building Advanced Grid Layouts, introduces advanced features of CSS Grid, such as the row and column axes, how to align and justify grid content, and advanced grid templates.

Chapter 4, Understanding and Creating Responsive and Fluid Grid Layouts, covers what responsive and fluid layouts are, what best practices exist, and how to build the layouts with CSS Grid.

Chapter 5, Implementing Layouts With Flexbox and CSS Grid, explores the differences and similarities between CSS Grid and Flexbox and their specific use cases.

Chapter 6, Benefits of Grid Layouts and When Not to Use Them, discusses the benefits and drawbacks of grid layouts related to design and usability and introduces alternative layout methods.

Chapter 7, Polyfilling CSS Grid's Missing Features, introduces PostCSS and JavaScript to implement missing features and better understand how they will work once introduced.

Chapter 8, Grids in the Wild – How Frameworks Implement Grids, discusses the different approaches to the grids of eight different CSS frameworks while explaining how to implement standard use cases.

Chapter 9, Quick Reference and Cheat Sheet, gives a condensed overview of all CSS Grid features, terminology, and the most important frameworks and offers code snippets for standard use cases.

To get the most out of this book

We recommend some knowledge of the basics and advanced CSS and JavaScript features, such as custom CSS properties or Promises. Knowing how Flexbox works is also recommended. A solid knowledge of HTML is assumed.

Software/hardware covered in the book	Operating system requirements
CSS Grid	Windows, macOS, or Linux
Flexbox	
PostCSS	
JavaScript	

Since these technologies primarily run in the browser, they can be used on any operating system. NodeJS, used to execute some code snippets and create a web server for the accompanying project, and NPM, used to install JavaScript dependencies, are available for all major operating systems too.

*To handle different versions of NodeJS, either a Docker setup or **Node Version Manager (NVM)** is recommended. We also require a modern browser that supports CSS Grid and offers grid tooling and a grid debugger. Having multiple browsers installed helps us to see the differences in the development tools and get used to them.*

If you are using the digital version of this book, we advise you to type the code yourself or access the code from the book's GitHub repository (a link is available in the next section). Doing so will help you avoid any potential errors related to the copying and pasting of code.

Download the example code files

You can download the example code files for this book from GitHub at `https://github.com/PacktPublishing/Mastering-CSS-Grid`. If there's an update to the code, it will be updated in the GitHub repository.

We also have other code bundles from our rich catalog of books and videos available at `https://github.com/PacktPublishing/`. Check them out!

Download the color images

We also provide a PDF file that has color images of the screenshots and diagrams used in this book. You can download it here: `https://packt.link/0FCcj`.

Conventions used

There are a number of text conventions used throughout this book.

`Code in text`: Indicates code words in text, database table names, folder names, filenames, file extensions, pathnames, dummy URLs, user input, and Twitter handles. Here is an example: "The total number of `fr` determines the size of each `fr`."

A block of code is set as follows:

```
.container {
  display: grid;
  grid-template-columns: 1fr 3fr;
  grid-template-rows: 1fr 4fr 1fr;
}
```

When we wish to draw your attention to a particular part of a code block, the relevant lines or items are set in bold:

```
header {
  grid-column-end: span 2; /* Make it reach to the end of the second
column */
}

footer {
  grid-column-end: span 2; /* Make it reach to the end of the second
column */
}
```

Any command-line input or output is written as follows:

```
$ npm install
$ npm run serve
```

Bold: Indicates a new term, an important word, or words that you see on screen. For instance, words in menus or dialog boxes appear in **bold**. Here is an example: "When we open the inspector and hover over the grid container in the **Elements** tab, we can see what we already knew from our color experiment."

> **Tips or important notes**
> Appear like this.

Get in touch

Feedback from our readers is always welcome.

General feedback: If you have questions about any aspect of this book, email us at customercare@packtpub.com and mention the book title in the subject of your message.

Errata: Although we have taken every care to ensure the accuracy of our content, mistakes do happen. If you have found a mistake in this book, we would be grateful if you would report this to us. Please visit www.packtpub.com/support/errata and fill in the form.

Piracy: If you come across any illegal copies of our works in any form on the internet, we would be grateful if you would provide us with the location address or website name. Please contact us at copyright@packt.com with a link to the material.

If you are interested in becoming an author: If there is a topic that you have expertise in and you are interested in either writing or contributing to a book, please visit authors.packtpub.com.

Share your thoughts

Once you've read *Mastering CSS Grid*, we'd love to hear your thoughts! Scan the QR code below to go straight to the Amazon review page for this book and share your feedback.

https://www.amazon.in/review/create-review/error?asin=180461484X

Your review is important to us and the tech community and will help us make sure we're delivering excellent quality content.

Download a free PDF copy of this book

Thanks for purchasing this book!

Do you like to read on the go but are unable to carry your print books everywhere?

Is your eBook purchase not compatible with the device of your choice?

Don't worry, now with every Packt book you get a DRM-free PDF version of that book at no cost.

Read anywhere, any place, on any device. Search, copy, and paste code from your favorite technical books directly into your application.

The perks don't stop there, you can get exclusive access to discounts, newsletters, and great free content in your inbox daily

Follow these simple steps to get the benefits:

1. Scan the QR code or visit the link below

https://packt.link/free-ebook/9781804614846

2. Submit your proof of purchase

3. That's it! We'll send your free PDF and other benefits to your email directly

Part 1 – Working with CSS Grid

In this part, you will learn how to work with CSS Grid. You will learn the basic and advanced features of CSS Grid. In addition, from the second chapter, you will practice with a dedicated project that will accompany you throughout the book, called AwesomeAnalytics, a realistic example of a project that heavily uses CSS Grid.

This part has the following chapters:

- *Chapter 1, Understanding the Basic Rules and Structures for CSS Grid*
- *Chapter 2, Project Introduction: What We'll Work on and First Tasks*
- *Chapter 3, Building Advanced Grid Layouts*

1

Understanding the Basic Rules and Structures for CSS Grid

Welcome to the first chapter of this book titled *Mastering CSS Grid*. As the title suggests, this book helps us to become pros at this layout technique and learn about all its specialties and details. Throughout the book, we'll work on various tasks using grid layouts in an overarching project called **Awesome Analytics**.

In the first chapter of this book, we will start introducing you to CSS Grid. We must first establish its basic CSS rules to understand how the grid model works. To do that, we'll look at how grids are structured and how we can visually represent them. We'll learn about the CSS rules used to create grid layouts, how to combine them to achieve different arrangements, and how to use shortcut rules to shorten our code.

A look at how the development tools of Google Chrome and other Chromium-based browsers visualize grids will help us understand how we can debug and understand existing grids. This chapter will not work with our overarching project just yet—we'll first cover some theory.

So, in this chapter, we will cover the following topics:

- Understanding the basic rules related to CSS Grid
- Using grid templates
- Grid flow
- Understanding special grid-related units, keywords, and functions
- Using shortcuts

Technical requirements

For this chapter, we'll need roughly the same things as for most chapters, as follows:

- A modern browser that supports CSS Grid and offers grid debugging and a grid toolset
- An **integrated development environment** (**IDE**) or text editor, such as WebStorm, VS Code, or Vim, with HTML and CSS syntax highlighting
- Internet access is an advantage but not necessary

We can find several of the code examples on GitHub in this repository: `https://github.com/ PacktPublishing/Mastering-CSS-Grid/tree/main/chapter1`.

All screenshots and examples have been made with a Chromium-based browser.

Understanding the basic rules related to CSS Grid

First, we need to know what grids are and what their purpose is. In short, grids aim to arrange items in a consistent manner. Grids provide clarity about content structure and sizing and allow us to steer where things are placed. Grids provide structure.

To achieve this understanding, we first have a look at some standard grid terminology, before creating our first CSS grid.

Defining grid terminology

We first need to establish some words we'll use throughout the book. The following diagram will explain to us the most important terms:

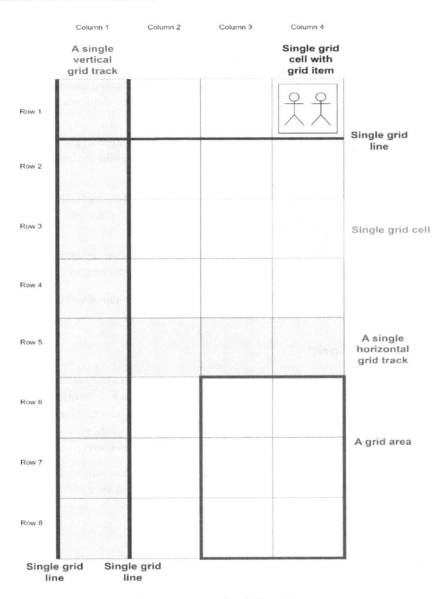

Figure 1.1 – A grid and all its terms

We see many different elements here, as follows:

- The **grid** is the whole structure. It consists of all arranged elements, the layout, and its attributes.

- A grid is made up of **grid cells**. These grid cells can have different sizes, depending on the row and column definitions we give the grid. A grid cell doesn't necessarily have content.

- A grid has several **grid lines**. These are the lines that separate grid cells and make up the structure of the grid. They can be horizontal or vertical. In the diagram, three grid lines are marked: the two surrounding *Column 1* and a single line between *Row 1* and *Row 2*.

- These grid lines can become **gaps**. Gaps are also sometimes called **gutters**. Gaps are used to separate grid tracks and allow us to add white space between elements. Gaps between rows don't have to be the same size as gaps between columns.

- Between two adjacent parallel grid lines, we see rows and columns of grid cells, also known as **grid tracks** or simply **tracks**. Two such tracks are marked in blue in the diagram: *Row 5* and *Column 1*.

- When we place content within a grid, we speak of them as **grid items**. Grid items can be images, div tags, text nodes, or any other HTML element we want to place and arrange. A grid item can be seen in *Row 1*, *Column 4* in the diagram.

- When we want to name specific groups of one or more cells, we speak of a **grid area**. Those grid areas are delimited by four grid lines and are, therefore, rectangles.

With these terms, we now have a common language to use when we talk about grids. We'll use these terms throughout the book when defining grids.

Creating our first grid

In many ways, CSS Grid behaves like Flexbox. It needs a grid container and elements to align. In most cases, such as general page layouts or when working with teaser elements to link to additional content, we use <div> elements. Teaser elements can be built with <article> elements, too. We don't have to, though! When working with semantic HTML, we might as well use the elements that fit best: <main>, <aside>, <header>, <footer>, <nav>, and more.

To start, let's consider the following HTML structure. It resembles a standard **Document Object Model (DOM)** that we would use to structure any website and features most of the elements we would typically use when we develop a page's layout:

```
<div class="container">
  <header><!-- Header with a logo, navigation, etc. -->
    </header>
  <aside><!—Partially related things like social buttons --
  ></aside>
  <main><!-- Main content, headings, teasers, etc. -->
    </main>
  <footer><!-- Footer with contact, FAQ, etc. --></footer>
</div>
```

We see four elements that we want to align in a grid, as follows:

- A header that might contain a logo or navigation
- An element that will contain content not directly related to the main page content
- An element for the actual content
- A footer that displays things such as contact details, information about the company, a link to the FAQ, and similar additional controls

For ease of illustration, we will apply the following CSS upfront (the code has nothing to do with CSS Grid just yet and only serves illustration purposes):

```
/* 01_page_layout.html, Micro-resetting */
body { padding: 0; margin: 0; }
* { box-sizing: border-box; font-size: 25px; }

/* Making things visible on the page */
.container {
  border: 2px solid #555;
  padding: 8px;
  min-height: 100vh;
}
header {
  border: 2px solid #dd0808; /* Dark red */
  background-color: #ff6666; /* Light red */
}
aside {
  border: 2px solid #0ba7c6; /* Dark cyan */
  background-color: #74ddf2; /* Light cyan */
}
main {
  border: 2px solid #6f09e5; /* Dark purple */
  background-color: #b880f7; /* Light purple */
}
footer {
  border: 2px solid #c4be0d; /* Dark yellow */
  background-color: #f7f380; /* Light yellow */
}
```

This CSS code will color our containers and ensure we can track which element goes where. When loaded up in a browser, this results in four colored stripes along the screen. That's what we expected. After all, our DOM does not have any content.

Things get interesting, though, when we add the following CSS code:

```
.container {
  display: grid; /* Marks this class as a grid container */
}
```

When reloading, we see that CSS Grid has evenly distributed the four containers vertically. Since the outer `<div>` element has a fixed height, CSS will calculate the height of every element and rescale it to fit. Since we have not yet defined anything other than `This is a grid`, each element takes up the same amount of space:

Figure 1.2 – Our HTML is styled and displayed as a grid

CSS Grid has entirely taken over the placing and sizing of statically and relatively positioned elements within the grid. This, in turn, means that any other inline positioning method does not apply anymore. Any use of `display: inline-block`, `display: table-cell`, `float`, or `vertical-align` will have no effect. However, we can still use `position: fixed`, `position: absolute`, or `position: sticky` because the elements are not static anymore. Elements that have `position: relative;` attached to them can be moved around and are still affected by the grid.

There's also the possibility to define an inline grid by using `display: inline-grid;`. The main difference is that the grid container behaves like an inline container instead of a block container. Therefore, we now know that `display: grid` defines a grid that behaves like a block element.

Let's remove the colors briefly and see how the browser development tools indicate that we use a grid. Usually, Chrome shows grids with dashed lines. When we open the inspector and hover over the grid container in the **Elements** tab, we can see what we already knew from our color experiment. We can also click on the grid button that appears in the inspector to turn on grid debugging, which will show us the grid lines.

In the following screenshot, we can see the full grid representation in Chrome's development tools:

Figure 1.3 – Chrome's inspector showing us the different grid slots

Just as in the color experiment we did before, we see four grid rows, indicated by purple dashed lines. These lines also indicate the grid lines and would become larger once we introduce gaps. The blue areas we see are our grid cells. Currently, they don't contain any grid items. The green border around the grid is our padding. It's not related to the grid.

Arranging grid elements

So far, CSS Grid has taken care of arranging things for us—in our example, it automatically created four rows because there were four elements, spaced them evenly, and placed them in the same order as they appeared in the DOM.

However, often, we don't want this, especially when wanting responsive layouts. For example, on a mobile, social media buttons might move to the bottom of the page and become sticky elements, whereas on a desktop they should stay in one place, such as the sidebar.

To be able to move elements, we first need to state the number of grid rows and grid columns explicitly. We achieve this by using the `grid-template-rows` and `grid-template-columns` rules, which go into the `container` element and will pre-create a grid structure for us. We specify the number of grid columns and rows by providing their size, separated by spaces. The size may vary from row to row and column to column.

The total number of grid cells may be larger than the total amount of elements we'd like to arrange. We can, for example, define a grid with three rows and three columns and only arrange five items within it—a case that's common in galleries or news websites. The remaining grid cells remain empty.

For the time being, let's work with `1fr`. `fr` is a unit that has been introduced to CSS with CSS Grid and works exclusively with grids. `1fr` essentially means: *Take one unit of free space for this grid element.* We will discuss the `fr` unit later in this chapter. So, if we used it for grid rows, this means taking one unit of free space for this grid row. The same applies to columns too.

Let's change our example to a 2x3 grid of evenly spaced grid elements by applying the following CSS code to the `container` class:

```
.container {
  display: grid;
  grid-template-columns: 1fr 1fr;
  grid-template-rows: 1fr 1fr 1fr;
}
```

As we can see, we used `1fr` twice in `grid-template-columns`, resulting in two equally sized columns, and three times in `grid-template-rows`, resulting in three equally sized rows. When inspected, Chrome shows us that it has now created a grid structure, as indicated in the following screenshot:

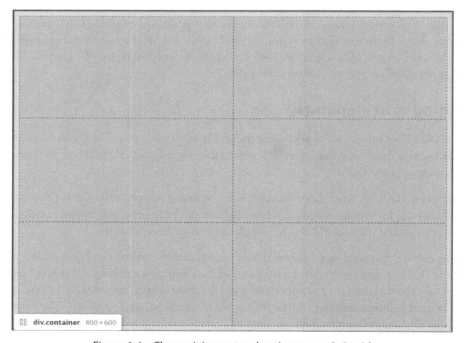

Figure 1.4 – Chrome's inspector showing us our 2x3 grid

CSS Grid assigns integers to all grid lines for us to use as coordinates. These integers increase from left to right and top to bottom, starting at 1. When we think of the grid as a coordinate system, its origin is in the top-left corner. This allows us to place grid items starting from the top left to the bottom right.

However, CSS Grid offers a second origin that lets us place items from the bottom-right to the top-left corner. It does so by also assigning negative integers to the same grid lines, starting at the bottom-right corner with -1.

Our grid so far would receive the numbers illustrated here:

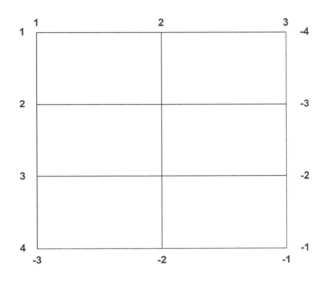

Figure 1.5 – Grid line numbering

Currently, all columns are the same size. If we want one column twice the size of the other, we increase the value of that column to 2fr. For example, if we wish to have a 1/4 sidebar and 3/4 main content slot, we adjust the grid-template-column rule to 1fr 3fr. Then, if wanted to have a 1/6 header, 1/6 footer, and the other 2/3 (4/6 in a six-column layout) for the main content, we would use the grid-template-rows: 1fr 4fr 1fr rule.

We see that the size of the grid rows and columns depends on the total number of free space units. If we think of a grid as 100% wide and 100% tall, we can calculate the size of each row and column as percentages. For example, in a layout with four columns of size 1fr, each column takes up 25% of the space.

In a two-column layout with sizes 1fr and 3fr, however, the total number of free space units is 4, resulting in 1fr being 25% wide and 3fr equaling 75% width. The total number of fr units determines the size of each fr unit.

Let's adjust our example to this new layout:

```
.container {
  display: grid;
  grid-template-columns: 1fr 3fr;
  grid-template-rows: 1fr 4fr 1fr;
}
```

This won't affect the assigned numbers (they just stay the same), but we can see that this has the desired effect when inspecting, as illustrated in the following screenshot:

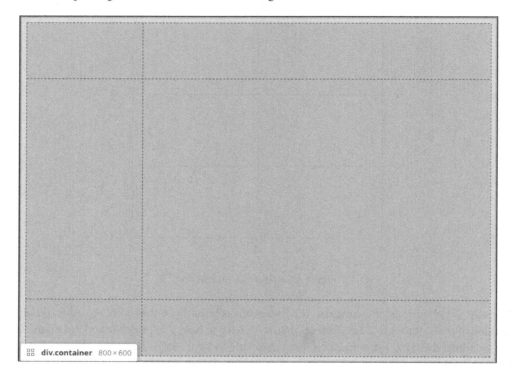

Figure 1.6 – Chrome's inspector shows us our adjusted 2x3 grid

By re-applying the colors, we can now see the default arrangement for this grid. By default, CSS Grid fills grid elements from left to right, top to bottom. This grid resembles a painting by Piet Mondrian and is not exactly what we'd like:

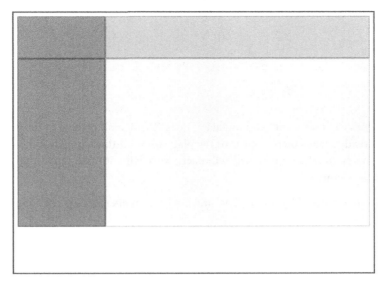

Figure 1.7 – Our accidental neoplasticism painting, using CSS on HTML

But we still have not explicitly arranged the elements yet. For that, we use four different CSS rules: `grid-column-start`, `grid-column-end`, `grid-row-start`, and `grid-row-end`. We apply these to the elements we want to position—so, in our case, `header` (marked red), `footer` (marked yellow), `aside` (marked cyan), and `main` (marked purple).

By default, `grid-row-start`, `grid-row-end`, `grid-column-start`, and `grid-column-end` will have the `auto` value, meaning that CSS Grid will figure out the beginning row and column itself, again with the left-to-right, top-to-bottom method. Most of the time, this is enough. We can, however, define where to place any element explicitly.

Looking at the grid outline in *Figure 1.6*, we notice that the header and footer both have to span two columns. We achieve this with the `span` keyword for `grid-column-end` and `grid-row-end`. `span` tells the browser to enlarge the element until it encounters a grid cell with that name or for the amount specified. (But wait—grid cells can have names? Yes, they can. We'll have a look at this a bit later in this chapter.)

So, `grid-column-end: span 2;` means *enlarge the element to a width of two columns*, and `grid-column-end: span something;` means *enlarge the element to the gap named "something"* (we will have a look at gap names later on too). If the element already starts at the second column, this will not do much. However, if it begins in the first column, it will fill two adjacent grid cells.

Let's place the header and footer first since they work very similarly:

```
header {
  grid-column-end: span 2; /* Make it reach to the end of
    the second column */
```

```
}

footer {
  grid-column-end: span 2; /* Make it reach to the end of
    the second column */
}
```

Let's see if this does what we want. And indeed, it does. The default placing of the main and aside grid elements already makes them appear in the place we want them to. Since the header and the footer elements both take up two grid cells each, we're left with two remaining grid cells for the main and aside elements.

These grid cells are occupied by the aside and main elements in the order of appearance in the HTML code:

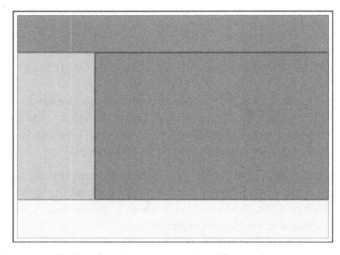

Figure 1.8 – The header, sidebar, content, and footer elements arranged

Adding some breathing room (or gaps)

Right now, all the elements are aligned snuggly. However, we don't always want this. Especially for elements arranged in a grid in the page content, we might wish to have some space in between. There are two approaches to this. Either we can use paddings and margins to try to get the spacing right or we can use CSS Grid's column-gap and row-gap rules.

Usually, when working with paddings and margins as grid gutters, there is a risk of inconsistencies because we need to specify values for each grid element individually. Furthermore, we might want to use paddings and margins for other purposes, such as adding more margin to text or giving images a border effect. To mitigate these risks, CSS Grid offers two rules regarding gaps between elements: column-gap and row-gap.

These two rules are defined on the container level and govern the space between all rows and all columns. We can use any unit we'd like—so, px, rem, em, or even %. If the latter, the browser does the percentage calculation on the container's size. So, if our container is 100px high and we define a 5% row gap, we have a 5px gap between every row.

However, if we do not define the height or width of the container, its size would be determined by its content and the gaps. So, for example, if the gaps are 5% of the container size, we have a *circular dependency*: the gap is 5% of the width and at the same time is contributing to the width.

The browser would first calculate the gap size by calculating 5% of the container's size, assuming the gap has a current width of 0. It then sets the size of the gap, enlarging the container. The browser would then realize that the gap is now smaller than 5% of the size of the container, re-calculate the gap, and so on.

Mathematically speaking, this is the limit of a series. If you're not familiar with calculus, you can skip the following part. We can define the total width of a container as the sum of the gap, *g*, and its element's width, *e*. We can define the series and its limit as follows:

$$s = Gap\ size\ in\ percentage$$

$$g = Sum\ of\ the\ gaps$$

$$e = Width\ of\ elements\ without\ gap$$

$$g_0 = 0$$

$$g_n = s * (g_{n-1} + e)$$

$$g = \lim_{n \to \infty} g_n$$

This limit might either converge to a single value or diverge off to infinity, if *s* is greater than or equal to 100%. Limits are hard to calculate, especially if they are of complex series. CSS Grid circumvents these calculations by simply downsizing the grid cell widths so that the total width doesn't change. This effect is often undesired. Elements will overlap the container if no explicit size is given to it.

In summary, to avoid unexpected behavior in element sizing, it's recommended to use non-relative units for gaps. With that knowledge, we can start practicing gaps.

Let's add a 16px row gap and a 4px column gap to our modern art-like example and see how it behaves. We'll apply the following code:

```
.container {
    /* Grid definition */
    row-gap: 16px;
    column-gap: 4px;
}
```

And the result looks just like what we expected:

Figure 1.9 – Our grid now has spacing in it

Notice that the inner padding of the grid container was already there. This is because row-gap and column-gap only affect the space between rows and columns, not around them.

We now know how to define basic grids. This allows us to define grids for most use cases already. However, these rules often need extra context by using explicit class names and perhaps even comments in the code. Otherwise, they're hard to maintain, which might cause frustration and delay development. Let's learn how we can be more explicit about the intent of our code.

Using grid templates

Working with larger grids can get confusing. For now, we used two rules on the container to define our grid size and then some seemingly arbitrary numbers to denote where an element should be placed in both rows and columns. For developers not familiar with the code, these seemingly arbitrary numbers and sizes could be hard to understand.

They would need to spend more time understanding the grid since it's not very self-descriptive. However, CSS Grid offers us possibilities to be more explicit. We'll now have a look at how to name rows, columns, and entire grid areas.

Naming grid rows and columns

To add more clarity to our grid definitions, CSS Grid allows us to name columns and rows.

When defining columns and rows with `grid-template-columns` and `grid-template-rows`, we can add names in between grid sizes with a syntax like this:

```
grid-template-columns: [sidebar-start] 1fr [sidebar-end content-start]
3fr [content-end];
```

Everything in square brackets is considered a name. We can also see that we've assigned two names to the middle grid line between the sidebar and the content, which we can separate by using spaces. Using explicit two names, such as `sidebar-end` and `content-start`, for the same grid line allows us to decouple the name from the structure: the sidebar doesn't necessarily have to end where the content starts.

So, instead of using numbers when placing elements, we can use these names to explicitly state where an element's placement starts and where it ends. If we wanted to align the header of our example with the new names, we would replace the numbers with the corresponding names, as shown here:

```
header {
  grid-column-start: sidebar-start;
  grid-column-end: span content-end;
}
```

Unlike the case where we used numbers, we also added a `grid-column-start` rule to the code. Otherwise, CSS Grid wouldn't know where the element starts (it defaults to `auto`) and would assume that it should only span a single column.

By naming rows and columns, we make our code more readable. In the template definition, we can see what the rows and columns are meant to contain. In addition, we now have more context on the grid items as well: the header, for example, spans from the start of the sidebar to the end of the content. Someone reading this code for the first time would understand its placement better, especially in a complex grid.

We can also define and use grid areas to place grid items. With grid areas, we have an almost visual representation of our grid within the code. The CSS rule we use to define grid areas is `grid-template-areas`.

This rule is sometimes accompanied by `grid-template-rows` and `grid-template-columns` to ensure we have size definitions for rows and columns, if necessary. This is especially necessary for fixed-size grid cells—for example, a `100px`-wide sidebar or a `250px`-high footer. If we work with `fr` only, using `grid-template-rows` and `grid-template-columns` isn't obligatory.

We know, for example, the size of our grid columns: `1fr 3fr`. And we also know the sizes of our rows: `1fr 4fr 1fr`. If we wanted to give the grid areas names, we would probably use a system as illustrated in the next screenshot:

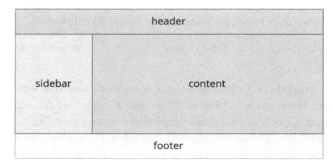

Figure 1.10 – Our grid with explicit names for every area

Using the six rows and four columns, we can also translate this to a system where we name each grid cell, as shown in the next screenshot:

header	header	header	header
sidebar	content	content	content
sidebar	content	content	content
sidebar	content	content	content
sidebar	content	content	content
footer	footer	footer	footer

Figure 1.11 – Our grid with explicit names for every cell

Our grid sizes (`1fr 3fr` and `1fr 4fr 1fr`) are represented by the number of grid cells we have for rows and columns. We can then, more or less, translate the system shown in the previous screenshot as CSS code:

```
.container {
 display: grid;
 grid-template-areas:
   "header header header header"
   "sidebar content content content"
   «sidebar content content content»
   «sidebar content content content»
```

```
    "sidebar content content content"
    "footer footer footer footer"
  ;
}
```

What CSS Grid will do now is automatically calculate the `grid-template-rows` and `grid-template-columns` rules. However, instead of having two columns and three rows of different sizes, CSS Grid will create four columns and six rows, each cell being the same size.

If we now want to place elements within the grid, we use the `grid-area` rule on our elements. So, to place the header, sidebar, content, and footer, we use the following code:

```
header {
   grid-area: header;
}
aside {
   grid-area: sidebar;
}
main {
   grid-area: content;
}
footer {
   grid-area: footer;
}
```

This will take care of the entire `grid-column-start`, `grid-column-end`, `grid-row-start`, and `grid-row-end` configuration for us and places the elements correctly. We can see the new structure of the same-sized grid cells when inspecting and how the elements span them according to the template:

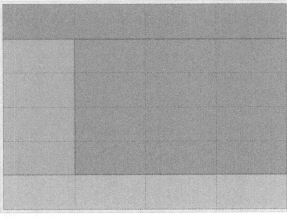

Figure 1.12 – How CSS Grid represents grid-area templates

Usually, this is the most straightforward way to configure grids. It gives us a visual representation of our grid in the code and lets us assign elements to grid areas using a single CSS rule, making it very obvious where an element will go in the grid.

However, we can also combine it with `grid-template-rows` and `grid-template-columns` to give the areas specific sizes. If we, for example, wanted to make the sidebar `150px` wide and the header and footer `200px` tall, we would add the following definitions next to the `grid-area` definitions:

```
.container {
  display: grid;
  grid-template-areas:
    "header header header header"
    "sidebar content content content"
    «sidebar content content content»
    «sidebar content content content»
    «sidebar content content content»
    «footer footer footer footer»
  ;
  grid-template-rows: 200px 1fr 1fr 1fr 1fr 200px;
  grid-template-columns: 150px 1fr 1fr 1fr;
}
```

This would result in a grid, as shown in the following screenshot:

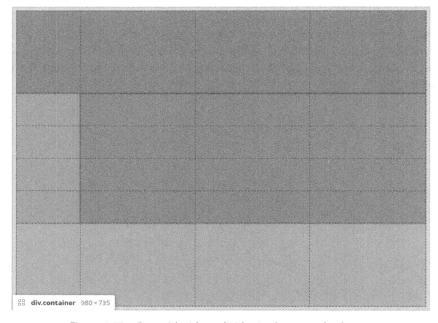

Figure 1.13 – Our grid with explicitly sized rows and columns

When we use `grid-template-area` together with `grid-template-rows` and `grid-template-columns`, however, there is no need to define larger grid areas. We can thus simplify our `grid-template-area` definition, and therefore our grid, to the following:

```
.container {
  display: grid;
  grid-template-areas:
   "header header"
   "sidebar content"
   "footer footer"
  ;
  grid-template-rows: 200px 1fr 200px;
  grid-template-columns: 150px 1fr;
}
```

And that works just as well:

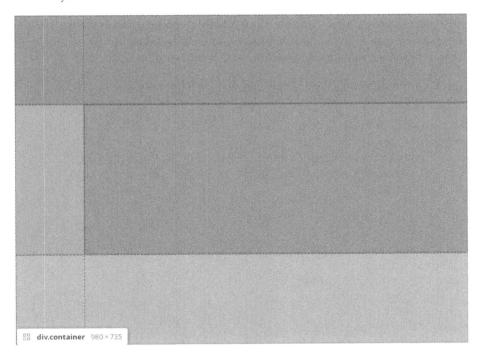

Figure 1.14 – Our grid with explicitly sized rows and columns and a reduced number of rows

Instead of six rows and four columns, we now only have three rows and two columns.

To summarize, grid areas allow us to specify our grid in a visual way without forgoing structural simplicity or flexibility.

Grid flow

So far, we've seen elements being placed by CSS Grid with the same rule: it starts from the top left and fills the grid with elements, row by row, to the bottom right. However, there's a way that we can control how CSS Grid places new items within the grid, which is called `grid-auto-flow`.

The possible values for this function are set out here:

- `row` (the default value): This fills elements row by row, from left to right. If an element does not have enough space to be placed in a row, it is moved to the next one.

- `column`: Behaves the same as `row`, except for the direction—it will fill columns first, top to bottom, and move to the next column once the previous one is full.

- `dense`: Tries to fill in any holes in the grid, no matter their placement. This is interesting if we have many different-sized elements that need no particular order, such as randomized mood images on restaurant websites.

- `row dense` and `column dense`: These values are combinations of the previous three. They will first try to fill in rows and columns, respectively, and then fill any resulting holes. Since `row` is the default value, `row dense` is equivalent to just using `dense`.

Let's inspect how the different values behave. For that, we'll have a look at this code:

```
<style>
  .container {
    display: grid;
    grid-template-columns: 100px 100px 100px 100px 100px;
    grid-template-rows: 100px 100px 100px 100px
      100px 100px;

  }
  .container > div {
    background-color: darkblue;
    display: flex;
    justify-content: center;
    align-items: center;
    color: #ffffff;
    font-size: 24px;
    font-weight: bold;
  }

  .large {
    grid-column-end: span 2;

    grid-row-end: span 2;
```

```
    }
</style>
<div class="container">
    <div class="small">1</div>
    <div class="large">2</div>
    <div class="large">3</div>
    <div class="large">4</div>
    <div class="large">5</div>
    <div class="small">6</div>
    <div class="small">7</div>
    <div class="small">8</div>
    <div class="small">9</div>
    <div class="small">10</div>
    <div class="small">11</div>
    <div class="small">12</div>
    <div class="small">13</div>
</div>
```

This code will create a 5x6 grid with equally sized, quadratic cells. This contains thirteen squares, composed of nine small (1x1) and four large (2x2) squares. Because of the lack of space, we use an extra row for any spill-over grid cells we might have.

We told CSS Grid to first add a small square, then add four large ones, and then add the other eight small ones. We have not defined the `grid-auto-flow` property for now, so it defaults to `row`. Therefore, CSS Grid will start with the first row, add the small square, then two large ones, and then go to the second row, notice that there's not enough space, move on to the third row, add two more large ones, and then fill the rest up with small ones. And indeed, it does:

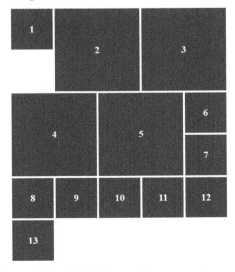

Figure 1.15 – CSS Grid arranging squares by rows

There is a noticeable gap in the top left of the grid. Also, the extra row we've added has proven useful by housing the extra square.

We can expect roughly the same behavior if we swap the value of grid-auto-flow from rows to columns:

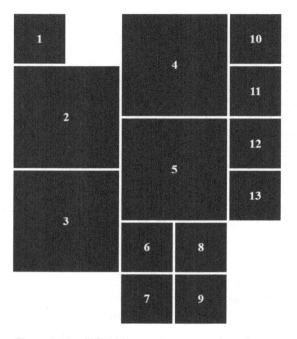

Figure 1.16 – CSS Grid arranging squares by columns

Now, we've ended up with three gaps. Since CSS Grid cannot fit the third large square, it moves to the second column and repeats the filling process.

Those gaps are annoying, though, aren't they? With dense, we can tell CSS Grid to fill these gaps. The plain value of dense is only a short form of row dense, so we don't need to differentiate those cases. However, it will produce a—well, dense layout:

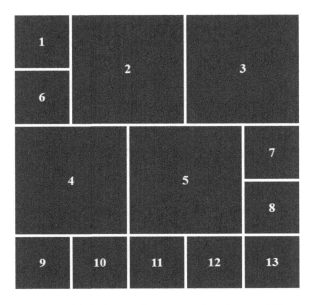

Figure 1.17 – CSS Grid arranging squares in a dense grid by rows

A dense column layout, achieved by using `column dense`, works the same way:

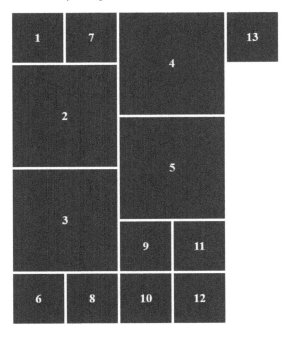

Figure 1.18 – CSS Grid arranging squares in a dense grid by columns

The layout is similar: some parts are rotated and mirrored, and the rest is filled up, column by column. Thinking about it, we can get pretty artsy with grids. Maybe there's some pixel art made with CSS Grid out there—who knows?

Grid flow gives us even more control over how a grid behaves, should we not know its content in advance. Think of user-generated content or randomly selected items. Grid flow fills any resulting gaps for us and guarantees a pretty grid.

Understanding special grid-related units, keywords, and functions

Let's now look at the units and CSS functions that CSS Grid has introduced. Many of these are specifically for CSS Grid; however, some might be useful for Flexbox layouts and other use cases.

The fractional unit

The only actual unit that was introduced with CSS Grid is `fr`—this stands for **fractional unit** and denotes a fraction of the total space. Think of it like a cooking recipe—for example, two parts of oil mixed with three parts of flour. So, when we want to have a total mixture of 500 grams, we can divide it by five and multiply by the number of parts. So, with 500 grams, we have 200 grams of oil (two parts) and 300 grams of flour (three parts). Now, replace `parts` with `fr`, and you've understood how the unit works.

When defining grid templates, we can mix in other units, such as `px` or `rem`, to denote fixed-size grid cells. CSS Grid will then take the total width, deduct the fixed-size cells, and then calculate the parts again. Returning to the cooking example, say that our recipes tell us to mix two parts of oil with three parts of flour, bake, and then add 100 grams of rosemary as decoration.

If our finished product weighs 600 grams, and we need to calculate the amount of flour and oil, we first subtract the 100 grams of rosemary from the 600 grams and then calculate the weight of the parts again.

The main difference between percentages and fractional units is their basis of calculation. While percentages use the entire size of the grid to calculate their exact values, `fr` uses what is left over after all fixed-size elements are subtracted.

Sizing keywords and functions

Not only can we use units when defining grid column and row sizes, but we can also give them a general behavior. For that, CSS Grid offers four different keywords and three functions we can use. Most of them are related to the content of the grid cell and will be calculated once the size of the content is known, allowing us to have different-sized grids for each content variant.

The four keywords are `min-content`, `max-content`, `fit-content`, and `auto`. We can use these keywords as values for `grid-template-columns` and `grid-template-rows` instead of using any value with a unit.

The three functions are `min()`, `max()`, and `minmax()`. We can also use these as a substitute for any value with a unit.

First, we can tell the cell to always fit its absolute possible minimum size with `min-content`. This can be useful if we have images and text aligned in a grid, and the image sizes should define the grid sizes. For the following screenshot, we used an image with a fixed width of 200x200 pixels.

The grid columns are defined as `min-content 1fr 4fr`. The `min-content` sizing keyword ensures that the grid cell's width does not go below `200px`, the smallest non-wrappable content:

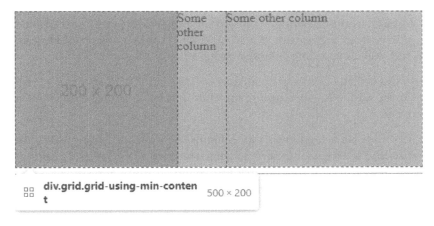

Figure 1.19 – An image resizing a grid cell

As well as images, `min-content` also takes text into account. If the minimum width of a grid cell, for example, is determined by the longest word in that cell, that word's pixel width will then be the minimum size. This can have funny effects when paired with `word-break: break-all;` as the minimum width is then calculated by the widest character:

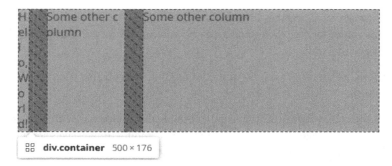

Figure 1.20 – CSS Grid breaks the text—the widest character, "W", defines the cell's width

The second keyword we can use is `max-content`, which will calculate the maximum possible content size and use this as the grid-cell sizing. So, instead of using the longest word, this will calculate the width of the entire sentence and use that. When paired with images, it will use the image's `max-width` or `max-height` value, depending on if we're sizing a row or column.

The third keyword is `fit-content`, a mixture of `min-content` and `max-content`. It will behave like the `fr` unit, but with a minimum value of `min-content` and a maximum value of `max-content`.

To illustrate, let's think about a grid with four columns and a total of `200px` width. Each column is evenly spaced with `1fr`, except for the first column, which has a sizing of `fit-content(50px)`. We now put an image of `80px` width in that first column. Instead of resizing the image to `50px` width, it will increase the size of the cell to `80px` and reduce the size of all the others by `10px` each.

To summarize, we would use the following CSS code:

```
.fit-content-grid {
    display: grid;
    width: 200px;
    grid-template-columns: fit-content(50px) 1fr 1fr 1fr;
}
```

And we apply it to the following HTML structure:

```
<div class="fit-content-grid">
    <img src="assets/80.png" alt="80x80">
    <div>A</div>
    <div>B</div>
    <div>C</div>
</div>
```

We can see how the image stays the same size in the following screenshot:

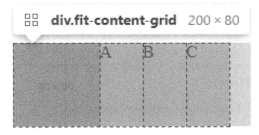

Figure 1.21 – A grid using fit-content to allow a cell to grow if the content does not fit

We can see that the entire width stays at 200px. The columns containing letters are significantly smaller than the one containing an image. The cell has expanded to fit the content.

However, if we removed the image—for example, with JavaScript—the cell size would go back to 50px. If we used max-content instead, it would result in a column width of 0px since there is no content.

The last keyword is auto. This also behaves a lot like the fr unit but with a little twist. It is interchangeable with 1fr if only 1fr is used. Consider the following grid declaration:

```
.grid {
  display: grid;
  grid-template-columns: 1fr 1fr 1fr;
}
```

This declaration behaves the same as the following one:

```
.grid {
  display: grid;
  grid-template-columns: auto auto auto;
}
```

The following screenshot shows the equivalence:

Figure 1.22 – Two grids: one of them uses fr units, and the other uses the auto keyword

Both grids are the same width and share the same number of columns. The top one uses `fr` units, and the bottom one uses the `auto` keyword. We can see that all columns are the same size.

However, when we mix the two, `auto` receives a different share of the available space than the columns using `fr`: instead of taking up a unit of space, the `auto`-sized cell will resize to fit its content and the `fr` cells will take up that remaining space. This behavior is equivalent to using a fixed unit value: `fr` will always divide the leftover space.

To illustrate this behavior, let's consider the following declaration:

```
.grid {
  display: grid;
  width: 500px;
  grid-template-columns: auto 1fr 3fr;
}
```

The size of the first column depends on its content. An image with a width of `120px` means that the grid cell will be `120px` wide. `1fr` of space would therefore be `95px`, a quarter of the remaining space. Likewise, if we use an image with a size of `40px`, the first column will be `40px` wide and `1fr` of space would equal `115px`, a quarter of the remaining `460px` of the entire grid.

The same applies to text. When we consider the previous grid definition and apply it to the following HTML, CSS Grid will make the first column the largest and squeeze in the other two, which will only take up as much space as their content needs:

```
<div class="grid">
  <div>
    Lorem ipsum dolor sit amet
    Lorem ipsum dolor sit amet
    Lorem ipsum dolor sit amet
  </div>
  <div>
    Short
  </div>
  <div>
    Text
  </div>
</div>
```

The result looks like this:

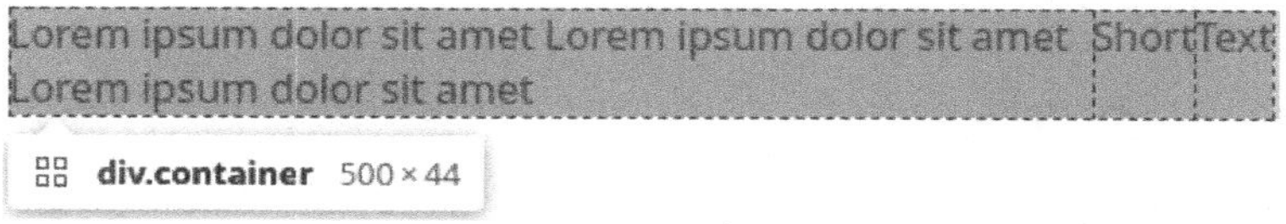

Figure 1.23 – Spacing with auto and the fr unit

If we want to explicitly state a minimum and maximum size for our grid cells, we can use a function called `minmax()`. This function does precisely what one would think: it sets a minimum and a maximum for the size of a value. When paired with the `fr` unit, we can give cells relative sizes but keep them at a minimum and maximum size. Remember the example with `word-break: break-all;`?

The `min-content` keyword, in combination with `word-break: break-all;`, resized the column to the width of the largest character, which is undesirable. We can mitigate such issues by using `minmax()` and assigning it a minimum value, as shown here:

```
<style>
.container {
    width: 500px;
    display: grid;
    grid-template-columns: minmax(50px, min-content) 1fr 3fr;
    gap: 25px;
}
div {
    word-break: break-all;
}
</style>
<div class="container">
  <div>
    Hello, World!
  </div>
  <div>
    Some other column
  </div>
  <div>
    Some other column
  </div>
</div>
```

From this code, the first column has a width of `50px`, the defined minimum size:

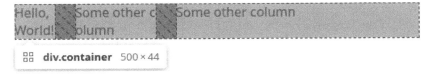

Figure 1.24 – Spacing with minmax

However, if larger content is found within the cell, such as an image, it will be enlarged:

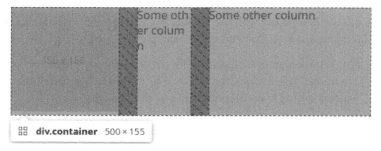

Figure 1.25 – Spacing with minmax and larger content in the first cell

We can also use the `min()` and `max()` functions for grid sizing. `min()` takes the smaller of two values and is often used with a relative and an absolute value, while `max()` takes the larger of two values, respectively.

For example, a column with `min(50vw, 200px)` sizing would result in a width of `50%` up to a screen size of `400px`. From `401px` onward, the column would stay at `200px` since that would be smaller than `50%` of `401px`, behaving like a combination of `max-width` and `width`.

Likewise, a column with `max(50vw, 200px)` sizing would result in a `200px`-wide column for all screen sizes smaller than `400px`. It thus behaves like a combination of `min-width` and `width`.

Repetitive column and row definitions

Imagine a gallery of images: it should be `800px` wide and `1600px` tall. Each image should take up `100px` by `100px`, resulting in 8 columns and 16 rows, all equally sized. If we wrote out this grid definition, it would look like this:

```
.gallery-container {
  width: 800px;
  height: 1600px;
  display: grid;
  grid-template-columns: 1fr 1fr 1fr 1fr 1fr 1fr 1fr 1fr;
  grid-template-rows: 1fr 1fr 1fr 1fr 1fr 1fr 1fr 1fr 1fr
    1fr 1fr 1fr 1fr 1fr 1fr 1fr;
}
```

This grid definition has several issues. The first is its readability. The brain can only quickly count about four items at a glance—a concept known as subitizing—and so when more than four or five similar items occur at once in an unfamiliar pattern, the brain doesn't immediately know the number of items and has to count manually.

The second problem is its maintainability. Code repetition is usually not good for maintainability since it forces us to change the same thing multiple times. For example, imagine that we now got the requirement to fix the image width to `100px` but keep the container at `100vw`.

To do that, we would adjust every row and column to be `100px` instead of `1fr`. The resulting code would be even less readable since each cell now takes five instead of three characters to define. The result would look roughly like this:

```
.gallery-container {
  width: 100vw;
  display: grid;
  grid-template-columns: 100px 100px 100px 100px 100px
    100px 100px 100px;
  grid-template-rows: 100px 100px 100px 100px 100px 100px
    100px 100px 100px 100px 100px 100px 100px 100px 100px
      100px;
}
```

Grid definitions such as these do work—don't get me wrong—but there's a tool that allows us to define multiple columns and rows in a much cleaner way: the `repeat()` function. Instead of writing `100px` 24 times, we would rewrite the code using `repeat(number, size definition)`, as shown in the next code snippet:

```
.gallery-container {
  width: 100vw;
  display: grid;
  grid-template-columns: repeat(8, 100px);
  grid-template-rows: repeat(16, 100px);
}
```

Essentially, the `repeat()` function replaces the use of multiple identical columns.

We can even mix it with other cell definitions. For example, a `grid-column-template` value of `100px repeat(10, 1fr) 100px` would result in 10 equally sized columns, surrounded by 2 columns of `100px` width each:

Figure 1.26 – The repeat() function mixed with other sizing definitions

When we need to define large amounts of alternating sizes, such as `50px 100px 50px 100px 50px 100px`, we can also use the `repeat()` function: `repeat(3, 50px 100px)`. Any valid size definition works, except `repeat()` itself. Sadly, we cannot nest `repeat()` calls, so something such as `repeat(3 100px repeat(3, 1fr) 100px)` won't work.

The repeat() function already seems very useful, but it gets much fancier with its two accompanying keywords, auto-fill and auto-fit. We use these instead of numbers to define how many grid cells we want. So, instead of repeat(3, 100px), we would write repeat(auto-fill, 100px) or repeat(auto-fit, 100px).

The auto-fill value will add as many grid cells as possible to a row or column. For example, if a container is 375px wide and we define the grid-template-columns rule as repeat(auto-fill, 100px), there will be three columns with a left-over value of 75px. The number of rows and columns is, therefore, dependent on the size of the container. The following code example illustrates this:

```
<style>
  .container {
    display: grid;
    grid-template-columns: repeat(auto-fill, 100px);
    gap: 5px;
    height: 50px;
    margin-bottom: 100px;
  }
  .small {
    width: 375px;
  }
  .large {
    width: 750px;
  }
  .container div {
    background-color: darkred;
    height: 20px;
  }
</style>

<p>Width: 375px;</p>
<div class="container small">
  <div></div>
  <!-- Repeat 10x -->
</div>

<p>Width: 750px;</p>
<div class="container large">
  <div></div>
  <!-- Repeat 10x -->
</div>
```

The result of the previous code would look like this:

Width: 375px;

Width: 750px;

Figure 1.27 – The repeat() function mixed with other sizing definitions and using auto-fill

On the other hand, we have `auto-fit`. This keyword tries to fill the entire grid width (when used for `grid-template-columns`) or height (when used for `grid-template-rows`). This value is generally practical when working with `minmax()` and `fr` as the size definitions, as we allow the grid cells to grow and shrink.

The `repeat(auto-fit, minmax(100px, 1fr)),)` value, for example, will result in a minimum column width of `100px`. If the container is smaller than the current amount of columns times `100px`, it will remove one column, rearrange the layout, and fill the entire width again by enlarging the columns. These values already allow us to build very responsive grids that are useful for article listings or image galleries.

The following screenshot shows the difference in behavior:

Width: 375px;

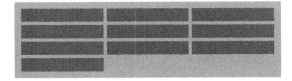

Width: 750px;

Figure 1.28 – The repeat() function using auto-fit

We can see that the columns now fill the entire container, whereas they were the same size when using `auto-fill`, `auto-fit` adapts the width of all columns.

CSS Grid offers us many possibilities to define the sizes of grid rows and columns and even allows us to add responsiveness without the need for media queries. To summarize, CSS Grid offers us an extra unit to define relative sizes, keywords to react size grid cells according to their content, and functions to keep sizes in defined ranges and to simplify repetitive grid definitions, with even more keywords to steer the number of grid cells.

Using shortcuts

A complex grid definition can result in a lot of code. Luckily, we can shorten much of the code by using shortcuts and combined definitions. Let's look at some now.

The grid attribute

The most general and, by far, the most powerful shortcut we can use is simply called `grid`. This attribute receives a ton of arguments and is a shortcut for these attributes:

- `grid-auto-flow`
- `grid-auto-rows` (we'll cover this in-depth in a later chapter, so don't worry too much about that now)
- `grid-auto-columns` (we'll also cover this in a later chapter)
- `grid-template-areas`
- `grid-template-columns`
- `grid-template-rows`

Not necessarily in that order, though. The official formal `type` definition of this shortcut is as follows:

```
grid =
  <'grid-template'>                                     |
  <'grid-template-rows'> / [ auto-flow && dense? ]
    <'grid-auto-columns'>?   |
  [ auto-flow && dense? ] <'grid-auto-rows'>? /
    <'grid-template-columns'>
```

This looks complicated and, given, a lot like TypeScript. It tells us that the `grid` attribute can either receive an entire grid template or separate definitions for grid rows or columns. Optionally, we may also specify the grid flow with a flag (either at the row or column definition) and add values for `grid-auto-rows` and `grid-auto-columns`. Grid rows and columns are separated by a forward slash.

The shortcut may receive one of the following three combinations:

- A grid definition that we would usually use with grid-template-areas

- grid-template-rows, the auto-flow keyword (optionally with dense), and grid-template-columns (equivalent to using grid-auto-flow: columns;)

- The auto-flow keyword (optionally with dense), grid-template-rows, and grid-template-columns (equivalent to using grid-auto-flow: rows;)

Mind the position of the auto-flow keyword in the last two combinations. The keyword's position determines how the grid flows.

To illustrate, let's have a look at an example:

```
.grid {
  display: grid;
  grid-auto-rows: 100px;
  grid-template-columns: repeat(4, 1fr);
  grid-auto-flow: row dense;
}
```

This grid has four columns, all equally sized, and uses automatically generated rows of 100px height. The grid-auto-flow property is set to dense to fill gaps and rows, so it fills rows first.

But we can rewrite this with the grid attribute to the following:

```
.grid {
  display: grid;
  grid: auto-flow dense 100px / repeat(4, 1fr);
}
```

The rewritten code is noticeably shorter than the first. Less code means we don't have to send as many bytes over the wire, making requests and rendering faster, and we can see what the grid looks like at a glance.

The shortcut syntax isn't as self-explanatory as the expanded syntax, but it can save us valuable time once it's in our muscle memory.

The grid-template attribute

If we want to use both grid-template-rows and grid-template-columns and combine these into a single attribute, we can use grid-template. This attribute allows us to specify each row and column and even grid-template-areas more compactly.

The most basic way to use `grid-template` is to specify the rows, add a forward slash, and then add the columns. For example, if we want to specify three rows of `150px`, `1fr`, and `200px`, as well as four columns of `1fr` each, we could write this as follows:

```
grid-template: 150px 1fr 200px / repeat(4, 1fr);
```

Notice how we can use any valid `grid-template-rows` and `grid-template-columns` values. We can also mix in `grid-template-areas` values. For that, we specify the grid areas as rows with their height and add column sizes after a forward slash.

To illustrate how we can leverage this shortcut, let's have a look at our page example that used `grid-template-areas`:

```
.container {
  display: grid;
  grid-template-areas:
    "header header"
    "sidebar content"
    "footer footer"
  ;
  grid-template-rows: 200px 1fr 200px;
  grid-template-columns: 150px 1fr;
}
```

We can rewrite this using `grid-template` to the following definition:

```
.container {
  display: grid;
  grid-template:
    "header header" 200px
    "sidebar content" 1fr
    "footer footer" 200px /
    150px 1fr
  ;
}
```

We have now integrated `grid-template-rows` and `grid-template-columns` into the `grid-area` definition. By adding the height values for each row next to the row, we're able to tell immediately how tall a given row is. We added the column widths at the end of the `grid-template` value, separated with a single forward slash.

The grid-row and grid-column attributes

Instead of having four different CSS rules to define the span and placement of an item within a grid, we can arrange it using `grid-row` and `grid-column`. Both use the same argument as `grid-row-start` and `grid-row-end`, and `grid-column-start` and `grid-column-end`, respectively.

So, we'd originally place an element like this:

```css
.item {
  grid-row-start: 2; /* Make it begin in the second row */
  grid-row-end: span 3;
  grid-column-start: 4;
  grid-column-end: span 5; /* Make it reach to the ninth
    column */
}
```

However, we can shorten it to this:

```css
.item {
  grid-row: 2 / span 3;
  grid-column: 4 / span 5;
}
```

We can also use named columns, like so:

```css
.item {
  grid-row: navigation / footer;
  grid-column: sidebar / content;
}
```

Any valid value for the expanded attributes is also valid for the shortcuts.

The gap attribute

Last but not least, there is a shortcut for gap definitions called gap. Instead of using row-gap and column-gap, we can either use gaps with a single value to denote a valid size for both row and column gaps or specify row gaps and column gaps separately with two different values, much like padding and margin.

Let's assume we have the following grid definition with row gaps and column gaps:

```css
.grid {
  display: grid;
  grid-template-areas:
    "header header"
    "sidebar content"
    "footer footer"
  ;
  row-gap: 15px;
  column-gap: 30px;
}
```

We can then use the gap attribute to shorten the code, like so:

```css
.grid {
  display: grid;
  grid-template-areas:
    "header header"
    "sidebar content"
    "footer footer"
  ;
  gap: 15px 30px;
}
```

If we used the same values for row-gap and column-gap, we could even shorten the gap value to a single value, much like margin and padding.

Shortcuts help us to reduce the verbosity of our code. They can help us to be less repetitive and communicate our grid with more clarity. Some of these shortcuts, especially grid, might need more effort to write but can save us much time once we're familiar with them. Using them isn't mandatory, either. Some developers prefer shortcuts; some don't.

Summary

In this chapter, we've now looked at the basic terms, structures, rules, attributes, units, and functions of CSS Grid. We've seen that a grid doesn't have to look like just a bunch of rows and columns, with CSS Grid allowing us to build complex layouts with relatively small tools.

With grid-template-rows, grid-template-columns, grid-area, and grid-template, we can specify what the grid looks like, how large different grid tracks are, and how many of them there are. Moreover, we can precisely define where an item will be placed inside the grid with grid-area, grid-row, grid-column, and their specific start and end variants, such as grid-column-start or grid-row-end. Then, gap definitions help us separate items without the need for complex padding and margin definitions on the items.

To practice the things we've learned now, we will have our first look at Awesome Analytics, our overarching project, in the next chapter. We will learn how to apply grids to existing structures and how to work with CSS Grid to achieve the layouts we'd like.

2
Project Introduction: What We'll Work on and First Tasks

Now that we have learned the basics of CSS Grid, it's time to start getting more practical.

This chapter introduces the project that accompanies us throughout the book. This example project is called **Awesome Analytics**. Awesome Analytics is a made-up analytics app that shows all kinds of randomly generated graphs. Dashboards and a layout tailored to professional users let us practice different kinds of grids and how we approach them.

In each following chapter, we will further develop and improve the design of this app. With a starting task and a possible solution, we will strengthen our knowledge of the grid basics, implement an overall layout, and arrange dashboard elements with different sizes.

As for the details, we'll look at the following topics:

- Introducing Awesome Analytics – our gibberish analytics tool
- Setting up Awesome Analytics locally
- Our first tasks: setting up the page layout and arranging the dashboard widgets
- A deep dive into Awesome Analytics
- Possible solutions to our tasks

Technical requirements

We need a few more things for this chapter than in the last chapter:

- A modern browser that supports CSS Grid, offers grid debugging, and provides a grid toolset
- An **Integrated Development Environment** (IDE) or a text editor such as WebStorm, VS Code, or VIM with HTML and CSS syntax highlighting.
- Internet access is necessary to access the code
- Git (optional; we can also download the folder from GitHub)
- Node.js with at least version 14 and npm with at least version 6

If Node.js is not currently installed on your system, or you've got the wrong version, nvm (the **Node Version Manager**) is a fantastic tool to handle different Node.js versions on one system.

All the code for this chapter can be found on GitHub in this repository: `https://github.com/PacktPublishing/Mastering-CSS-Grid/tree/main/chapter2`.

Introducing Awesome Analytics – our gibberish analytics tool

Awesome Analytics is an HTML/CSS/JavaScript-based example website built without a JavaScript or CSS framework (but it uses a few tools to ease development as well as a few assets, such as fonts and icons).

Awesome Analytics, for now, only consists of a single page: the dashboard. An analytics dashboard is a perfect playground for our purpose. When we think of analytics tools by popular search engine companies, we first consider widgets. And often, these widgets are arranged in a grid. These widgets can be of various sizes and rarely leave gaps when they self-arrange.

Let's look at the current layout of Awesome Analytics in the following figure.

Figure 2.1 – Awesome Analytics as it currently stands

Currently, Awesome Analytics doesn't have any layout whatsoever. All elements stack on top of each other, which is intentional! In this chapter, we implement the grid layout from scratch.

The page has a logo in the header bar, a sticky collapsible sidebar, and 18 charts created with ChartJS and Faker. These charts are entirely random and don't represent anything useful. Awesome Analytics, therefore, has no function whatsoever. Its sole purpose is for us to style it with grids and further develop its layout.

There are already a few things we might notice when looking at this screenshot:

- Any icons, titles, and links are already positioned correctly. We, therefore, don't need to bother with these.

- The navigation has a right border of one pixel, meaning it should go on the left.

- The header is already in the correct position.

- The charts seem to be responsive. Otherwise, they wouldn't take up the entire width and squish themselves to the least height possible.

- All charts seem to be within a single container with some extra spacing, represented by the large gray area surrounding them. The charts themselves seem to be distinct containers, too, indicated by the dark borders around them.

With the knowledge about what Awesome Analytics is and how its current state looks, we have a general idea of the challenges we might face. The app lacks layouts, but its overall styling is in place. We must implement a layout for the page and arrange the chart boxes.

Setting up Awesome Analytics locally

Now it's time to get this project up and running locally.

We first need to ensure that we've got Node.js and npm installed. If they're not installed on our system, we can head to `https://nodejs.org/en/download/` and download Node.js and npm. npm is included when installing Node.js. Once installed, we can check out the code on our local machine.

For that, we have three different options. We can either clone the code for the entire book and work in the chapter directory, do a sparse checkout and only clone the project, or download the code folder from GitHub without using Git.

Since the GitHub repository also provides other code pieces and project progress for other chapters, cloning the entire repository is recommended. For that, we enter the following code in our command-line interface. On OS X and Linux, the command line interface is the Terminal app. On Windows, we may use PowerShell or WSL:

> **A note on Terminal code**
>
> To keep it consistent, we use the dollar sign to denote single lines in terminal code. We also use the dollar sign in terminal code snippets on GitHub. This sign might be different on your terminal. Zsh, for example, uses the percent sign instead.

```
$ mkdir become_a_css_grid_pro
$ git clone https://github.com/PacktPublishing/Mastering-CSS-Grid.git
become_a_css_grid_pro
$ cd become_a_css_grid_pro/chapter2/AwesomeAnalytics
```

Next, we will install all dependencies with npm and run the `serve` command to start the application:

```
$ npm install
$ npm run serve
```

Our console should now tell us that the app is available on `http://localhost:3000/`. An error that might occur is that the port is already in use. To fix this, we need to ensure that we don't have any other Node.js app or web server running that might occupy port `3000`.

To do this, we must stop any other process potentially occupying the port. We can find these using either Netstat (Windows, OS X, and Linux) or by stopping all other Node.js processes and servers.

When we now open `http://localhost:3000/` in our browser, we're greeted by Awesome Analytics. Awesome! (Analytics.)

Our local version of Awesome Analytics is now up and running. Time to get our hands dirty and have a look at our first task.

Receiving our first task – implementing the grids

After we've set up everything, it's time to get started. Imagine working for a company that implements Awesome Analytics. There are stakeholders, such as users, a sales department, and, of course, management. Imagine working in a cross-functional team of a few developers, UX experts, and a product owner.

Our stakeholders are pleased with the progress so far. They love the implementation of corporate identity and corporate design. They have also looked at the gibberish charts and checked whether they were as nonsensical as they anticipated, and indeed they were. However, they noticed that the dashboard is missing a critical element: the entire layout for the charts and the page itself.

As the newly hired expert for CSS Grid and grid layouts, we get called in to an important meeting. There, the product owner, the design expert, and the most important person, the end user, are discussing the issue at hand. The product owner rises from their chair, a smile on their face, greets us, and promises everyone at the table that this expert will fix all layout problems they ever had or will have in the future. The discussion continues.

Everyone agrees that a grid layout is best for both the page and the charts. The charts, however, have different sizes depending on the end user's needs. The sidebar should not have a fixed width, nor should the charts be pushed out of the right side of the screen if it's expanded. The design expert says that every chart should occupy a minimum of ¼ of the available width, resulting in four columns. Each row of charts should be precisely 400 px tall so that the charts don't look squished, at least horizontally.

The end user at the table is asked whether they use any device other than a laptop for working with Awesome Analytics. They admit to often being on their phone and tablet, but never for work purposes. The design doesn't need to be fully responsive; medium to large screens is enough. We will cover responsiveness in *Chapter 4, Understanding and Creating Responsive and Fluid Grid Layouts*. They also add that they might want more charts in the future and perhaps would like to change the size of any chart later.

We've now been asked to apply a layout to this page. What our stakeholders would like to see has been designed by experts and looks like this:

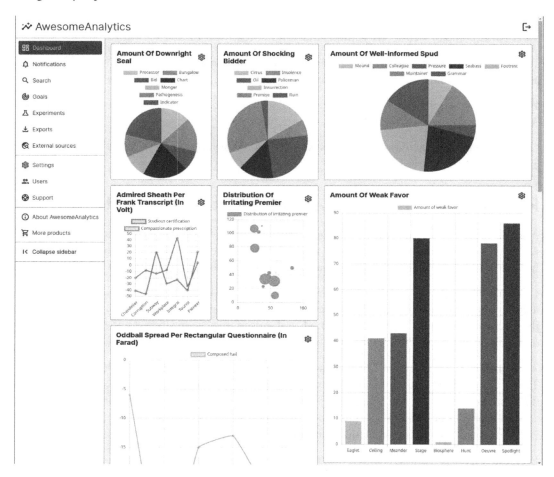

Figure 2.2 – The desired result at the end of this chapter

We return to our workstation, drink some water, and get going.

Exploring the code of Awesome Analytics

The first thing we do next is to open up the project in our favorite code editor or IDE. There, we try to get an overview of the structure and a feel for the code base. We'll notice that there is only a single HTML file, `index.html`. Our dashboard.

When we open up `index.html`, we'll find a total of 10 references to CSS files. At the very bottom of the page, we find two references to JavaScript files. We look at `index.html` top to bottom, going into detail where we need to.

The CSS structure

We start at the very top of `index.html` and have a look at the `<head>` tag. We see all CSS files arranged in groups.

Let's have a look at the references:

```
<!DOCTYPE html>
<html>
  <head>
    <title>Awesome Analytics - An example app for CSS
      Grid</title>
    <!-- General setup -->
    <link rel="stylesheet" href="node_modules/
      minireset.css/minireset.min.css">
    <link rel="stylesheet" href="assets/css/brand.css">
    <link rel="stylesheet" href="assets/css/icons.css">
    <link rel="stylesheet" href="assets/css/
      typography.css">
    <link rel="stylesheet" href="assets/css/general.css">

    <!-- Components -->
    <link rel="stylesheet" href="assets/css/
      page-header.css">
    <link rel="stylesheet" href="assets/css/sidebar.css">
    <link rel="stylesheet" href="assets/css/
      main-page-content.css">
    <link rel="stylesheet" href="assets/css/chartbox.css">

    <!-- Grid -->
    <link rel="stylesheet" href="assets/css/grid.css">
  </head>
```

The first referenced file is `minireset.css`. This library removes all basic browser styles for modern browsers and only weighs 484 KB – mini indeed.

The second file, `brand.css`, defines the essential CSS variables, such as colors, font sizes, and spacing values:

```css
:root {
  --color-gray-0: #fff;
  --color-gray-1: #eee;
  --color-gray-2: #ccc;
  --color-gray-3: #999;
  --color-gray-4: #666;
  --color-gray-5: #333;
  --color-gray-6: #181818;

  --color-brand-dark: #0008C1;
  --color-brand-light: #2146C7;
  --color-brand-alt-dark: #E6CBA8;
  --color-brand-alt-light: #FDF0E0;

  --font-size-base: 16px;
  --font-size-xxl: 1.953rem;
  --font-size-xl: 1.563rem;
  --font-size-l: 1.25rem;
  --font-size-m: 1rem;
  --font-size-s: 0.8rem;
  --font-size-xs: 0.64rem;

  --line-height-snug: 1.1;
  --line-height-standard: 1.3;
  --line-height-relaxed: 1.75;

  --spacing-xxl: 64px;
  --spacing-xl: 32px;
  --spacing-l: 16px;
  --spacing-m: 8px;
  --spacing-s: 4px;
  --spacing-xs: 2px;

  --border-standard: 1px solid var(--color-gray-3);
}
```

Not all of them are in use, however, examples being some of the font sizes, colors, and spacings.

The third file of the category is `icons.css`. It imports the icon library from the installed dependency:

```css
@import "../../node_modules/@fontsource/
  material-icons/index.css";
```

```css
@import "../../node_modules/@fontsource/
  material-icons-outlined/index.css";
```

The following file, `typography.css`, defines how titles, paragraphs, and links look. It makes use of the defined font sizes and line heights, and also imports the font we installed with npm:

```css
@import "../../node_modules/@fontsource/inter/300.css";
@import "../../node_modules/@fontsource/inter/400.css";
@import "../../node_modules/@fontsource/inter/700.css";

body {
  font-family: "Inter", sans-serif;
}

.link, a, a:link, a:visited {
  color: var(--color-brand-dark);
  text-decoration: none;
  display: flex;
  align-items: center;
}
.link:hover, a:hover {
  color: var(--color-brand-light);
  text-decoration: none;
}

.link > .icon, a > .icon {

  margin-inline-start: var(--spacing-m);
}

.h1 {
  font-weight: 300;
  font-size: var(--font-size-xxl);
  line-height: var(--line-height-snug);
}

.h2 {
  font-weight: 300;
  font-size: var(--font-size-xl);
  line-height: var(--line-height-snug);
}

.h3 {
  font-weight: 300;
  font-size: var(--font-size-l);
```

```
  line-height: var(--line-height-snug);
}

p, .p {
  font-weight: 300;
  font-size: var(--font-size-m);
  line-height: var(--line-height-standard);
}

.bold {
  font-weight: 700;
}
```

The last file of this group, `general.css`, contains some basic CSS that doesn't fall into any other file or group:

```
body {
  min-height: 100vh;
}
```

It doesn't contain much but is meant to contain any styling for the body and the HTML tag.

The next group contains components. They define how the page header works, how the sidebar behaves, and how the chart boxes look. The first file, `page-header.css`, is responsible for the page header:

```
.page-header {
  padding: var(--spacing-l);
  display: flex;
  align-items: center;
  justify-content: space-between;
  border-bottom: var(--border-standard);
}

.page-title {
  display: flex;
  align-items: center;
}

.page-title .material-icons-outlined {
  margin-right: var(--spacing-m);
}
```

The second file in this group takes care of the sidebar and is the most complex one. It also contains styles for the collapsed state and handles transitions:

```css
.sidebar {
  border-right: var(--border-standard);
}

.sidebar nav {
  position: sticky;
  top: 0;
}

.sidebar li {
  padding: var(--spacing-m);
  margin: var(--spacing-m);
  border-radius: var(--spacing-s);
  line-height: var(--line-height-snug);
}
.sidebar li:first-child {
  margin-top: 0;
}

.sidebar li.active {
  background-color: var(--color-brand-light);
}

.sidebar li.active a,
.sidebar li.active a:visited,
.sidebar li.active a:link,
.sidebar li.active a:hover {
  color: var(--color-gray-0);
}

.sidebar li a {
  height: 24px;
}

.sidebar .group {
  padding-top: var(--spacing-m);
  border-bottom: var(--border-standard);
}

.sidebar .text {
  max-width: 400px;
```

```
    transition: all ease-in-out .2s;
    white-space: nowrap;
    overflow: hidden;
}
.sidebar .icon {
    transition: all ease-in-out .2s;
}

.sidebar.collapsed .icon {
    margin-right: 0;
}
.sidebar.collapsed .text {
    max-width: 0;
}

.sidebar .collapse-icon {
    display: block;
}
.sidebar .expand-icon {
    display: none;
}
.sidebar.collapsed .collapse-icon {
    display: none;
}
.sidebar.collapsed .expand-icon {
    display: block;
}
```

Then there is `main-page-content.css`, which takes care of the container for the charts:

```
.main-page-content {
    background-color: var(--color-gray-1);
    padding: var(--spacing-1);
}
```

And next, there is `chart-box.css`, which styles the individual chart boxes:

```
.chart-box {
    background-color: var(--color-gray-0);
    border: var(--border-standard);
    border-radius: 4px;
    padding: var(--spacing-1);
    min-width: 0;
    min-height: 0;
    display: flex;
    flex-direction: column;
```

```
}

.chart-box header {
  display: flex;
  justify-content: space-between;
  text-transform: capitalize;
}

.chart-box .chart-container {
  margin: var(--spacing-m);
  flex: 1 1 1px;
}
```

The last CSS file, however, is `grid.css`. This file is currently empty. The code for our grid will go in there.

The HTML structure

Let's look at the HTML. The body contains three elements: a `<header>`, an `<aside>`, and a `<main>` element. These three elements are the ones we identified in the first screenshot.

The `<header>` element contains an `<h1>` tag for the logo and a singular link with a logout icon:

```
<!-- Page header -->
<header class="page-header">
  <h1 class="h1 page-title">
    <span class="material-icons-outlined h1"
      aria-hidden="true">insights</span>
    AwesomeAnalytics
  </h1>

  <a href="/">
      <span class="material-icons-outlined h1">
        logout</span>
  </a>
</header>
```

The `<aside>` element contains `<nav>`, which itself contains several unordered lists with icons and links as their list items:

```
<!-- Side bar -->
<aside class= "sidebar collapsed">
  <nav>
    <ul class="group">
      <li class="active">
        <a href="/" class="p">
```

```
      <span class="material-icons-outlined icon"
        aria-hidden="true">dashboard</span>
      <span class="text">Dashboard</span>
    </a>
  </li>
  <li>
    <a href="/" class="p">
      <span class="material-icons-outlined icon"
        aria-hidden="true">notifications</span>
      <span class="text">Notifications</span>
    </a>
  </li>
  <li>
    <a href="/" class="p">
      <span class="material-icons-outlined icon"
        aria-hidden="true">search</span>
      <span class="text">Search</span>
    </a>
  </li>
  <!-- ... -->
</ul>
<ul class="group">
  <!-- ... -->
</ul>
 <ul class="group">
  <!-- ... -->
</ul>
<ul class="group">
  <!-- ... -->
</ul>
  </nav>
</aside>
```

`<main>` contains all the charts. However, all chart boxes look the same – they've got a generic title, an empty canvas, and a settings icon in a link that leads nowhere. However, the CSS classes of these chart boxes are curious. Sometimes, they only have the `chart-box` class.

Sometimes this class is accompanied by either `chart-box-wide` or `chart-box-tall` or, at times, both. In the following code snippet, we can see an example for all the different sizes and also see how the DOM of the chart boxes doesn't differ. Their content is provided by JavaScript:

```
<!-- Main page content with charts -->
<main class="main-page-content">
  <div class="chart-box">
    <header>
      <h2 class="h3 bold">Title</h2>
```

```
      <a href=""><span class="material-icons-outlined"
        aria-hidden="true">settings</span></a>
    </header>
    <div class="chart-container">
      <canvas></canvas>
    </div>
  </div>

  <div class="chart-box chart-box-tall chart-box-wide">
    <header>
      <h2 class="h3 bold">Title</h2>
      <a href=""><span class="material-icons-outlined"
        aria-hidden="true">settings</span></a>
    </header>
    <div class="chart-container">
      <canvas></canvas>
    </div>
  </div>

  <div class="chart-box chart-box-wide">
    <header>
      <h2 class="h3 bold">Title</h2>
      <a href=""><span class="material-icons-outlined"
        aria-hidden="true">settings</span></a>
    </header>
    <div class="chart-container">
      <canvas></canvas>
    </div>
  </div>

  <div class="chart-box chart-box-tall">
    <header>
      <h2 class="h3 bold">Title</h2>
      <a href=""><span class="material-icons-outlined"
        aria-hidden="true">settings</span></a>
    </header>
    <div class="chart-container">
      <canvas></canvas>
    </div>
  </div>

  <!-- ... -->
</main>
```

The `chart-box-tall` and `chart-box-wide` classes define the size of the different chart boxes.

We receive another mockup from the design department, showing us what was meant by these `tall` and `wide` chart containers.

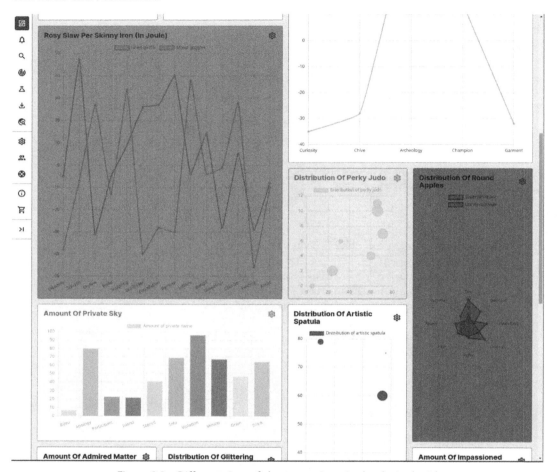

Figure 2.3 – Different sizes of chart containers in the desired grid

The UX department has added colors to explain the different sizes.

- The cyan chart seems to be a standard one
- The yellow chart box is a wide one, spanning two columns

- The purple one shows us a tall one spanning two rows

- The red box appears to be a tall and wide one, spanning two rows and columns

However, knowing the contents of `chart-box.css`, the sizing isn't covered by the existing CSS – we can achieve this with CSS Grid.

The JavaScript structure

Finally, while there is some JavaScript, there are only two files:

- The first, `sidebar.js`, takes care of collapsing the sidebar with a single click listener and the toggle of a class.

- The second file, `createCharts.js`, uses ChartJS, a color-utility library called `lighten-darken-color`, and `@faker-js/faker` to generate charts for us. It fills the generic titles and uses the canvases to display fake and random data.

> **Note**
>
> Though it contains a pretty large library, Faker is convenient for projects like these and can generate test data with minimal code. It offers vast possibilities, from creating user-related data such as names, email addresses, physical post addresses, randomly distributed data of any type, and even scientific values.

We now know how Awesome Analytics is structured and where to look for information, such as possible spacings for gaps or which class names to use. With this knowledge, we're prepared to implement what the stakeholders of Awesome Analytics have asked us to implement.

Fixing Awesome Analytics' layout problem – a possible solution

Let's recap the task. Awesome Analytics does not have any layout, and the chart boxes are stacked on top of each other. So, our task is to align the different parts of the page (header, sidebar, and main content) into a grid and to align the chart boxes so they're in a grid as well, keeping in mind that there are differently sized chart boxes.

Each chart box should occupy one grid cell. Some are marked as *wide*, meaning that they are two grid cells wide, and some are marked as *tall*, meaning they occupy two rows. Chart boxes can be tall, wide, both, or neither. We don't know up front whether there are more chart boxes to come.

Analyzing the problem

We know from the screenshot in *Figure 2.3* that the base layout should have two rows – one for the header and one for the sidebar and content – and two columns – one for the sidebar and one for the content. In addition, the header should span two columns, as shown in the following figure:

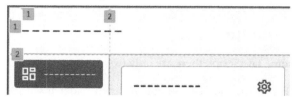

Figure 2.4 – What the finished header should look like, showing the grid structure

We can see that the header bar starts above the sidebar and spans across the content section, essentially two columns wide.

We also know that the header will likely never grow but that the sidebar grows in width when expanded. From the screenshots, we see that the sidebar text is never wrapped. We also know that a chart box grid cell is 400px tall, and each column has ¼ of the available width.

There is also a gap between the chart boxes, roughly the size of the gap between the sidebar and the first column and the header and the first row.

With that information, we can start implementing the layout and the chart box arrangement.

Creating the page layout

We'll start with the outer grid for the layout. We want a total of two rows and two columns. The first row should likely have a height value of min-content, as we want it to be as narrow as necessary. The second row should then have a height of 1fr, allowing it to grow indefinitely.

The columns behave similarly to the rows. As we recall from the first chapter, min-content calculates the minimum size it can give to an element so that the content doesn't overflow. In our case, when also applied to columns, it likely breaks the text at the first space it encounters, resulting in two lines of text for some links. The mockups show us that the text doesn't break, however, so we need a different solution.

We can give it the size auto instead. auto ensures that the column is sized not to break lines. The second column, the main content, should have a width of 1fr to occupy the rest of the page.

To define the entire grid structure, we'll use the grid-template shortcut, define the name of the top row as header, and name the bottom row consisting of the columns' sidebar and content.

Our grid container element is the `<body>` element itself. The code that we add to `grid.css` would therefore look like the following:

```
body {
  display: grid;
  grid-template:
    'header header' min-content
    'sidebar content' auto;
  grid-template-columns: auto 1fr;
}
```

When we load the page, we see that the sidebar has now ended up on the right side of the header. To move it back, we also need to tell the header that it should occupy the header grid area:

```
.page-header {
  grid-area: header;
}
```

The page layout is already done now:

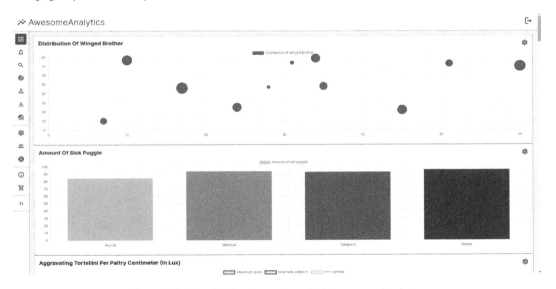

Figure 2.5 – The finished page layout of Awesome Analytics

Since we used the grid definitions `auto` and `1fr` and knowing that the `fr` unit receives the larger share of the available space, the sidebar is also expandable. However, it does not grow beyond its content size.

Arranging the chart boxes

Now, we take care of the chart boxes. These should be arranged in four columns in as many rows as necessary. These rows, however, should be 400px in height. The container for this grid is the element with the .main-page-content CSS class.

For the column definition, we can use grid-template-columns with 1fr of space for four columns. We can use the repeat keyword to define the number of equally sized columns.

For the row definition, we use grid-auto-rows with a value of 400px. We can use the --spacing-1 variable to define the gap, as it contains just the right pixel value for the spacing to be pixel-perfect.

Our finished grid definition now looks like this:

```
.main-page-content {
  display: grid;

  grid-template-columns: repeat(4, 1fr);
  grid-auto-rows: 400px;
  gap: var(--spacing-1);
}
```

In this code, we used grid-auto-rows for the first time. This property adds the number of necessary rows to contain all content. The pixel value we specify determines the size of each row. We will look into this attribute more in *Chapter 3, Building Advanced Grid Layouts*.

We'll now notice that the chart boxes all have the same size. So, we need to tell those with the .chart-box-wide and .chart-box-tall classes to span two columns or rows, respectively. We achieve this with the grid-column and grid-row CSS rules, both receiving a value of span 2:

```
.chart-box-wide {
  grid-column: span 2;
}

.chart-box-tall {
  grid-row: span 2;
}
```

We're almost there. The last thing we notice when scrolling through the page is gaps. Because of the order of the chart boxes, the grid automatically arranges them per row, skipping specific grid cells if the next element doesn't fit.

So, we alter the CSS for .main-page-content to also contain grid-auto-flow: row dense; to tell it that it should try to compact the elements.

The entire finished CSS now looks like this:

```
body {
  display: grid;

  grid-template:
    'header header' min-content
    'sidebar content' auto;

  grid-template-columns: auto 1fr;
}

.page-header {
  grid-area: header;
}

.main-page-content {
  display: grid;

  grid-template-columns: repeat(4, 1fr);
  grid-auto-rows: 400px;

  gap: var(--spacing-1);

  grid-auto-flow: row dense;
}

.chart-box-wide {
  grid-column: span 2;
}

.chart-box-tall {
  grid-row: span 2
}
```

When we load the page now, we see that it looks exactly like the mockups the UX department sent us in *Figure 2.2*. Amazing! The other developers on our team review the code and approve it, the product owner tests and closes the ticket, and the end user is happy. Awesome!

Summary

In this chapter, we've learned about the project we'll be working on throughout the book: Awesome Analytics. Although its data is gibberish, Awesome Analytics is a realistic example we can use to practice our CSS Grid skills and shows us how to create complex user interfaces with CSS Grid.

We've practiced the basic rules of CSS Grid with our first task of implementing the page layout and a self-arranging grid for the chart boxes and have satisfied all the stakeholders. Our result looks just like the mockups. To achieve this result, we've used grid areas, sizing keywords, and the `repeat` function, and we've altered grid flow and added rows automatically. In the following chapters, we'll further build upon this knowledge and create even more complex user interfaces.

Since we know the repository, we know how to navigate through the code base and which tools we'll use in the next chapter.

The next chapter will show you how to place elements inside grid cells, the advanced usage of grid areas, and how nested grids and sub-grids can help us implement more detailed and refined layouts that cover more use cases.

3

Building Advanced Grid Layouts

The last two chapters were about learning the basics of CSS Grid and getting used to them. We've practiced adding grid layouts to pages and automatically arranging items. Since we've gained experience, we will now look into more advanced features of CSS Grid, one of which is not even available in all browsers yet, as of 2022.

In this chapter, we will look at advanced grid areas, the placement of grid items within grid cells, and subgrids, and how they differ from nested grids. And we'll further develop parts of Awesome Analytics, our overarching project.

We'll look at the following topics:

- What are the row axis and column axis?
- Arranging grid items and grid cells with the *align* and *justify* properties
- Defining and using advanced grid templates
- Creating subgrids
- Emulating subgrids with nested grids
- Masonry layouts
- Practicing with Awesome Analytics

Technical requirements

For this chapter, we'll need roughly the same tools as we used in *Chapter 2, Project Introduction: What We'll Work on and First Tasks*:

- A browser, preferably Chromium-based, such as Google Chrome, Brave, or Vivaldi, but Firefox or Apple Safari works, too.

- A browser that currently supports subgrids. We can check which browsers support subgrids on Caniuse: `https://caniuse.com/?search=subgrid`.

- An **integrated development environment** (**IDE**) or text editor, such as WebStorm, VS Code, or VIM, with HTML and CSS syntax highlighting.

- Internet access is necessary to access the code.

- Git (optional, we can also download the folder from GitHub).

- Node.js with at least version 14, and npm with at least version 6.

If Node.js is not currently installed on your system, or you've got the wrong version, **nvm** (the **Node Version Manager**) is a fantastic tool to handle different Node.js versions on one system.

All the code for this chapter can be found on GitHub in this repository: `https://github.com/PacktPublishing/Mastering-CSS-Grid/tree/main/chapter3`.

Understanding the row axis and column axis and how to influence them

When discussing a grid, we often also discuss where something is positioned on which axis. What many people know from other applications, or even from mathematics, are the standard X and Y axis, with X being the horizontal axis (that is, the larger X, the more on the right it is) and Y being the vertical axis.

However, things become more complicated when we take different scripts into account. Most language scripts nowadays use a **left-to-right** system, or **LTR** for short. But some scripts, such as the Arabic script, the Hebrew alphabet, or Thaana, use a **right-to-left** system, or **RTL** for short.

For some applications, a top-to-bottom approach might also be desirable for text, images, and other content. When we speak of an axis, we usually use the **row axis** (or **inline axis**) and **column axis** (or **block axis**).

In standard writing mode, the row axis is horizontal from left to right and corresponds with the X axis, whereas the column axis is equivalent to the Y axis.

Some CSS Grid properties also use `start` and `end` as possible values. Depending on the writing mode, the start of a grid item, grid container, or grid cell is usually at the top and left, whereas the end is on the opposite side of these elements.

We can adjust the text direction and, therefore, the grid direction with the `direction` CSS property, which takes the following values:

- `ltr` is the default value and stands for *left to right*

- `rtl` stands for *right to left*

We can also use the `dir="rtl"` HTML attribute on the HTML tag of our application to change the text direction.

In addition to changing the text direction on the horizontal axis, we can also adjust its placement on the vertical axis. For that, CSS Grid offers the `writing-mode` CSS property, which takes one of the following values:

- `horizontal-tb` is the default value and aligns the elements and the text horizontally.

- `vertical-rl` means *from top to bottom, then right to left*, and basically rotates the entire grid by 90 degrees clockwise.

- `vertical-lr` means *from top to bottom, then left to right*, and rotates the grid by 90 degrees clockwise.

- `sideways-rl` means *from bottom to top, then right to left*. The value is experimental as of 2023.

- `sideways-lr` means *from bottom to top, then left to right*. The value is experimental as of 2023.

All of these values influence the direction and orientation of the row axis and column axis. The `vertical-*` and `sideways-*` values switch them; when applied, the row axis becomes equivalent to the *Y* axis, and the column axis becomes equivalent to the *X* axis.

A note on the readability of the chapter

From this point on, we'll use mainly the row and column axes and rarely talk about the *X* and *Y* axes anymore. For the sake of simplicity, we'll assume a horizontal left-to-right writing mode.

With this knowledge, we can influence the direction and alignments of grids to our will and define the rules of how grid items behave within it. Next, we'll learn how to align and justify elements within those grids.

Arranging grid items and grid cells with alignment and justification rules

By default, all grid items are arranged within the grid cells in a stretched manner. Think of the Awesome Analytics dashboard. The following figure of the dashboard illustrates this behavior:

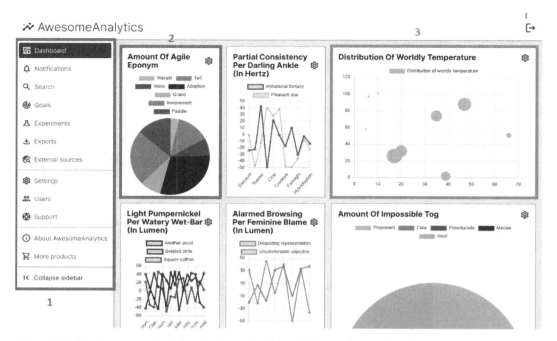

Figure 3.1 – The Awesome Analytics dashboard with its sidebar and some chart boxes marked with colors

The sidebar (**1**), marked with a red border, stretches to fill the entire height. We can see this with the white and gray backgrounds. Its content wouldn't take up that much space, in any case. The same behavior applies to the chart boxes.

We see in the first row that a pie chart fits in a single grid cell, as shown in the chart box marked with blue (**2**), but the chart stretches to its available space when defined as such, as illustrated by the chart box marked in orange (**3**).

In most cases, this is the expected and desired behavior. However, in some cases, we'd like grid items only to take up as much space as their content, and in other cases, we don't even want the grid to fill the entire space available. Not spanning the entire available space is especially interesting for responsive page layouts built with grids.

To achieve these behaviors, CSS Grid lets us steer where it should place and justify items and where it should place and justify the entire grid within its container.

Aligning and justifying items

First, we will look at the placement and justification of individual grid items. A practical example is tags or pills. We often see these at the beginning or end of blog posts to indicate some kind of category or to lead to related content.

Consider the following HTML code:

```
<!-- File: chapter3/01_placing_grid_items.html -->
<div class="tag-container">
  <div class="tag">Some</div>
  <div class="tag">Random</div>
  <div class="tag">Tags</div>
  <div class="tag">That</div>
  <div class="tag">Take up space</div>
  <div class="tag">And could also take up quite a lot of space</div>
  <div class="tag">But</div>
  <div class="tag">Could also be short</div>
  <div class="tag">Just like</div>
  <div class="tag">Some</div>
  <div class="tag">Of</div>
  <div class="tag">The pills</div>
  <div class="tag">In</div>
  <div class="tag">This</div>
  <div class="tag">Example</div>
  <div class="tag">Banana</div>
</div>
```

We can see 16 tags defined as single `div` tags with a `tag` class in a container element with the `tag-container` class. (Going off on a tangent, I think 16 tags are way too many. I'm sure content experts agree here: that many tags blur the focus, and I'm pretty sure the content that actually needs 16 tags isn't the most focused to begin with. Anyway, back to CSS Grid.)

Let's apply a grid structure to them and add some styling for the `tag` pills by giving them a rounded border and a background color:

```
.tag {
  background-color: #aec6cf;
  padding: 10px;
  font-family: sans-serif;
  border-radius: 20px;
}

.tag-container {
  display: grid;
  gap: 5px;
  grid-template-columns: 1fr 1fr 1fr 1fr;
}
```

This code puts all 16 tags in a grid of four columns with automatically defined rows, as illustrated in the following figure:

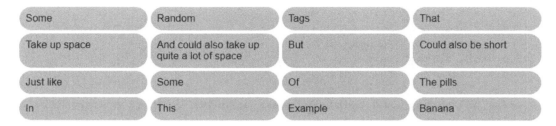

Figure 3.2 – All 16 tags aligned in a grid

As described in the section introduction, the stretching of the elements happens regardless of how it looks. Especially in the second row from the top and the first three columns from left: the **Take up space** and **But** grid items are stretched over the entire width of the columns and even take up more vertical space than necessary since the grid item with the content **And could also take up quite a lot of space** needs two rows and stretches the entire track.

The design doesn't even resemble a pill design. Instead, it looks more like a grid of randomly arranged words (which it basically is), somehow reminding us of website navigation from the early 2000s.

It all boils down to how the items are stretched in height and width. If we didn't want to stretch them, we could add containers around the pills, effectively decoupling them from the grid. If we wanted to align and justify them, we could use Flexbox. However, this method would add a lot more HTML and CSS to our code, which isn't necessary.

Consider the following CSS code as a possible Flexbox solution to the preceding problem:

```
.tag {
  background-color: #aec6cf;
  padding: 10px;
  font-family: sans-serif;
  border-radius: 20px;
  flex: 1 0 25%;
  max-width: calc(25% - 5px);
  box-sizing: border-box;
}

.tag-container {
  display: flex;
  flex-direction: row;
  flex-wrap: wrap;
  width: 100%;
  gap: 5px;
}
```

We can see that the amount of CSS has grown from 11 lines necessary for the arrangement to a total of 16 lines. We needed to add explicit `box-sizing` to the `tag` class and calculate a maximum width that takes the gap into account to arrive at a four-column layout.

More complex layouts require additional DOM as well. We will further discuss the differences with Flexbox in *Chapter 5, Implementing Layouts with Flexbox and CSS Grid*. There's an alternative to the extra-container-and-flexbox method. CSS Grid offers four properties: `align-items`, `justify-items`, `align-self`, and `justify-self`. Those seem familiar: Flexbox uses similar ones as well.

Unlike the Flexbox versions, the `align-*` and `justify-*` properties used in CSS Grid are not dependent on any main axis. Instead, they always align with the same axis:

- The `align-*` properties align along the column axis, so the *Y* axis on the screen in the standard writing mode
- The `justify-*` properties align along the row axis, meaning the *X* axis on the screen in standard writing mode

We can either align and justify all items within a grid with the `*-items` properties defined on the grid container or align and justify individual grid items with the `*-self` properties defined on the items themselves.

A note on readability

We mean both variants when talking about `justify-*` and `align-*`. So, `justify-*` stands for `justify-items` and `justify-self`, whereas `align-*` stands for `align-items` and `align-self`.

The same applies to `*-items` and `*-self`, meaning both variants. So, `*-items` stands for `justify-items` and `align-items`, whereas `*-self` stands for `justify-self` and `align-self`.

Using the align properties

The `align-*` properties can take one of five different values:

- `stretch` stretches the grid item to fill the entire grid cell and is the default value.
- `start` aligns the grid items with the start of the grid cell on the column axis, meaning the top of the grid cell.
- `end` aligns the grid items with the end of the grid cell on the column axis, meaning the bottom of the grid cell.
- `center` aligns the items with the center of the grid cell on the column axis and ensures equal space from the item to the start and end of the grid cells.

- `baseline` aligns the grid items along the text baseline of the entire row. This value is especially useful for differently sized text that should all be on the same line.

Let's try. By adding `align-items: center;` to the `.tag-container` class, CSS Grid aligns all elements to the center of their row.

The following figure shows the result:

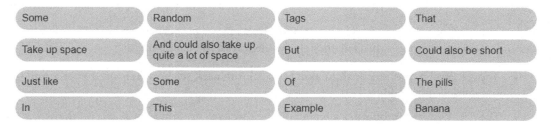

Figure 3.3 – The pill layout with its items being centered

In the second row, we can see the effect: although the **And could also take up quite a lot of space** item enlarges the row, the other items keep the same height and are centered in their row.

Similar effects with different placements can be observed when using `start` or `end`. However, `baseline` behaves differently.

The following figure explains what is meant by the **text baseline**.

Figure 3.4 – The baseline and several other keywords related to text sizing explained

The baseline is marked in red. It defines where all characters, except those with a descender, are aligned. This line is used to align all the text when using `align-items: baseline;` or `align-self: baseline;`.

Let's try this as well. To illustrate, we assign some top and bottom padding to some pills to ensure we can observe the effect of `align-items: baseline;`. `;`. The result is illustrated in the following figure:

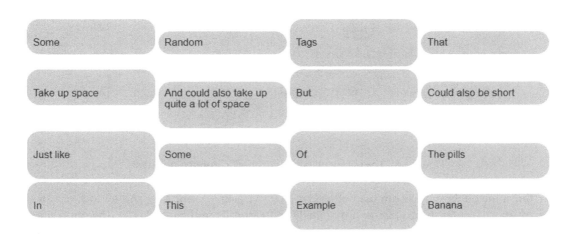

Figure 3.5 – Aligning items to the text baseline

We can see how the items are adjusted to a common baseline per row in the second to last row. The baseline value also offers two modifiers: `first baseline` and `last baseline`. These two modifiers use the first or the last baseline in the case of multi-line text.

> **A note on browser compatibility**
>
> As of 2023, the `last baseline` modifier has only limited browser support. While fully supported by all browsers for the `align-self` and `align-items` properties, support for `align-content` is limited.

Using the justify properties

The `justify-*` properties align grid items on the row axis. They take one of four different values:

- `stretch` stretches the item to fill the entire width of the grid cell and is the default value
- `start` aligns the item with the start of the grid cell, meaning its left side (LTR)
- `end` aligns the item with the end of the grid cell, meaning its right side (LTR)
- `center` aligns the item with the center of the grid cell, ensuring equal spacing on the left and right side

To practice, we add `justify-items: center;` to the container. The following figure shows the effect:

Figure 3.6 – The pill layout with horizontally centered grid items

To finish the pill layout, we can use both `justify-items: center;` and `align-items: center;` to center the grid items horizontally and vertically in their grid cells. The result can be observed in the following figure:

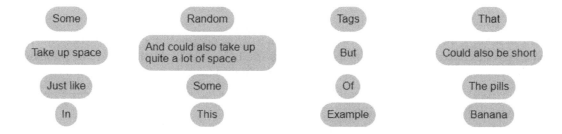

Figure 3.7 – The pill layout centered vertically and horizontally using the justify and align properties

When we take the **And could also take up quite pace** item as a reference, we can observe that the items on the same row and same column are centered.

Using shortcuts

To shorten the code, we can use `place-items` as a shortcut for `align-items` and `justify-items`, as well as `place-self` as a shortcut for `align-self` and `justify-self`. These shortcuts work by either specifying the same value for both `align-*` and `justify-*` or assigning them specific values, separated by a space. For example, if we wanted to use a single property for the finished, all-centered pill layout, we use `place-items: center;` instead of `justify-items: center;` and `align-items: center;`.

However, different values mean we need to specify them individually, as the following code snippet shows:

```
.tag-container {
    align-items: baseline;
    justify-items: start;
}
```

```
/* is equivalent to */

.tag-container {
  place-items: baseline start;
}
```

The `place-*` shortcuts always take the value of `align-items` first, then the value of `justify-items`.

Aligning and justifying the entire grid within its container

Sometimes, our grid is smaller than our container. Think of a grid layout for an entire page on an ultra-wide screen with a screen ratio of 21:9. These screens usually have a resolution of a whopping `3440px` in width and `1440px` in height. They are arguably not very common, and that is the exact reason most websites are not optimized for them.

On such an ultra-wide screen, a 12-column grid with a gap of `30px` would result in columns roughly `260px` wide. Too wide for most content. At some point in time, grid systems started to emerge, one being `960px` in total width with 12 columns and a gap of `20px`, making each column `60px` wide. These grid systems allowed UX experts and developers to speak a common language and simplified development with a large palette of ready-to-use code templates. Even frameworks started implementing them.

In 2020 or 2021, the trend shifted to grids with a total width of around `1200px` (still only a third of an ultra-wide screen, mind you) and `30px` gaps. Even with the perhaps most used screen resolution on a desktop of a `1920px` width, `1200px` is still only roughly 60% of the available width.

We notice that, on larger screens, we usually don't need the entire screen width for content. This has good reasons: first, most content wouldn't fit. For example, an image or video with a ratio of 16:9 spread over a `1920px` width would be full-screen. Other ratios, such as 4:3 or 1:1, would overflow the viewport, making it impossible to see the entire image or video simultaneously.

The second reason is text width: from books, newspapers, and smartphones, users are used to reading short lines of text. The Baymard Institute, an independent web UX research institute, has studied the optimal line length and concluded it to be between 50 and 75 characters. We can read about its findings in this article: `https://baymard.com/blog/line-length-readability`.

Additionally, Schneps et al. have shown in their 2013 paper that people with dyslexia show improved reading speeds on smaller devices with no cost to comprehension. We can read their excellent paper on the website of the US National Library of Medicine's National Center for Biotechnological Information: `https://www.ncbi.nlm.nih.gov/pmc/articles/PMC3734020/`.

Spanning a paragraph over 1920px, or, even worse, 3440px, would cause frustration and even look visually broken. The third reason is page navigation. The larger the distance between objects, the more I have to move my mouse cursor, and the less connected individual components feel.

Most CSS frameworks offer a container class with a maximum width of the used grid system that positions its content as horizontally centered. Often, these work with either Flexbox or the ol' reliable margin: 0 auto; for centering to avoid having extra containers.

However, with CSS Grid, there's no need for extra containers or margin tricks to achieve a centered layout that does not span the entire screen width.

To illustrate, let's have a look at the following HTML:

```html
<!-- File: chapter3/03_placing_grid_content.html -->
<!DOCTYPE html>
<html>
  <head></head>
  <body>
    <div class="container">
      <header class="header">
        <!-- Header + navigation -->
      </header>
      <aside class="sidebar">
        <!-- Sidebar -->
      </aside>
      <main class="main">
        <!-- Content -->
      </main>
      <footer class="footer">
        <!-- Footer -->
      </footer>
    </div>
  </body>
</html>
```

It's a standard page layout: a container element with a header, a sidebar, and a footer. We apply the following CSS code to the HTML:

```css
* { box-sizing: border-box; }

body, html {
  min-height: 100vh;
  padding: 0;
  margin: 0;
}
.container {
```

```
    border: 10px solid #333;

    min-height: 100vh;
    display: grid;
    grid-template:
      "header header" 100px
      "sidebar content" 1fr
      "footer footer" 100px
      / 200px 1fr
    ;
}
header {
    border: 2px solid #dd0808; /* Dark red */
    background-color: #ff6666; /* Light red */
    grid-area: header;
}
aside {
    border: 2px solid #0ba7c6; /* Dark cyan */
    background-color: #74ddf2; /* Light cyan */
    grid-area: sidebar;
}
main {
    border: 2px solid #6f09e5; /* Dark purple */
    background-color: #b880f7; /* Light purple */
    grid-area: content;
}
footer {
    border: 2px solid #c4be0d; /* Dark yellow */
    background-color: #f7f380; /* Light yellow */
    grid-area: footer;
}
```

This sets up a standard page layout that spans the entire width and height of the browser and gives the elements some color (namely red for the header, cyan for the sidebar, purple for the content, and yellow for the footer), so we can distinguish the elements.

We also added a thick border to the container to see where it is. It also aligns all elements within the grid. We get the following result on a 1,920 x 1,080 display:

Figure 3.8 – A page layout spanning the entire screen width

We see that the sidebar in cyan, which takes up 200px of space, is relatively narrow compared to the content element in purple. The sidebar feels lost and is almost out of sight on large displays.

Ideally, the content column wouldn't take up 1fr of space but a value of 1000px. The following figure illustrates what the size change would look like:

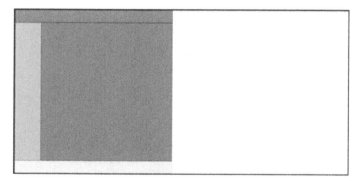

Figure 3.9 – The layout with a fixed-size content column

We see a significant portion of whitespace on the right of the layout. The dark border around the entire figure shows us that our grid content only occupies about half of the available space. However, the content sticks to the left side of the screen.

Depending on the design we might implement, this isn't always the desired outcome. However, CSS Grid offers us two properties to align and justify the content of a grid: align-content and justify-content.

They function similarly to align-items and justify-items, as they use the same axis (align-content aligns along the column axis, and justify-content works along the row axis) and have similar values. However, they align and justify the entire grid instead of items within it.

Justifying grid content on the row axis

Let's have a look at `justify-content` first. This property takes one of seven different values:

- `start` is the default value and justifies the grid content to the start of the container, meaning the left side.

- `end` justifies the grid content to the end of the container, meaning the right side.

- `center` centers the entire grid in its container.

- `stretch` stretches the grid content to fit the container if no explicit values are given.

- `space-around` adds an even amount of space between grid columns and half of the same space around them, much like Flexbox's `justify-content: space-around;`.

- `space-between` adds an even amount of space between grid columns but no space around them.

- `space-evenly` adds the same amount of space between all grid columns and around them.

Let's experiment a bit with these values. Let's assume we'd like to center the content first to adjust it further. We add the following code to the grid container definition of `.container`:

```
.container {
  display: grid;
  /* ... */
  justify-content: center;
}
```

When we reload the page on the same screen size, we see the grid now arranged in the center, as illustrated by the following figure:

Figure 3.10 – The grid layout, centered

We notice that the space around the grid is now even on both sides and that the size of the colored grid cells hasn't changed. However, we might feel that the grid feels a little lost in the center and that the sidebar feels cramped with the content. Therefore, we now replace `center` with `space-around` and have another look at the result, shown in the following figure:

Figure 3.11 – The grid layout, its columns being aligned on the column axis with space around

We see that there is now a significant portion of whitespace between the sidebar in cyan and the content in purple. We also see that the header and footer still span the entire grid content width. The next value we'd like to try is `space-between`. The result is shown in the following figure:

Figure 3.12 – The grid layout, its columns aligned on the column axis with space between

We can see that the grid content now spans the entire grid container again. The red header bar spans from the far-left side to the far-right side. However, the columns haven't changed in size and are now separated by a lot of whitespace.

The last value we'd like to try is space-evenly. The result is shown in the following figure:

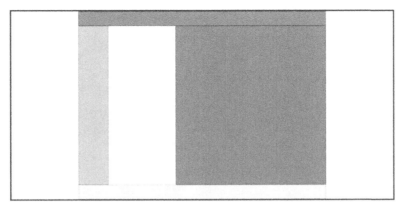

Figure 3.13 – The grid content is spaced evenly

We now see that the whitespace between the columns is the same size as the whitespace to the left and right of the grid.

Aligning content along the column axis

To align and justify items on the vertical axis, meaning the column axis in standard writing mode, we use align-content. It takes the exact same values, namely start, end, center, stretch, space-around, space-between, and space-evenly, and works the same as justify-items, only in the vertical direction.

The align-content property is handy for small pages or sections of pages that don't use the entire available height.

Let's have a look at our original grid container definition again:

```
.container {
  border: 10px solid #333;

  min-height: 100vh;
  display: grid;
  grid-template:
    "header header" 100px
    "sidebar content" 1fr
    "footer footer" 100px
    / 200px 1fr
  ;
}
```

We see that the second row, containing the sidebar and the content, takes up `1fr` of space, meaning the grid container takes up all available space. So let's set it to an explicit height of `600px` and look at the result:

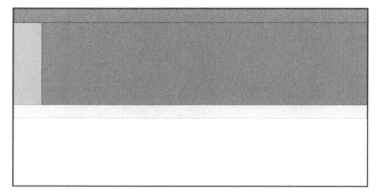

Figure 3.14 – The grid layout, reduced in height

We see that the grid content has a reduced height, and the rest of the grid is filled with whitespace. In addition, we see that the grid content is sticking to the top of the grid container, indicating the default value of `align-content` being `start`.

When we add `align-content: center;` to the grid definition, the grid content will be centered vertically, as shown in the following figure:

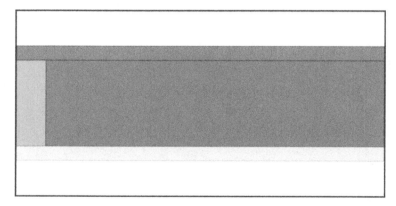

Figure 3.15 – The vertically centered grid content

We see an equal amount of whitespace at the top and bottom of the grid.

Using shortcuts

There is also a shortcut for align-content and justify-content called place-content. This property works similarly to the place-items shortcut: it takes values for both align-content and justify-content. It can define a single value for both properties or distinct values for each property, separated by a space.

Let's assume the following grid container definition:

```
.container {
  border: 10px solid #333;

  min-height: 100vh;
  display: grid;
  grid-template:
    "header header" 100px
    "sidebar content" 1000px
    "footer footer" 100px
    / 200px 1fr
  ;
  align-content: center;
  justify-content: space-between;
}
```

We can shorten the usage of align-content and justify-content, as shown in the following code snippet:

```
.container {
  border: 10px solid #333;

  min-height: 100vh;
  display: grid;
  grid-template:
    "header header" 100px
    "sidebar content" 1000px
    "footer footer" 100px
    / 200px 1fr
  ;
  place-content: center space-between;
}
```

A single value in place-content, such as center, would set both align-content and justify-content to center.

We have now learned how to precisely steer the arrangement of grid items within grid cells and the entire grid container. With these techniques, we use less HTML, don't have to use Flexbox to center things, and can add more complexity to our layouts.

Defining and using advanced grid templates

So far, we've looked at explicitly named grid areas defined with `grid-template-areas`. We looked at how we can define header bars that span multiple columns, arrange items automatically or explicitly in these areas, and learned how to leverage grid areas to create standard layouts.

However, there's more to grid areas. We can define cells that will always be empty, name grid areas by their grid lines, or even arrange nested child elements in parent grids using grid areas. First, we'll look at always-empty grid cells.

Defining empty cells in grid area templates

Sometimes, we want grid cells always to stay empty. This is the case for layouts that use the entire width of the grid container for header and footer bars but not for the main content area.

Let's look at the following HTML code:

```
<div class="container">
  <header class="header">
    <!-- Header + navigation -->
  </header>
  <main class="main">
    <!-- Content -->
  </main>
  <footer class="footer">
    <!-- Footer -->
  </footer>
</div>
```

To place all the items in the grid, we use the following CSS:

```
.container {
  border: 10px solid #333;

  min-height: 100vh;
  display: grid;

  grid-template:
    "header" 100px
    "content" 1fr
    "footer" 100px
```

```
      / 1fr
    ;
}

header {
    border: 2px solid #dd0808; /* Dark red */
    background-color: #ff6666; /* Light red */
    grid-area: header;
}
main {
    border: 2px solid #6f09e5; /* Dark purple */
    background-color: #b880f7; /* Light purple */
    grid-area: content;
    max-width: 1000px;
}
footer {
    border: 2px solid #c4be0d; /* Dark yellow */
    background-color: #f7f380; /* Light yellow */
    grid-area: footer;
}
```

We see that the header, content, and footer elements are all in a single column that spans the entire grid. We do want the header and footer to span the entire width, but the main content should only be 1000px wide and be centered. Using place-content for this endeavor would be difficult, if not impossible, since we can only adjust the size of entire columns, not single cells.

However, we can add two more columns. The header and footer should span all three, and the content should only occupy the center. The two adjacent grid cells on the horizontal axis should always stay empty. To achieve empty grid cells, we use the dot character (.) as the grid area's name, as illustrated in the following CSS code:

```
.container {
    border: 10px solid #333;

    min-height: 100vh;
    display: grid;

    grid-template:
        "header header header" 100px
        ". content ." 1fr
        "footer footer footer" 100px
        / 1fr 1000px 1fr
    ;
}
```

Since the grid areas specified for the header, main, and footer haven't changed, these grid cells will stay empty. Also, browsers refuse to use the dot character when assigning grid areas with `grid-area`, making it impossible to occupy the cells on purpose.

The result of this code is shown in the following figure:

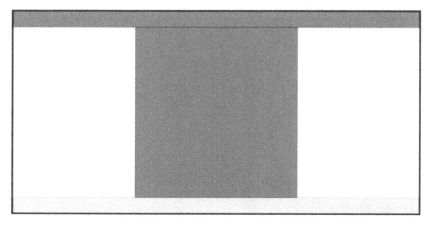

Figure 3.16 – A centered main element with a full-width header above and a footer below

We can see that there is whitespace around the purple main element and that it is centered, the exact result we wanted to achieve.

However, there are limitations to the dot notation. When auto-arranging grid items, CSS Grid does not automatically respect grid areas and their naming. We saw in *Chapter 1* that elements occupy only the single next free grid cell within the grid's flow if no grid area is specified.

Even if the grid area they would fall in spans multiple grid cells, only a single cell is occupied. This is also true if they're meant to be empty and use the dot notation as their name! The dot notation only keeps us, developers, from putting things there.

A note on using the same name for multiple grid areas

Technically, the following grid area definition creates two different grid areas that are named the same:

```
grid-template:
  "header header header" 100px
  ". content ." 1fr
  "footer footer footer" 100px
  / 1fr 1000px 1fr
;
```

Usually, grid areas with the same name need to be connected; otherwise, browsers would deem the grid template invalid and simply ignore it. For example, the following grid template is an illegal one because it uses two grid areas with the same name:

```
grid-template:
  "navigation" 1fr
  "content" 1fr
  "navigation" 1fr
  / 1fr
;
```

However, we can create as many grid areas named . as we'd like since they're meant to be empty and cannot be used.

Naming grid areas implicitly

Apart from using grid templates, there is another way we can implicitly name grid areas. We can also assign names to grid areas using named rows and columns. To recap what we learned in *Chapter 1, Understanding the Basic Rules and Structures for CSS Grid*, we can assign names to grid lines using the following syntax:

```
grid-template-columns: [sidebar-start] 1fr
  [sidebar-end content-start] 3fr [content-end];
```

In this example, we assigned the name `sidebar-start` to the first grid line, the names `sidebar-end` and `content-start` to the center grid line, and `content-end` to the rightmost grid line. We can do the same for rows:

```
Grid-template-rows: [header-start] 100px
  [header-end content-start] 1fr [content-end];
```

As we can see in these two definitions, we've assigned a horizontal and a vertical grid line with content-start and a horizontal and a vertical grid line with content-end. The intersection points of these grid lines create a grid area named content.

We can see what exactly happened in the following illustration:

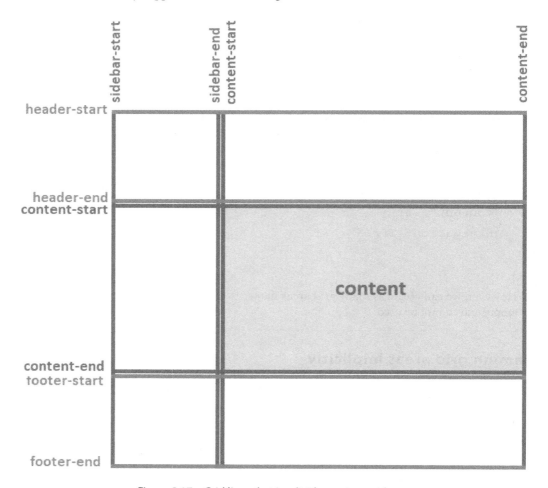

Figure 3.17 – Grid lines that implicitly create a grid area

We can see that the content-* grid lines enclose a rectangle in the second row and second column. Since the grid lines start with content, the grid area is named as such.

Since we can assign as many names to grid lines as we'd like, we can use these to encase all kinds of grid areas. This behavior also works the opposite way: explicitly named grid areas implicitly create grid lines with *-start and *-end variants.

Let's assume we want to rebuild the following grid template with named grid lines:

```
.container {
  display: grid;
  grid-template:
    "header header" 100px
    "sidebar content" 1fr
    "footer footer" 100px
  / 300px 1fr;
}
```

We've got a top row that spans two columns named header, a single cell named sidebar, a single cell named content, and a row that spans two columns named footer.

We, therefore, need two columns and three rows. We can start by assigning names to all grid lines encapsulating the header:

```
.container {
  display: grid;
  grid-template-columns: [header-start] 300px 1fr
    [header-end];
  grid-template-rows: [header-start] 100px [header-end]
    1fr 100px;
}
```

We then add the sidebar the same way:

```
.container {
  display: grid;
  grid-template-columns: [header-start sidebar-start]
    300px [sidebar-end] 1fr [header-end];
  grid-template-rows: [header-start] 100px
    [header-end sidebar-start] 1fr [sidebar-end] 100px;
}
```

Next, we add the content area:

```
.container {
  display: grid;
  grid-template-columns: [header-start sidebar-start] 300px
  [sidebar-end content-start] 1fr [header-end content-end];
  grid-template-rows: [header-start] 100px [header-end
    sidebar-start content-start] 1fr
      [sidebar-end content-end] 100px;
}
```

This code is starting to become less and less readable. The last thing missing is the footer. So we add it the same way:

```
.container {
  display: grid;
  grid-template-columns: [header-start sidebar-start
    footer-start] 300px [sidebar-end content-start] 1fr
      [header-end content-end footer-end];
  grid-template-rows: [header-start] 100px [header-end
    sidebar-start content-start] 1fr [sidebar-end
      content-end footer-start] 100px [footer-end];
}
```

We see that the grid lines have up to three names. Every area is encapsulated with its respective grid lines and implicitly creates the grid area.

We've already noticed that the code for these grid area definitions is becoming less and less readable the more grid areas we add. The `grid-template` property should therefore be favored since it is much more readable.

However, if we generate grids via code, say, from a **Content Management System (CMS)** or based on user-generated content, creating a grid template with the `grid-template` syntax is much more challenging. For example, suppose we offer the user a grid they can place elements in.

By placing an element, we only need to know its starting and ending grid rows and assign a name. Implicitly named grid lines simplify the automatic creation of grid areas while keeping the advantages of naming, which significantly helps to debug in cases of misarranged grid items, and changes to existing layouts, as well as easing onboarding new developers to the project.

Practicing creating flexible layouts with JavaScript

Let's create a flexible grid area structure with JavaScript. We can place this JS code wherever we'd like in our app. Let's assume the following HTML structure:

```
<!—File: chapter3/05_flexible_grid.html →
<div cla"s="flexible-g"id">
  <div
    cla"s="flexible-grid-i"em"
    data-na"e="fi"st"
    data-row-sta"t""1"
    data-row-wid"h""1"
    data-col-sta"t""1"
    data-col-wid"h""2"
  >
    First element
  </div>
```

```
<div
  cla"s"="flexible-grid-i"em"
  data-na"e"="sec"nd"
  data-row-sta"t""2"
  data-row-wid"h""1"
  data-col-sta"t""2"
  data-col-wid"h""1"
>
  Second element
</div>
<div
  cla"s"="flexible-grid-i"em"
  data-na"e"="th"rd"
  data-row-sta"t""1"
  data-row-wid"h""1"
  data-col-sta"t""3"
  data-col-wid"h""1"
>
  Third element
</div>
</div>
```

We see a grid container with three elements. Each of the three elements has several `data-*` attributes, denoting the element's name, which row and column it starts in, and how large it is. We'll use these data attributes to generate a grid with JavaScript automatically. If you're not familiar with JavaScript, don't worry. We'll keep it at a minimum.

First, we need to get the grid and all its elements. We also create two empty arrays for row grid lines and column grid lines:

```
const grid = document.querySelect'r('.flexible-g'id')
const gridElements = Array.from(grid.querySelectorAll
  ('.flexible-grid-item'))

let rowGridLines = []
let columnGridLines = []
```

Next, we loop over all the grid items and extract their names, grid row start, grid row end, grid column start, and grid column end:

```
for (const element of gridElements) {
  const name = element.dataset.name

  const rowStart = parseInt(element.dataset.rowStart) - 1
  const rowEnd = parseInt(element.dataset.rowWidth) +
    rowStart
```

```
const colStart = parseInt(element.dataset.colStart) - 1
const colEnd = parseInt(element.dataset.colWidth) +
  colStart

/* More code here... */
}
```

We subtract 1 from the rowStart and colStart variables to make them zero-indexed. We then check that we don't already have any elements at their respective grid lines and assign empty arrays to fill them later.

With this approach, each unused grid line has a value of undefined, and each used grid line has an array of its names as its value:

```
for (const element of gridElements) {

  /* rowStart, rowEnd, etc. */

  if (!rowGridLines[rowStart]) {
    rowGridLines[rowStart] = []
  }

  if (!rowGridLines[rowEnd]) {
    rowGridLines[rowEnd] = []
  }

  if (!columnGridLines[colStart]) {
    columnGridLines[colStart] = []
  }

  if (!columnGridLines[colEnd]) {
    columnGridLines[colEnd] = []
  }

  /* More code here... */
}
```

We then add the grid line names to their respective positions in these arrays and assign the grid area to the grid element:

```
for (const element of gridElements) {

  /* All previous loop code */

  rowGridLines[rowStart].push(name + '-start')
```

```
    rowGridLines[rowEnd].push(name  + '-end')

    columnGridLines[colStart].push(name  + '-start')
    columnGridLines[colEnd].push(name  + '-end')

    element.style.gridArea = name
}
```

We then create the grid row and grid column templates by concatenating the grid line names with spaces, surrounding them with square brackets, and adding a value of 1fr for each grid row and column:

```
const rowTemplate = rowGridLines.map(r => {
  if (r) {
    return '[' + r.join(' ') + ']'
  }

  return ''
}).join(' 1fr ')

const columnTemplate = columnGridLines.map(r => {
  if (r) {
    return '[' + r.join(' ') + ']'
  }

  return ''
}).join(' 1fr ')

grid.style.gridTemplateColumns = rowTemplate
grid.style.gridTemplateRows = columnTemplate
```

This code automatically creates grid rows and columns and aligns the elements accordingly.

With this JavaScript code, we could create React, Vue, or Svelte (or any other framework, really) components that automatically create grids for us, depending on their child components. This approach gives us much flexibility, and we can adjust the grids on the fly with JS.

Arranging nested child elements in parent grids

We all know the struggle: sometimes, designs can't be sensibly implemented with semantic HTML – for example, on a news site. We might have a grid layout with four columns and an infinite number of rows.

For example, the first five articles might always be the recently published ones, followed by the most read articles. We could divide these article groups into sections to add labels for screen readers and semantically separate the two categories.

One solution would be to add a grid to every section. However, this would result in a gap of three empty grid cells in the first section. CSS Grid offers a solution to this: `display: contents;`. It tells the browser to ignore this element and use its children as grid elements instead.

Let's consider the following HTML structure:

```html
<div class=»container»>
  <section class=»recent-articles»>
    <article></article>
    <article></article>
    <article></article>
    <article></article>
    <article></article>
  </section>
  <section class="most-read-articles">
    <article></article>
    <article></article>
    <article></article>
    <article></article>
    <article></article>
    <article></article>
    <article></article>
    <article></article>
    <article></article>
    <article></article>
    <article></article>
  </section>
</div>
```

It corresponds with the example we've discussed: we've got a section with the 5 most recent articles and a second section with 11 more articles that are the most read. Let's apply the following CSS:

```css
.container {
  display: grid;
  grid-template-columns: 1fr 1fr 1fr 1fr;
  width: 100%;
  grid-auto-rows: 200px;
  gap: 24px;
  box-sizing: border-box;
  min-height: 100vh;
  border: 10px solid #333; /* Border to indicate
    grid boundaries */
}

.recent-articles article {
  border: 2px solid #c4be0d; /* Dark yellow */
```

```
  background-color: #f7f380; /* Light yellow */
}

.most-read-articles article {
  border: 2px solid #0ba7c6; /* Dark cyan */
  background-color: #74ddf2; /* Light cyan */
}
```

We've added some color to the articles and defined a four-column grid with automatically created rows that are 200px tall. This structure would now try to align the sections within the grid, resulting in what we see in the following illustration:

Figure 3.18 – A failed attempt to arrange semantic HTML in a grid

We see a yellow and a cyan bar in the top-left corner of our grid, indicating the zero-height article elements of this color. This is not what we'd like. Ideally, the article elements themselves would be aligned in the grid. We can achieve this by applying the following CSS code:

```
section {
  display: contents;
}
```

This results in the following grid structure:

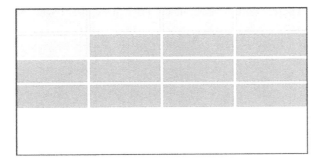

Figure 3.19 – The article grid working as intended

We see that the first 5 articles in yellow occupy the first row and parts of the second row, followed immediately by 11 cyan articles, without any empty grid cell in between. Exactly what we wanted.

> **A note on the browser compatibility of display contents**
>
> As of 2022, `display: contents;` is supported in all major browsers. However, there are some limitations. In most browsers (namely Opera, Firefox, Chrome, Edge, and any Chromium-based browsers), buttons lose their accessibility when `display: contents;` is applied to them. In Safari, buttons work, but it is tables that become inaccessible.

With this knowledge, we can create any grid structure we'd like. We can even go as far as dynamically creating grids and keeping them debugging-friendly.

Creating subgrids

Subgrids are a feature similar to `display: contents;`. They allow us to arrange child elements in a parent grid. However, the approach of the `subgrid` feature is different; an element with a subgrid has its own grid that inherits grid lines from its parent grid. We can use a subgrid either for rows, columns, or both.

To apply a subgrid to a child element, we apply `display: grid;` to it and use `subgrid` as a value for either `grid-template-columns`, `grid-template-rows`, or both.

> **How to practice**
>
> For this section, we need to have either the latest versions of Firefox or Safari because, as of 2023, no Chromium-based browser supports subgrids.

Understanding how subgrids work

At the beginning of this section, we mentioned that a subgrid creates a grid on a child element that inherits grid lines from a parent grid. To illustrate what this means, let's have a look at the following figure:

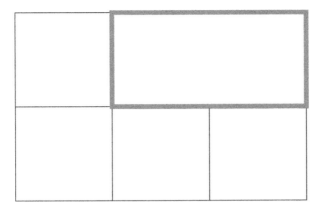

Figure 3.20 – A three-by-two grid with a grid item spanning the rightmost two cells of the first row

We can see a three-by-two grid with a single grid item that spans two grid cells on the first row. We indicated this with a red border. All grid lines of the grid are marked in black.

The grid item we see currently works as an independent container. If we were to mark it as a grid by using `display: grid`, we could define the grid however we'd like without any connection to the parent grid. However, the third vertical grid line from the left would theoretically go right through the middle of the element.

By applying `grid-template-columns: subgrid;` to the grid item (assuming it already has `display: grid;` applied to it), we would make the vertical grid lines available to this grid item, resulting in what we can see in the following figure:

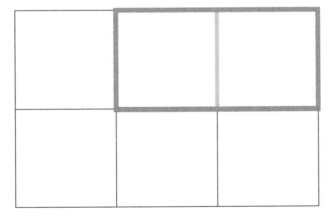

Figure 3.21 – The previous grid, with the inherited grid line visible

Since the grid item inherits the grid lines from the parent, it now has two columns. We can use these columns as if they were defined by the grid item's – well – subgrid.

The same behavior of the subgrid applies to rows and horizontal grid lines by applying `grid-template-rows: subgrid;` to the same container. In the previous example, the grid item only spans a single row and would not inherit anything. However, larger elements spanning multiple grid rows would inherit the horizontal gridlines, too.

Understanding what is inherited

As we know, a grid can consist of more than simple row and column definitions. There are also gaps and, if defined, names for grid areas and lines. When we apply a subgrid, these properties are inherited as well.

This means that all grid line names and implicitly defined grid areas are also available to the subgrid. However, this requires both rows and columns to be defined as subgrids.

Understanding subgrids' current state of development (as of 2023)

The `subgrid` feature is currently only supported in Firefox and Safari as of 2023. However, there is an open ticket on the Chromium bug tracker that should implement `subgrid` for Chromium and, therefore, all Chromium-based browsers, such as Google Chrome and Microsoft Edge. The bug has been open since 2016, so let's hope it'll be implemented soon.

Subgrids are a powerful tool that allows us to separate the grid structure even more from the HTML structure and keep layouts consistent when using nested grids. For example, we can now use an arbitrary container within the grid and overwrite its rows or columns while explicitly keeping the other. Other use cases include alignment in otherwise separated elements, such as tag lists, titles, or images on card elements.

Masonry layouts

Before the days of CSS Grid, masonry layouts were hard to achieve. The npm library `masonry-layout`, arguably very popular, still has around 200,000 weekly downloads according to the statistics on `https://www.npmjs.com/`, although it hasn't been updated since roughly 2018, as of 2022.

The library can arrange grid items in a masonry layout with a staggering 239 lines of code. It measures column widths, item widths, and a gutter, and applies a whole lot of CSS to achieve what is nowadays possible with CSS Grid.

A note on browser compatibility

As of early 2023, only Firefox offers masonry layouts behind a feature flag, so we won't be able to use it in production yet. Most of the masonry-related CSS attributes are in an experimental state.

We learn about this technology to be immediate experts once it's widely available.

Understanding what masonry layouts are

So, what exactly is a **masonry layout**? The name has nothing to do with building walls, although a masonry layout resembles brickwork. With differently sized elements stacked on top of each other, a brick wall-like structure emerges, which some design experts love and others detest.

Pinterest is one of the most popular sites that uses a masonry layout as of 2022. It arranges what it calls *ideas* (basically, one or more images with a title and some tags) in columns, and keeps images in their original ratio. These images lead to elements of all heights, but equal widths, as shown in the following illustration:

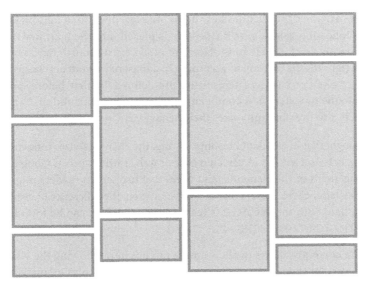

Figure 3.22 – An illustration of a masonry layout

One of the main features of the masonry layout is the equal-ish height distribution of elements. One could argue that 239 lines of JavaScript code could be replaced by simply dividing all elements into four groups and placing these next to each other, but that may not always work as intended.

To achieve a complete masonry layout, we want an equal height distribution. For that, the JS library we learned about in the beginning measures the height of all involved elements before rearranging them.

Using masonry layouts with CSS Grid and knowing about its pitfalls

We can use the experimental features of CSS Grid's masonry layout instead of using JS. To apply a masonry layout to either rows or columns, we can assign the masonry value to `grid-template-columns` or `grid-template-rows`. CSS Grid will then measure the sizes of all involved elements and align them accordingly.

Multiple related CSS attributes let us influence how CSS Grid arranges the elements:

- `align-tracks` can take one or more of the following values: `start`, `end`, `center`, `normal` (the same as `start`), `baseline`, `first baseline`, `last baseline`, `space-between`, `space-around`, `space-evenly`, or `stretch`. The `align-tracks` CSS property sets the alignment of all (when a single value is given) or individual grid tracks if a list is given. It works along the column axis.

- `justify-tracks` behaves the same way as `align-tracks`, only along the row axis.

- `masonry-auto-flow` defines how items are placed within a masonry layout. It can take one of the following values: `pack` (the item is placed into the masonry track with the most left-over space), `next` (the item is placed into the next masonry track, no matter the space), `ordered` (ignores the placement according to a masonry layout and keeps the HTML order), or `definite-first` (places items with a pre-defined slot first, before applying the masonry algorithm to the next items). A combination of `pack` or `next` and `definite-first` and `ordered` is also possible and mixes their behaviors.

Keep in mind, though, that in a default masonry setting, the elements' sizes influence their placement, which, in turn, impacts accessibility. A screen reader or web crawler, such as Googlebot, may not know about the rearrangement of the elements, and users that use screen readers might have an entirely different browser experience from users that don't. Worse even, the difference in visual order and logical order is not compliant with the WCAG 2.0 Technique C27, which can be found here: `https://www.w3.org/TR/WCAG20-TECHS/C27.html`.

However, there are currently efforts to allow authors to opt into following the visual rather than the logical order. The current state of the discussion is documented in this GitHub issue in the `csswg-drafts` respository of the W3C: `https://github.com/w3c/csswg-drafts/issues/7387`.

With this experimental knowledge, we are prepared for the release of CSS Grid's masonry layout for all major browsers. We can then eliminate any JS library and use CSS instead.

Practicing with Awesome Analytics

Now that we've learned about the advanced concepts of CSS Grid and how to create and steer advanced CSS Grid layouts, it's time to practice.

Receiving the task

After the first round of adding layouts to Awesome Analytics, the stakeholders were amazed. However, they asked for several improvements to the grid dashboard, the overall layout, and some visual adjustments.

They feel parts of the current design are old-fashioned and would like to improve a few things. First, they want to eliminate any gaps, as they feel that the chart boxes offer enough whitespace. Second, the gray background should be gone.

The design experts also feel that the app is missing a vertical rhythm. Ideally, all components (namely the header, all navigation points, and charts) should be aligned in rows of 40px with no gap. A standard chart box should be 10 rows tall and span 1 column, whereas tall chart boxes should span 20 rows. Wide chart boxes should span two columns.

Also, the management decided to ditch Chrome and only offer Firefox and Safari support. We pull the changes from our Git server and reload. What we see is this:

Figure 3.23 – Awesome Analytics without a grid layout

The development team tells you that they've already removed all the previous grid code and made the necessary adjustments to paddings, margins, and borders, so we only need to care of the grid layout.

Implementing a possible solution

We can find the starting code base for this exercise on GitHub: `https://github.com/PacktPublishing/Mastering-CSS-Grid/tree/main/chapter3`.

To get started, we download a copy via Git or the browser and follow the instructions in *Chapter 2, Project Introduction: What We'll Work on and First Tasks*, in the *Setting up Awesome Analytics locally* section. When we inspect the code, we see that not much has changed. Some of the original CSS code of margins and spacing has changed, but overall, it's the same.

We now need to apply a grid layout to the app. To practice, we'll use subgrids, as the requested support for Firefox and Safari only allows us to do just that. We begin by applying a grid to the body. Since we'll have a ton of rows, we use grid lines to create a header area implicitly.

Then, with two additional names for the content, we tell CSS Grid not to overlap the content with the sidebar. Finally, we directly assign the page header to the grid area `header`:

```
body {
  display: grid;
  grid-template-columns: [header-start] auto [content-
    start] 1fr 1fr 1fr 1fr [content-end header-end];
  grid-template-rows: [header-start] 40px 40px
    [header-end];
  grid-auto-rows: 40px;
}

.page-header {
  grid-area: header;
}
```

Next, we take care of the sidebar and the content. Since CSS Grid will determine the subgrid based on the parent grid, the elements need to have an explicit row count. CSS Grid does not create new grid tracks but inherits the ones defined on the parent grid. If the element with the subgrid does not define its row or column count, CSS Grid assumes one row worth of height and one column worth of width. It then places all elements in the available space, essentially overlapping them.

We, therefore, need to count rows. When we count all rows occupied by the chart boxes, we arrive at a total of 80 rows (2 tall and 4 short chart boxes mean *2 * 20 + 4 * 10 = 80* rows). So, for the sidebar to span the entire height, we tell it to span 80 rows.

Since the sidebar's links are deeply nested, first, mark the sidebar itself as a subgrid and use `display: contents;` on both the `nav` element and every `ul` element; make the `li` elements behave like the sidebar's grid items. The sidebar should span the entire 80 rows we counted earlier:

```
.sidebar {
  display: grid;
```

```
  grid-template-rows: subgrid;
  grid-row: span 80;
}

nav,
nav > ul {
  display: contents;
}
```

Now, we align the chart boxes. For that, we tell the element with the main-page-content class to align itself in the grid area called content and also span 80 rows. We then use subgrid as values for both grid-template-rows and grid-template-columns to use both the rows and columns of the parent grid:

```
.main-page-content {
  display: grid;
  grid-area: content;
  grid-row: span 80;
  grid-template-rows: subgrid;
  grid-template-columns: subgrid;
  grid-auto-flow: row dense;
}
```

Finally, we add sizing to the grid boxes by using grid-column and grid-row properties with their respective values:

```
.chart-box {
  grid-column: span 1;
  grid-row: span 10;
}

.chart-box-wide {
  grid-column: span 2;
}

.chart-box-tall {
  grid-row: span 20;
}
```

We reload and have a look at the result:

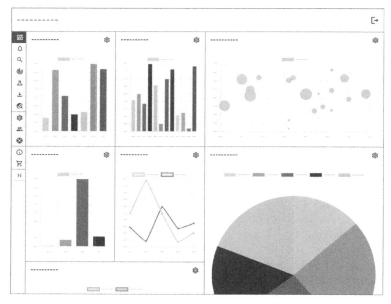

Figure 3.24 – Awesome Analytics with a new grid layout

We see that all grid items now align perfectly.

We've seen the utility of subgrid, especially in combination with `display: contents;`. We've now practiced implicit grid areas and have learned how to reduce the number of grids on our page.

Finally, we can also arrange the chart box titles by adding the following CSS code to `grid.css`:

```
.chart-box {
  display: grid;
  grid-template-rows: subgrid;
}

.chart-box header {
  grid-row: span 1;
  display: flex;
  align-items: center;
}

.chart-box .chart-container {
  grid-row: span 9;
}

.chart-box-tall .chart-container {
```

```
    grid-row: span 19;
}
```

Since standard chart boxes span 10 rows and tall ones span 20 rows, the inner `chart-container` elements have to span 9 and 19 rows. This additional change allows us to further the idea of the vertical rhythm. We can see the result in the following figure:

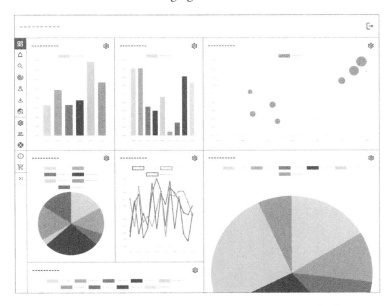

Figure 3.25 – Awesome Analytics with vertically aligned titles

We can see that the titles now occupy at max a single row within the parent grid. We may also change this to two rows if we think that two-line titles look too crowded.

Summary

We've now learned about advanced grid features, as well as experimental ones. We learned about the row axis and column axis, how to influence their direction and orientation, and how to align and justify grid items and the entire grid along them. We learned about implicitly defined grid areas and how to build grids dynamically, and we learned about subgrids, the content display mode, and masonry layouts. We've practiced most of these with Awesome Analytics.

This knowledge and practice already renders us advanced CSS Grid users and allows us to build almost any grid layout that design experts may come up with.

In the next chapter, we'll look at arguably one of the most essential topics of layouts on the web: how to define fully responsive grid layouts with the tools we already have and with the help of media queries. We'll also look into best practices when designing grids for multiple viewports and devices.

Part 2 – Understanding the CSS Grid Periphery

This part will give you a broader understanding of grids in general and CSS Grid in particular. You will learn how to build responsive grids, what responsiveness and fluidity mean in the context of layout building, and about potential pitfalls.

You will also learn about the differences and similarities between CSS Grid and Flexbox and that these two tools work best when mixed. Finally, you will learn about grid design and grid alternatives and receive a list of guidelines, allowing you to decide when to ditch grids entirely.

This part has the following chapters:

- *Chapter 4, Understanding and Creating Responsive and Fluid Grid Layouts*
- *Chapter 5, Implementing Layouts with Flexbox and CSS Grid*
- *Chapter 6, Benefits of Grid Layouts and When Not to Use Them*

4

Understanding and Creating Responsive and Fluid Grid Layouts

After learning about advanced grid structures and concepts and how to align individual elements, or even the entire grid content, the next concept to conquer is responsiveness. Since the invention of smartphones (and no, we do not mean the 1994 IBM Simon, which predates the first CSS release by a full 2 years!), more screen sizes have emerged.

I remember when specific versions of websites were developed for smartphones and even tablets once those started to become a thing. I remember some apps even having specific domains for their mobile versions. Nowadays, we use the same website for all devices and let CSS make the adjustments for us.

And let's also be thankful that the times of **Wireless Application Protocol** (**WAP**), used to transfer web content to cellphones such as the Nokia 6310 from 2001, are over…

In detail, this chapter covers the following topics:

- Understanding the challenges we could face when creating and designing layouts in general
- Understanding the difference between adaptive, responsive, and fluid layouts
- Learning responsive layout best practices
- Implementing responsive grid layouts in different ways with CSS Grid
- Practicing with our next task for AwesomeAnalytics

Technical requirements

For this chapter, we need the same setup as for *Chapter 2, Project Introduction: What We'll Work on and First Tasks*, as follows:

- A browser, preferably Chromium-based, such as Google Chrome, Brave, or Vivaldi, but Firefox or Apple Safari work, too

- An **integrated development environment** (**IDE**) or text editor, such as WebStorm, VS Code, or VIM, with HTML and CSS syntax highlighting

- Internet access is necessary to access the code

- Git (optional—we can also download the folder from GitHub)

- NodeJS with at least version 14 and npm with at least version 6

If Node is not currently installed on your system or you've got the wrong version, **Node Version Manager** (**nvm**) is a fantastic tool to handle different NodeJS versions on one system.

All the code for this chapter can be found on GitHub in this repository: `https://github.com/PacktPublishing/Mastering-CSS-Grid/tree/main/chapter4`.

Understanding the challenges of designing layouts

Let's switch our roles for a moment. So far, we've mainly looked at the implementation perspective of grids and layouts. Still, it is also helpful to understand the struggles and challenges design experts face when creating a design.

Let's imagine we're design experts and need to create a layout for a large website or app. What factors do we use when deciding on a layout approach?

Existing things

More often than not, design experts don't start entirely from scratch. Often, they receive existing guides for corporate identity/corporate design containing colors, typography definitions, stock images, logos, and spacings, or can get some inspiration from other products, such as native mobile apps, competitor websites, printed brochures, or even merchandise and giveaways.

Often, the company requesting a design has specific values that shape its work and culture. It might be an exciting art collective that wants to show and sell its modern art pieces, a care-taking facility wanting to convince clients about how calm, professional, and healing their institution is, or a tech company wanting to convince potential buyers of its engineering expertise.

A very exhaustive example of design guidelines is the guide created by the car brand Audi. We see parts of their responsive layout definitions in the following screenshot:

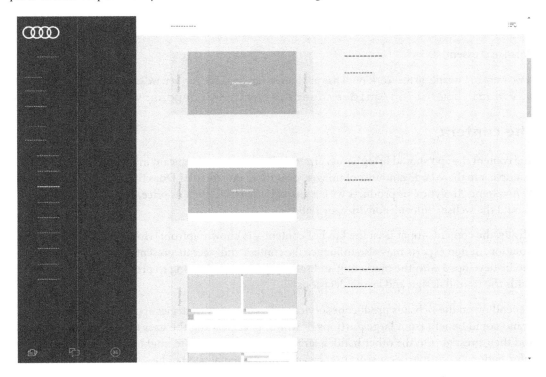

Figure 4.1 – Part of the responsive UI guidelines of the car brand Audi

We see different definitions: Audi defines a common language for parts of its layouts so that people working with them can communicate better.

These existing resources can offer either some guidance for making decisions about the layout or offer a ready-made solution. For example, if the new website should imitate the look and feel of the newly released native app, we can analyze the existing layout, adapt it where necessary, and scale it up for larger viewports.

The challenge here is to transport what is already there, be it values, CI/CD, or the spirit of existing products, in many different shapes without losing its mentality. For example, a large desktop screen might feel like a blank canvas to work with, but we must also not forget about the smaller viewports. What might feel relaxed and beautiful on large screens can feel crowded and overloaded on small ones.

Balance is essential.

If we want to investigate the work Audi has put into its design guide further, we can find it here: `https://www.audi.com/ci/en/guides/user-interface/responsive-ui.html`.

The content

The content the app should bring across arguably has the most significant influence on the layout. For example, are there large amounts of images, or is there mostly text? Does the app show graphs, such as Awesome Analytics, or products with a few key attributes, such as price, availability, and a name? Should the website inform, convince, or sell?

Ideally, the content—or at least the kind of content—is known upfront. However, depending on the situation, design experts may also influence the content and steer its presentation. A content strategy can be developed with the marketing and sales departments, leading to presentation principles that guide the overall design and layout decisions.

Depending on the website's product or service, different layout strategies apply. For example, a luxury brand could benefit from large portions of white space, leading the user to focus on the products and their prestige. On the other hand, a large grocery store website might want to convey as much information as possible because its users want a fundamental need to be solved.

Consider the example of the famous luxury brand Bottega Veneta in the following screenshot:

Figure 4.2 – A screenshot of a product detail page of Bottega Veneta's webshop

Here, we can see two main elements: the product image to the left, having a different background color, and a color selector for the product itself, paired with the product information. The rest of the page is empty—on purpose. More information would take away focus from the product image.

Another example is Walmart. Its product detail pages contain much more information, as shown in the following screenshot:

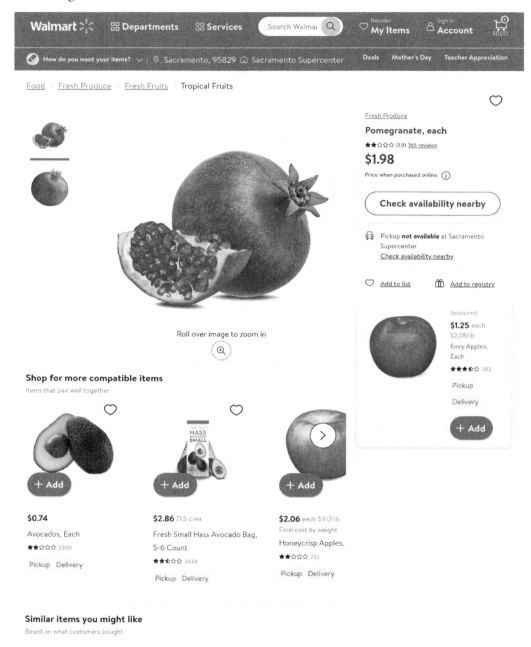

Figure 4.3 – A screenshot of a Walmart product detail page

When investigating the page from top to bottom and comparing it to Bottega Veneta, we notice that the header bar of the Walmart page contains much more information already. The product image takes up less space, and the product information is much more prominent. Similar items are listed above the fold, encouraging additional purchases.

In general, form and function go hand in hand.

The target groups

Of course, it is also helpful to know about the people who will use our app. For example, are they primarily smartphone users, or are they more likely to use the app in a work environment in front of a large screen? Will they use their keyboard to navigate or explore the content with gestures?

Consider smartphone users, for example. Most people use their devices on the go and perhaps can't or won't use their non-holding hand for navigating. For example, shopping-list apps should be usable with one hand because a bag of groceries likely occupies the other hand. The user also shouldn't need to switch their hands or change the device orientation in order to fulfill their needs.

Samantha Ingram has published an article in *Smashing Magazine*, teaching us about what they call the **Thumb Zone**. We can find this article here: `https://www.smashingmagazine.com/2016/09/the-thumb-zone-designing-for-mobile-users/`.

Essentially, there are areas on a smartphone that are easier to reach with a thumb than others. Depending on the user being left- or right-handed, these zones change. So, try for yourself: which areas on your smartphone are the hardest to reach when using it single-handed?

The zones for left-handed and right-handed users are roughly illustrated in the following screenshot:

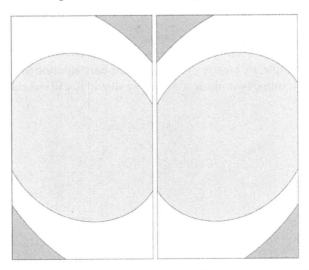

Figure 4.4 – An approximation of the screen areas reachable with a single hand on a smartphone

We can see that the area best reached is the center, marked in green. We best avoid placing content in the corners, marked in orange. The yellow zones aren't necessarily unreachable; they simply require you to stretch your thumb.

Another target group that is often neglected is older people. Often, they aren't used to using computers. Therefore, apps for them must have a much more intuitive structure and offer some form of guidance.

People with visual impairments who need to use a screen reader may not profit from a well-thought-out visual layout. Others that don't use a screen reader may profit from high-contrast mode, screen magnification, and other helpful criteria outlined in accessibility guidelines such as the **Web Content Accessibility Guidelines** (**WCAG**).

Additionally, users might already use similar apps and websites and are used to specific patterns. For example, learned behavior is likely why we still see floppy disk icons and immediately think of a *save* function. (I'm sure some people reading this book haven't even seen a physical floppy disk in their lives. If you haven't, you can consult a popular search engine).

These learned behaviors and ingrained patterns make certain apps frustrating or confusing, while others feel intuitive and easy to use. All of these thoughts play a role in making decisions for our design.

They influence how we present content, where the main navigation points are located, the sizes of icons and text, and many more aspects. In the end, these factors influence the overall layout, too.

The stakeholders

A considerable influence on the entire application comes from the stakeholders, be they management, investors, product owners, clients, sales departments, marketing departments, or even governments (think websites for universities, public libraries, or a local municipal office).

These stakeholders have goals, usually. For example, they may want to influence the project to a certain degree or need to use it in the end but are not interested in contributing to its creation and maintenance—for example, by creating bug reports or participating in user tests. We can use a stakeholder map to determine how much attention we should pay to stakeholders' opinions.

The following diagram shows an exemplary version of a stakeholder map:

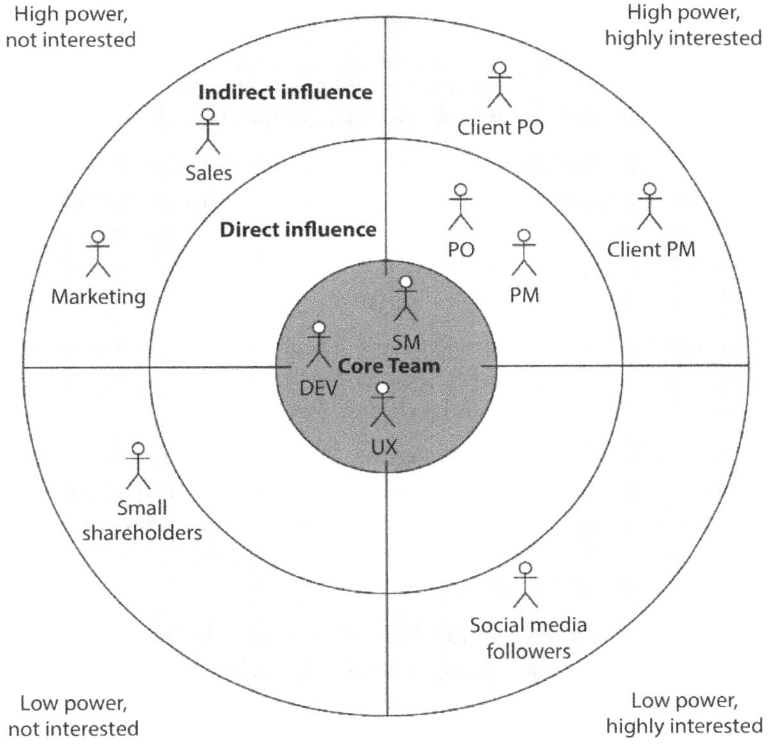

Figure 4.5 – A stakeholder map with example stakeholders

This diagram shows three different spheres of influence and four categories. Generally, each stakeholder is either part of the core team taking decisions daily, directly influencing these decisions, or can only steer the decisions by talking to people with direct influence.

Each stakeholder has either a lot of power, primarily due to their position, or not much power due to them not being involved in any decision-making processes. A stakeholder may also either be interested in the project or not interested at all. The twelve emerging categories (three spheres of influence times four interest/power combinations) determine the input's importance to the priorities and roadmap.

For example, a follower of one of our company's social media accounts may be highly interested in the progress of this brand-new application, but their messages will mostly go unheard. However, the PO can directly steer a feature's priority and decide which items go to the backlog.

Whoever the stakeholders may be, their needs will influence the design to some degree, according to the stakeholder map.

The web design principles

Last but not least, we also need to follow certain principles. There are various frameworks, but most agree on the following design principles:

- **Contrast**: The *contrast* principle tells us how different elements should be. If all elements look alike, they don't stand out. If they look too different, the visual design doesn't work anymore.

- **Balance**: *Balance* means things such as symmetry and "visual weight." For example, imagine a large image that fills the left half of your desktop screen with a title text in the right half. Since the image is large and likely colorful, it carries more visual weight than a 16px paragraph. To counter the imbalance, we can make the text larger, place an icon next to it, or increase the font weight.

- **Repetition**: The principle of *repetition* means to repeat concepts. For example, we usually use the same styles for headings, image captions, buttons, and icons. Repeating patterns let the user scan through a page quickly and recognize elements faster.

- **Rhythm**: A good *rhythm* is defined by spacing and arranging elements in repeating patterns. For example, a vertical rhythm could align all elements in a vertical grid of 8px, making all spacings a multiple of 8px, having line heights of 24px and font sizes of 16px, and possibly size images as a multiple of 8px as well. A horizontal rhythm works just as well. One way to define such rhythms in a general layout is a grid.

- **Hierarchy**: To structure a layout with a *hierarchy* means making the essential elements appear more important—for example, by size or color. Larger elements appear more important than small ones. Elements with a primary color draw more attention to them than elements with a secondary color.

- **Proximity**: The *proximity* principle tells us that elements close to each other appear as a single visual element and will likely share some attributes, such as information or functionality, with other elements of the same group. Therefore, we can use proximity to group elements, such as navigations, teaser cards, **call-to-actions** (**CTAs**), or product tiles.

These principles govern how we structure elements in a layout.

> ### A recommendation
>
> A great source of learning about design, in general, is *The Non-Designer's Design Book* by the award-winning author Robin Williams. In 238 pages, the author manages to teach us about design principles, such as repetition, colors, contrast, and proximity. Well worth the read!

With these challenges—namely, any pre-defined constraints or inspirations, the amount and type of content, the needs of the target groups and the stakeholders, and any design principles we follow—we can better understand the work of design experts.

Understanding the difference between adaptive, responsive, and fluid layouts

Three layout types can be used to optimize an application for all viewports: adaptive layouts, responsive layouts, and fluid layouts. Let's look at the similarities and differences and understand the terms.

Adaptive layouts

An **adaptive layout** consists of ready-made templates for each screen size we want to cover. We saw this a lot at the beginning of the mobile web with the rise of mobile and tablet versions of websites and the redirect popups that asked us whether we wanted a mobile-optimized version.

To illustrate, let's have a look at the following diagram:

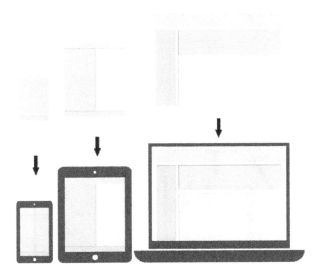

Figure 4.6 – Adaptive design illustrated

We can see that three distinct layouts are used for three different devices. The layouts may not even share the same elements, as we can see that the yellow box is missing on mobile devices. Also, the distinct layouts influence the order of elements: whereas the green box is the last item on the page on smartphones and tablets, it appears to be the second on desktop devices. Since the visual order has changed, likely did the DOM, resulting in different HTML for all devices.

While adaptive layouts generally work, they're not ideal: they neglect all screen sizes they're not optimized for and offer only rudimentary support. Often, they need extra maintenance because they don't even share the same code. The neglect of in-between screens can be mitigated by combining adaptive layouts with fluid and responsive design techniques, but the extra maintenance stays.

One might even argue that if we're using responsive and fluid techniques, we might ditch the idea of adaptive layouts altogether. However, modern frameworks allow us to adapt the components in terms of DOM or styling by checking for the viewport size.

While we don't use entirely adaptive layouts anymore, reacting to the viewport and generating a different DOM is still used today. Consider a hamburger menu on mobile devices, for example: implementing fully visible navigation on a desktop but hiding it behind a hamburger icon on mobile is a classic adaptive technique.

Responsive layouts

A **responsive layout** implements a universal design for an application that reflows according to the space available. It reorders its elements based mainly on the viewport width. This reordering can include displaying grids as lists of elements on smaller screens or enlarging elements to fill the entire viewport width instead of only parts. We can see this happening in the following diagram:

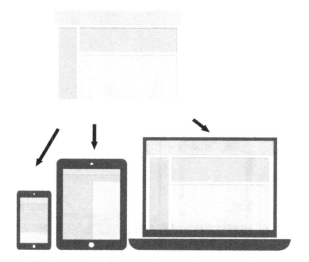

Figure 4.7 – A responsive layout illustrated across multiple devices

The order of items doesn't change in this responsive layout. We let them reflow. While the green box spreads the entire width on smartphones and tablets, it becomes a sidebar on desktop devices. Also, the yellow box becomes incorporated on all devices.

A purely responsive layout, by definition, does not replace, add, or remove any content on any viewport. Instead, it aims to reuse everything. By combining it with adaptive layout techniques, however, we're able to fit the content better and replace it with more sensible solutions.

Think of a **Save** button, for example. It may contain an icon and text. On smaller viewports, to save space, we might want to remove the text and enlarge the icon a bit for better visibility.

Fluid layouts

A **fluid layout** implements either all of or many of its sizes with relative units. For example, those units might be based on the screen size using vw (viewport width), vh (viewport height), and % units, or the font size by using the rem and em units, which in turn could be based on the viewport height as well.

In addition, fluid layouts often work with columns of relative size. We can, for example, define an element as four out of eight columns wide—the screen size will decide what that means in percentages or pixels.

The following diagram aims to illustrate what this means for different device sizes:

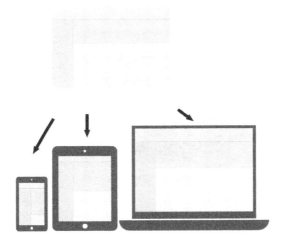

Figure 4.8 – A fluid layout shown on differently sized devices

We can see how the order or placement of items doesn't change over different screen sizes. They scale accordingly for smartphones, tablets, and desktop screens.

Purely fluid layouts are rarely found in the wild due to their complexity. They work for parts of pages but are often combined with responsive or adaptive techniques to create a layout for an entire page.

From this point on, we'll use the term *responsive* as a placeholder for any combination of the three approaches of purely responsive, purely fluid, and adaptive layouts. In practice, these approaches are usually mixed and called **responsive**.

With the knowledge of the terminology and the different approaches, we can clearly describe different parts of our layouts and make better decisions on what to apply where.

Learning responsive layout best practices

It is essential to learn about best practices to get the most out of our design and create something beautiful and valuable. The following few best practices aim to support creating responsive and fluid layouts.

Prioritizing content

Some content is more important to convey a message or sell a product than others. For example, let's look at Walmart's product detail page again and add boxes to different parts of the content, as shown in the following screenshot:

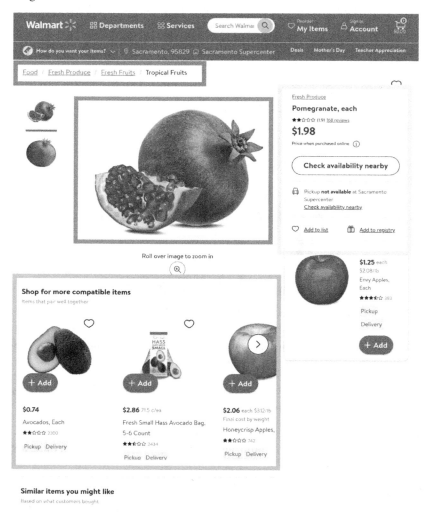

Figure 4.9 – The Walmart product detail page with boxes around parts of the content

We have four different kinds of content that Walmart decided to put above the fold. Being **above the fold** comes from the old days of newspapers and describes the placement you see on the very first page, above the center fold that hides away half of the page. On the web, being above the fold means being visible for the user on load without scrolling.

The first element, in light blue, is the breadcrumbs. They offer orientation for the user but are not of immediate importance when loading the page. In addition, they're relatively small compared to the rest of the elements.

The most prominent element, marked in green, is the product image. Humans are highly visual creatures. Visual stimuli can trigger emotions and let us remember the taste of things or even entire situations. The product image, placed in the absolute center of the page, is meant to convey a sizeable visual stimulus of the product.

The second most prominent element positioned to the right of the product image is the essential information about the product: its name, price tag, some reviews, and where to pick it up. It;s less prominent than the product image but still in the vertical center of the page, making it equally important.

The bottommost element is similar products, marked in pink. These items might be interesting to the user but are small enough not to draw too much attention. However, they use the visual stimulus of a product image as well. However, these are not entirely above the fold in this case. Further below is more information about these similar products, such as their names, price tags, and ratings.

The rest of the info about this product, such as nutrition facts, ingredients (surprisingly, Pomegranate contains pomegranate), specifications, and detailed reviews that we're currently looking at, is below the fold: the user needs to scroll several times to access them.

What Walmart has done here is a textbook showcase of content prioritization. It thought about the most critical aspects of the page, centered them, and made them take up large portions of the screen. We can observe this even better when looking at the mobile version of the same page in the following screenshot:

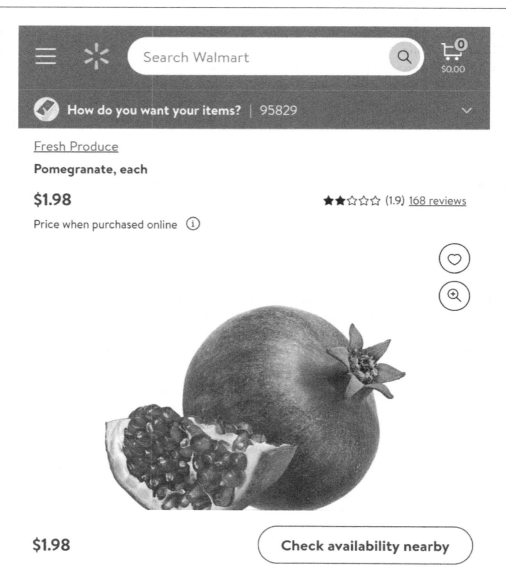

Figure 4.10 – The mobile view of the same Walmart product detail page

On mobile, the focus is just the same: the two most essential elements—the product information, such as the name and price tag, and the picture—are centered and take up a large portion of the screen.

Prioritising our content helps us decide the focus and, finally, the page's layout. We want the content to fulfill a function. Therefore, the content that best fulfills the function and contributes the most is the most important.

Applying mobile first

The **mobile-first** approach can be described as follows: start implementing from the narrowest viewport an app should be optimized for and work your way up to larger viewports instead of starting with the largest size and working your way down. This approach is built on the fact that an ever-increasing number of people use their mobile devices for surfing the web. Using media queries to take care of layouts on large screens reduces cascading on mobile devices, thus speeding up rendering.

However, we can apply this approach to design, too. For example, the main challenge of designing desktop-first and narrowing down is getting rid of information. Perhaps we've already prioritized our content and decided on the essential bits and pieces, only to learn that it will never fit the way we intended on small displays. If we, instead, started with mobile layouts, we could rethink our priorities and have much more freedom. When we then enlarge the layout to larger screens, we find that more information can fit in, and we can start adding the less critical pieces of information.

It boils down to the fact that narrowing down is more challenging than opening up. By starting small, we don't forcefully condense elements and thus make them less accessible, prominent, or *pop* (as some might say). Still, we give them the necessary place and space before surrounding them with less important bits.

In terms of implementing layouts, we also need to keep in mind that we can reorder things based on the viewport. A combination of media queries, Flexbox, and—most importantly—CSS Grid can help us save valuable bytes.

Designing with worst-case content in mind

Often, mock-ups and prototypes are designed with a perfect use case. Here are some examples of this:

- The title of the article detail page design fits precisely on a single line

- The comment count never goes beyond two characters

- The style of a user avatar will never contrast poorly with the rest of the design, let alone be pixelated or, worse, the logo of a competitor

What happens to the design if the content doesn't fit, in any case? For example, the word *information* can be 2 to 17 characters long, depending on our language. We must keep an eye on the content we use for our designs. Ideally, our layouts and designs work for the most extreme forms of content, such as very short or long page titles, different languages, or long usernames in the header bar.

Designing in that manner can be challenging, but even if we try to incorporate some edge cases, we can guarantee a good experience for many users. Ideally, though, the design should be independent of the content. Such an experience is often achieved by allowing content containers to grow. For example, a title can span multiple lines instead of being restricted to a single line of text.

Since the web—especially the mobile web—is mainly restricted to the horizontal axis, we can allow elements to grow on the vertical axis instead. First, however, we need to ensure that the most important content is still above the fold.

Combining adaptiveness, responsiveness, and fluidity

When we say that a layout is *responsive*, we often mean that it adapts to the available screen size. However, we've learned about adaptive and fluid techniques as well. We can apply these to achieve our layout goals but should use them where sensible.

For example, we can create a layout with a single column on mobile devices, four on tablets, and eight on desktop devices. This technique is essentially adaptive, combined with a fluid one. The columns are rarely defined in terms of pixels but often in terms of percentages of their container.

Fixed-width items can also be used, though: for example, a fixed-width sidebar with icons that need to be a specific size, as we've seen in Awesome Analytics. The key to a layout that works on all devices is to combine the methods and apply them where needed to either hide information, make it reflow, or resize.

We've learned about challenges, best practices, and terminology and have seen some examples. It's time to switch to the developer role again and get into the technical parts.

Implementing responsive and fluid layouts with CSS Grid

CSS Grid offers us two ways of defining responsive and fluid layouts: we can use media queries to create responsive layouts or sizing keywords to create fluid layouts. We can also combine media queries and the sizing keywords to achieve layouts better suited to fit our use case, as the possibilities are infinite.

We've covered the definitions of sizing keywords and their values in *Chapter 1, Understanding the Basic Rules and Structures for CSS Grid*, already, so we'll focus on their advanced usage in the context of fluidity and responsiveness.

Media queries and altering grid area templates

The first reflex to *responsive layout implementation* we might have would be to use media queries. Since becoming a **World Wide Web Consortium (W3C)** standard in 2012, they've been a staple of modern web development.

They have practically made fully adaptive layouts obsolete, as they allow us to react to the size of the user's device. We often use them to make columns full-width instead of only parts of the available size to adjust the layout. Adaptions to float rules help us steer the flow of elements and allow us to decide whether the sidebar stays a sidebar or becomes a top bar instead.

We can use media queries with CSS Grid just the same. However, we can adapt the grid layout so that the amount and sizes of columns and rows change for different screens.

To illustrate, we'll assume the following HTML structure:

```
<!-- chapter4/01_media_queries.html -->
<div class="container">
  <header><!-- Header with a logo, navigation, etc. -->
    </header>
  <aside><!-- Partially related things like social
    buttons --></aside>
  <main><!-- Main content, headings, teasers, etc. -->
    </main>
  <footer><!-- Footer with contact, FAQ, etc. --></footer>
</div>
```

It consists of a header, an aside element, a main element, and a footer. It's the same one we already worked with in *Chapter 1, Understanding the Basic Rules and Structures for CSS Grid*.

We'll also assume the following CSS code to give us a minimal basis:

```
/* chapter4/01_media_queries.html */
/* Micro-resetting */
body { padding: 0; margin: 0; }
* { box-sizing: border-box; font-size: 25px; }

/* Making things visible on the page */
.container {
  border: 2px solid #555;
  padding: 8px;
  min-height: 100vh;
}
header {
  border: 2px solid #dd0808; /* Dark red */
  background-color: #ff6666; /* Light red */
}
aside {
  border: 2px solid #0ba7c6; /* Dark cyan */
  background-color: #74ddf2; /* Light cyan */
}
main {
  border: 2px solid #6f09e5; /* Dark purple */
  background-color: #b880f7; /* Light purple */
}
footer {
  border: 2px solid #c4be0d; /* Dark yellow */
  background-color: #f7f380; /* Light yellow */
}
```

This code colors the boxes and gives a small border around the main content, showing us the boxes.

Now, let's add a single-column layout:

```
.container {
  display: grid;
  grid-template:
    "header" 100px
    "aside" 50px
    "main" 1fr
    "footer" 100px
  ;
}

header {
  grid-area: header;
}
aside {
  grid-area: aside;
}
main {
  grid-area: main;
}
footer {
  grid-area: footer;
}
```

Theoretically, we don't even need this layout. A single-column layout is achieved by block elements with a set height, too, rendering this approach redundant. However, we're taking advantage of CSS Grid here.

First, we're explicitly setting the positions of the elements instead of adding them implicitly. Second, we use the `fr` unit to make the main area span all the available space, taking over any sizing issues and positioning the footer at the bottom of the page.

When opening this example in the browser, we see the result as we expect it:

Figure 4.11 – The mobile layout as displayed by a browser with a mobile viewport

We can see the red header bar, a cyan box representing what will be the sidebar, a purple main content box, and a yellow footer box.

We can then add a second layout wrapped in a media query, like so:

```
@media screen and (min-width: 700px) {
  .container {
    grid-template:
      "header header" 100px
      "aside main" 1fr
      "footer footer" 100px
      / 200px 1fr
    ;
  }
}
```

The numbers used in this example are arbitrary, but they serve the purpose of illustrating the concept.

In this grid template, we've added a second column and started shifting the boxes. The sidebar should now be next to the main content area while the header and footer stay in place. By resizing our browser window, we can observe the effect of the grid template change, as shown in the following screenshot:

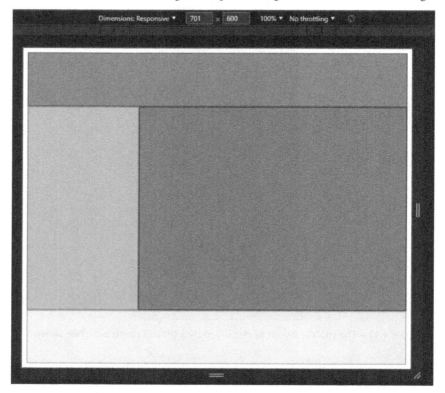

Figure 4.12 – The grid template, as shown on a screen width of 701px

With a screen size of 701px width, we can see that the layout shifts to having a sidebar, moving the cyan box to the left of the purple box. For larger screens, we may add empty cells around the second row, giving our main content container more white space and *room to breathe*.

The possibilities don't stop there, either. For example, we can deliver layouts for different device orientations with other media query values, such as `orientation: landscape` or `aspect-ratio: *`.

However, we must remember that elements' order and positioning only change visually. Therefore, to keep our project accessible, we should not deviate the visual order far from the order in which they appear in the DOM, as screen readers will narrate elements in their order of appearance in the DOM.

We also must remember that if we remove a grid area, we must remove the element from rendering using `display: none`.

Consider the following CSS code:

```css
.container {
  display: grid;
  grid-template:
    "header" 100px
    "main" 1fr
    "footer" 100px
  ;
}

header {
  grid-area: header;
}
aside {
  grid-area: aside;
}
main {
  grid-area: main;
}
footer {
  grid-area: footer;
}
```

It is almost identical to our initial layout, but the `"aside"` area is missing. The `aside` element has, therefore, no place to render. CSS Grid will add another row and column to render it, as shown in the following screenshot:

Figure 4.13 – The initial layout, missing a slot for the cyan aside element

We can only barely spot the little square at the bottom-right corner: it is the cyan `aside` element trying to find a spot to render itself, arguably without much luck.

Using sizing keywords and functions for fluid layouts

Apart from using media queries, we also can use sizing keywords to define fluid grid layouts. To recap, these are the sizing keywords and functions we can use:

- `min()`, `max()`, and `minmax()` to clamp values and choose smaller or larger values, depending on the desired behavior
- `repeat()`, in combination with `auto-fill` and `auto-fit`, to create columns and rows to fit the available space

The `minmax()` function can be used to define grid columns and rows that have a minimum and maximum size. It takes two arguments, the first being the lower bound and the second being the upper bound of the grid cell.

We can, for example, create a layout with four columns that each have a minimum width of `200px` and a maximum width of `500px` by using the following CSS code:

```
/* chapter4/02_fluid_columns.html */
.container {
  display: grid;
  grid-template-columns: repeat(4, minmax(200px, 500px));
}
```

The result already resembles a fluid layout: from a screen width of `800px` to `2000px`, the columns scale themselves; from `2000px` onward, the columns stay at `500px` width, whereas they start to overflow once the screen is less than `800px` wide.

Well, why wouldn't we use the `fr` unit for this approach, we may ask, which is a valid question. In itself, the `minmax()` function isn't very useful. However, with the `auto-fill` sizing keyword, we can add more columns (or remove them, depending on whether we enlarge or shrink our screen), depending on the screen size.

If we use `repeat(auto-fill, minmax(200px, 500px))` as the grid column template, we see something curious happen: the columns stay at `500px` width if there is more than one column. If the content is rendered in a single column, this column is resized to fit the screen unless the screen is smaller than `200px`, when it starts to overflow again.

To make the elements narrower than the specified `200px`, we can nest the `min()` function into the `minmax()` function. By applying `minmax(min(200px, 100%), 500px)`, CSS Grid will set the column size to either 100% or `200px`, whichever is smaller.

If we now also replace `500px` with `1fr` (resulting in `minmax(min(200px, 100%), 1fr)`), we end up with a genuinely fluid layout: the width of all columns is always such that they fill the screen. A new column is added once the width is a multiple of `200px`. Also, when we use `auto-fit` instead of `auto-fill`, there will only be as many columns (or rows) as there are elements to arrange.

We can see this in the following screenshot:

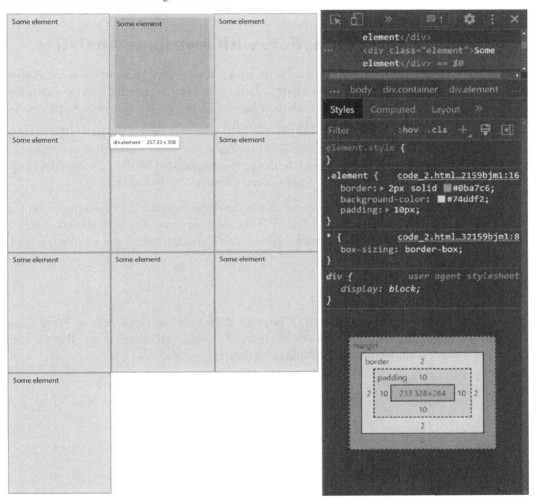

Figure 4.14 – A fluid layout with columns that can take up more than 200px

We see several cyan boxes arranged in a grid. The grid definition is `grid-template-columns: repeat(auto-fit, minmax(min(200px, 100%), 1fr));`, resulting in multiple columns. These columns scale up to automatically fit the available content, resulting in columns of 233px width.

Generally, a fluid layout defined with these techniques is best for arranging repeating content, such as articles or products, not entire page layouts. Usually, a good mix of the two approaches—responsiveness and fluidity—is necessary to achieve page layouts and content arrangement that work well on all devices.

Practicing responsive layouts with Awesome Analytics

We'll practice responsive and fluid layout approaches now that we've learned about them. In *Chapter 2, Project Introduction: What We'll Work on and First Tasks*, the end user at the meeting with the stakeholders said that they never used devices other than their laptops for work with Awesome Analytics. As it turns out, this particular end user isn't very representative.

In fact, the analytics of users have yielded that most users access the app from their smartphone or tablet device! However, since the layout and the design aren't optimized for these kinds of devices yet, they only see the desktop version on their phones and immediately close the tab.

The sales department is in panic: if potential clients cannot at least use the sign-up page on their mobile devices, we lose out on potential dozens of our local currency! The management shares the panic, thinking about all the office goodies they now don't have the money for, such as free apples or free coffee.

The task at hand

The plan is to act upon this panic immediately. Everyone at the table looks at us. After all, we've already saved the day twice with our knowledge of CSS Grid and layouts, so it doesn't matter that the entire design department is simultaneously on holiday for the next 3 weeks.

We look at the current sign-up page, as shown in the following screenshot:

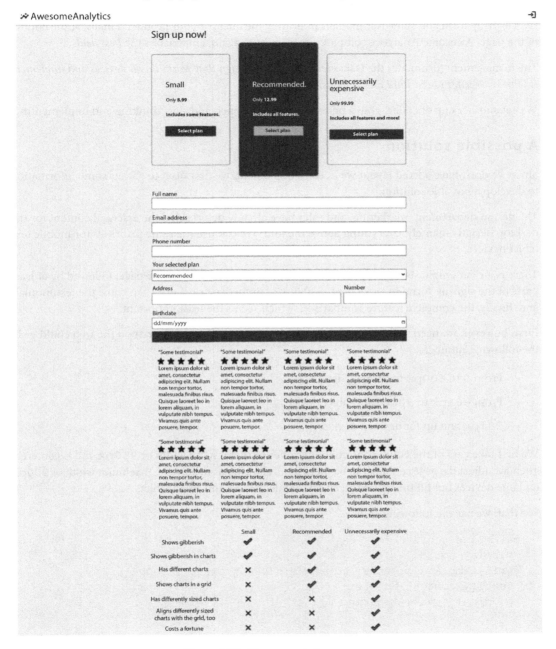

Figure 4.15 – The current sign-up page

The page offers some teasers for different plans. The marketing department has requested these since it has seen the same pattern on many competitor pages, such as **HalfwayDecentAnalytics**. We also see a sign-up form and some testimonials indicating the quality of our product. Finally, at the bottom of the page, Awesome Analytics compares its plans and, again, emphasizes the *best deal*.

The management formulates the task: *Please develop a design that works on all devices and implement it with knowledge about fluid and responsive designs!*

We get another cup of coffee, grab a pen and a piece of paper, and start thinking and implementing.

A possible solution

Since we don't have a fixed layout we need to implement, we first need to gather some information to develop a possible solution.

The design department, marketing, and sales have already determined the essential content for the desktop design—namely, everything above the fold. We can use the same priorities for mobile and tablet devices.

There is a clear emphasis on the possible plan boxes at the very top of the page, followed by at least parts of the sign-up form, to show the possibility of immediate sign-up. Then come the testimonials and, finally, the complete feature comparison, which seems the least important.

First, however, we need to decide which breakpoints we use. A quick search on the web could yield the following numbers:

- From 0 to 600px for mobile devices
- From 601px to 900px for tablet devices
- 901px and up for desktop devices

We first take care of the entire page container. We see that it has a width of 900px and is centered. Then, we adjust the page container to be more fluid, allowing us to keep the maximum width of 900px on large devices but fill the entire screen on mobile devices and small tablets.

For that, we use the following code:

```
.main-page-content {
  display: grid;
  grid-template-columns: minmax(min(900px, 100%), 900px);
  justify-content: center;
  padding: 0 var(--spacing-m);
}
```

Since the boxes at the top would take up a lot of space on mobile devices, we reordered them to show the recommended one first, followed by the other two boxes. However, we can keep the arrangement on tablet devices, meaning we surround its definition with a media query for the minimum width of the defined desktop size. We achieve this behavior with the following code:

```
.teasers {
  display: grid;
  grid-template:
    "b b" 250px
    "a c" 280px
    / auto auto
  ;
  gap: var(--spacing-m);
}

@media screen and (min-width: 901px) {
  .teasers {
    grid-template:
      ". b ." var(--spacing-m)
      "a b c" 600px
      ". b ." var(--spacing-m)
      / 1fr 1fr 1fr
    ;
  }
}

.plan-teaser:nth-child(1) {
  grid-area: a;
}

.plan-teaser:nth-child(2) {
  grid-area: b;
}

.plan-teaser:nth-child(3) {
  grid-area: c;
}
```

As illustrated in the following screenshot, we end up with an arrangement on mobile devices:

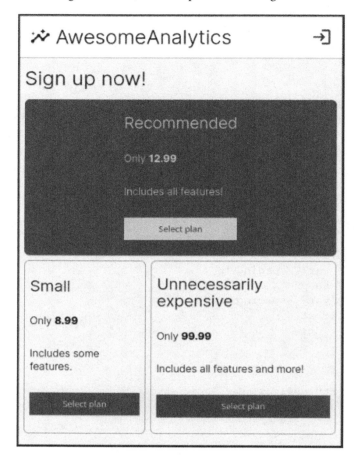

Figure 4.16 – The new mobile layout for the teaser boxes

We've arranged the grid so that the box with the most emphasis is on top, whereas the other two boxes share a single line below.

We then take care of the form. For that, we use a fluid variant, as the address fields allow us to keep them next to each other:

```
.form {
  display: grid;
  grid-auto-rows: 40px;
  grid-template-columns: 1fr 75px;
  gap: 10px;
}
```

```
.form label {
  align-self: end;
}
```

The following screenshot shows us the result on mobile devices:

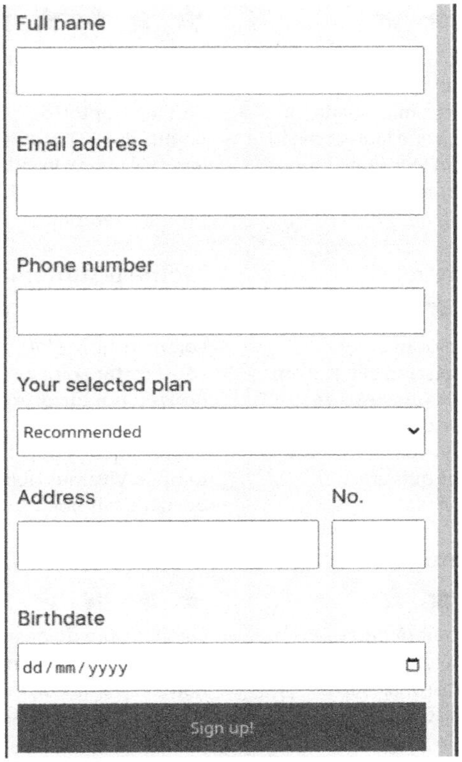

Figure 4.17 – The form, optimized for mobile devices

We can see that the form now fits perfectly and still maintains its proportions.

The testimonials currently have a fixed width of 225px and are arranged in four columns. Ideally, we'd like to keep the maximum width of 225px but alter the number of columns. Once the screen is smaller than 225px, the testimonials should not take up more than the available screen width.

We can achieve this with the following code:

```
.testimonials {
  display: grid;
  grid-template-columns: repeat(auto-fit,
```

```
    minmax(min(225px, 100%), 1fr));
}
```

And have a look at the result, shown in the following screenshot:

"Some testimonial"

Lorem ipsum dolor sit amet, consectetur adipiscing elit. Nullam non tempor tortor, malesuada finibus risus. Quisque laoreet leo in lorem aliquam, in vulputate nibh tempus. Vivamus quis ante posuere, tempor.

"Some testimonial"

Lorem ipsum dolor sit amet, consectetur adipiscing elit. Nullam non tempor tortor, malesuada finibus risus. Quisque laoreet leo in lorem aliquam, in vulputate nibh tempus. Vivamus quis ante posuere, tempor.

"Some testimonial"

Lorem ipsum dolor sit amet, consectetur adipiscing elit. Nullam non tempor tortor, malesuada finibus risus. Quisque laoreet leo in lorem aliquam, in vulputate nibh tempus. Vivamus quis ante posuere, tempor.

"Some testimonial"

Lorem ipsum dolor sit amet, consectetur adipiscing elit. Nullam non tempor tortor, malesuada finibus risus. Quisque laoreet leo in lorem aliquam, in vulputate nibh tempus. Vivamus quis ante posuere, tempor.

"Some testimonial"

Lorem ipsum dolor sit amet, consectetur adipiscing elit. Nullam non tempor tortor, malesuada finibus risus. Quisque laoreet leo in lorem aliquam, in vulputate nibh tempus. Vivamus quis ante posuere, tempor.

"Some testimonial"

Lorem ipsum dolor sit amet, consectetur adipiscing elit. Nullam non tempor tortor, malesuada finibus risus. Quisque laoreet leo in lorem aliquam, in vulputate nibh tempus. Vivamus quis ante posuere, tempor.

"Some testimonial"

Lorem ipsum dolor sit amet, consectetur adipiscing elit. Nullam non tempor tortor, malesuada finibus risus. Quisque laoreet leo in lorem aliquam, in vulputate nibh tempus. Vivamus quis ante posuere, tempor.

"Some testimonial"

Lorem ipsum dolor sit amet, consectetur adipiscing elit. Nullam non tempor tortor, malesuada finibus risus. Quisque laoreet leo in lorem aliquam, in vulputate nibh tempus. Vivamus quis ante posuere, tempor.

Figure 4.18 – The testimonials, optimized for mobile and tablet devices

The testimonials are now arranged as follows:

- In one column if the screen width is smaller than 466px

- Two columns if the screen width is between 467px and 691px

- Three columns if the screen width is between 691px and 916px

- Four columns if the screen width is above 916px

To understand how these breakpoints are calculated, we need to first take the padding of the page itself (8px on the left and right sides of the screen, so 16px) into account. If we subtract those 16px from all sizes, we arrive at the following breakpoint widths:

- Upto 450px

- Between 450px and 675px

- Between 675px and 900px

- 900px and above

Since we defined the column width as the minimum width of a minimum value between 225px and 100% of the parent's available width and a max width of 1fr of the parent width, each *breakpoint minus the padding* corresponds to a multiple of 225px.

Last, we take care of the table. Since the table labels overlap with the available space, we can rotate them on smaller screens with the following code. This isn't CSS Grid, but it's a handy thing to know, nevertheless:

```
.feature-comparison .table-label {
  white-space: nowrap;
  writing-mode: vertical-rl;
  transform: rotate(180deg);
}

@media screen and (min-width: 901px) {
  .feature-comparison .table-label {
    writing-mode: initial;
    transform: none;
  }
}
```

The result is shown in the following screenshot:

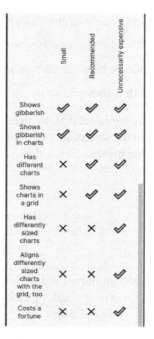

Figure 4.19 – The feature comparison table, optimized for mobile devices

With this, we have achieved a fully functioning layout for mobile and tablet devices while keeping the layout on desktop devices.

Summary

We now know some best practices for responsive and fluid designs and understand the struggles of design experts when coming up with designs. As developers, we understand the technical possibilities of design, but knowing some of the design principles and thought processes of UX experts helps in communicating with them.

We can give educated opinions on inclusivity and accessibility and ask the right questions when talking to stakeholders. We can ultimately support the entire team with our broad expertise. Since we've practiced creating responsive layouts and coming up with solutions, we've also practiced making informed decisions.

In the next chapter, we'll get back into the more technical aspects of CSS Grid and compare it to Flexbox. Then, we'll examine the limits of what's possible with CSS Grid and Flexbox and learn how to use one to support the other. Finally, we'll learn about the similarities and differences between Flexbox and Grid and practice again.

5

Implementing Layouts with Flexbox and CSS Grid

We can now almost consider ourselves experts in the usage of CSS Grid. We've looked at many details, practiced many aspects of the tool, and learned about different approaches to creating grids and how to design them. As a result, we now know what we can achieve with CSS Grid.

However, CSS knows another versatile and powerful tool for building layouts: Flexbox. Since Flexbox was first announced – I still remember that day – people have used it to replace all kinds of hacks and fixes. From vertically centering icons (remember this gem to center something in its container? `top: 50%; left: 50%; transform: translate (-50%, -50%);` — I'm shuddering while writing this…) to building entire pages, everything was positioned, aligned, and moved with Flexbox. At some point, people started using Flexbox for things they probably shouldn't have and for which CSS offers great alternative solutions, too, such as the `column-count` property for multi-column text.

But we can't blame the community for *over-using* Flexbox, as it has solved many problems people had in the past. The need for extra container elements only to solve specific design challenges and hacks with `float` or `position: absolute;` was solved by Flexbox. Similarly, CSS Grid solves some issues people had with building grid-like layouts with Flexbox, such as keeping rows at the same height.

As soon as CSS Grid was presented, people started advocating against Flexbox for entire page layouts and suggested code based on the latest release candidates of CSS Grid without it even being supported by major browsers yet. However, Flexbox still was, and technically still is, the de facto standard for a long time, although grid adoption is slowly growing.

Perhaps the most important lesson of this chapter can be said in advance so that we can keep it in mind: we must understand that CSS Grid does not replace Flexbox. It complements it.

In this chapter, we'll compare CSS Grid to Flexbox. In several small examples and a larger one at the end (the Awesome Analytics management members are having a meeting right now, believe it or not!), we will examine the differences and similarities and get a feeling for both tools, when to use which, and how to use them together.

In detail, this chapter will cover the following topics:

- Arranging media objects
- Arranging teasers and card elements
- Arranging forms and form elements
- Building page partials
- Practicing with Awesome Analytics

Technical requirements

For this chapter, we need the same setup as for *Chapter 2, Project Introduction: What We'll Work on and First Tasks*:

- A browser, preferably Chromium-based, such as Google Chrome, Brave, or Vivaldi, but Firefox or Apple Safari works, too
- An **integrated development environment** (IDE) or text editor such as WebStorm, VS Code, or VIM, with HTML and CSS syntax highlighting
- Internet access is necessary to get the code
- Git (this is optional, as we can also download the folder from GitHub)
- NodeJS with at least version 14 and npm with at least version 6

If Node is not currently installed on your system, or you've got the wrong version, nvm is a fantastic tool to handle different NodeJS versions on one system.

All the code for this chapter can be found on GitHub in this repository: `https://github.com/ PacktPublishing/Mastering-CSS-Grid/tree/main/chapter5`.

Arranging media objects

Media objects are an elementary example of flexible layouts. A media object is a media element (primarily images, though) with some content next to it that doesn't flow around it. Therefore, we don't deal with images aligned with `float` but with a two-column layout, of which one row determines the size of the other.

Usually, the media is rendered in its desired size, and the text takes the rest of the available space. Let's look at the example from the Bootstrap documentation to understand what this exactly means:

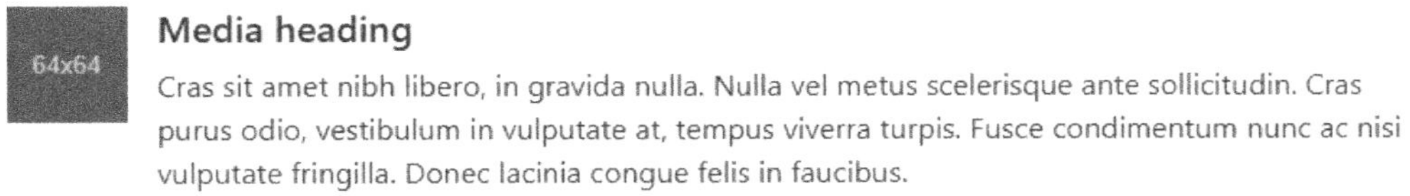

Media heading

Cras sit amet nibh libero, in gravida nulla. Nulla vel metus scelerisque ante sollicitudin. Cras purus odio, vestibulum in vulputate at, tempus viverra turpis. Fusce condimentum nunc ac nisi vulputate fringilla. Donec lacinia congue felis in faucibus.

Figure 5.1 – A media object as described by the documentation of Bootstrap

We can see the image on the left side being the exact desired size of 64 by 64 px and the text on the right not wrapping around it.

There are several spin-offs to the media object. For example, depending on the use case, the media could be positioned at the right end of the container, it could be nested (and therefore considered content itself), or the image could be centered vertically.

Let's first try to build a media object with CSS Grid before we try to achieve the same outcome with Flexbox. For both cases, we'll assume the same HTML structure:

```
<!-- chapter5/01_media_objects.html -->
<article class="media-object">
  <img src="https://via.placeholder.com/150"
    alt="Placeholder image">
  <div class="media-object-content">
    <h2>Media object heading</h2>
    <p>Lorem ipsum dolor sit amet</p>

    <article class="media-object">
      <img src="https://via.placeholder.com/150"
        alt="Placeholder image">
      <div class="media-object-content">
        <h2>Nested media object heading</h2>
        <p>Lorem ipsum dolor sit amet</p>
      </div>
    </article>
  </div>
</article>
```

The example uses an `<article>` element as the media object's container, a single placeholder image, and a `div` to contain the content. We also placed a nested media object in the content to cover that use case.

We'll use the following default styling for the media object:

```
/* chapter5/01_media_object.html */
.media-object {
  max-width: 700px;
```

```
  border: 1px solid #000;
  margin-bottom: 10px; /* Some spacing for screenshots etc. */
}
.media-object .media-object-content {
  padding: 10px;
}
```

The maximum width of 700px ensures readability, and the background colour will make nested media objects slightly darker so they are more visible, too.

The media object uses neither Flexbox nor CSS Grid now, meaning we would see the result as shown in the following figure:

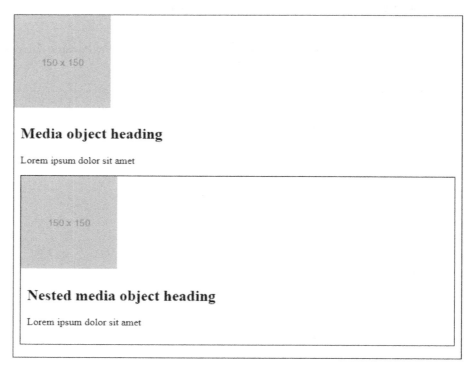

Figure 5.2 – The unaligned media object

The result is what we would expect: the content div functions as a block element that spans the entire width, pushing itself to the following line and rendering the entire element vertically. To rebuild the Bootstrap example, we must move the content to the right of the image.

Let's first apply CSS Grid to it to see how it behaves. We'll need two columns, one of size `auto` and one of size `1fr`, so the column containing the image does not grow beyond its content size:

```
.media-object {
  /* Previous declarations omitted for brevity */
  display: grid;
  grid-template-columns: auto 1fr;
}
```

This code does what we want, as shown in the following figure:

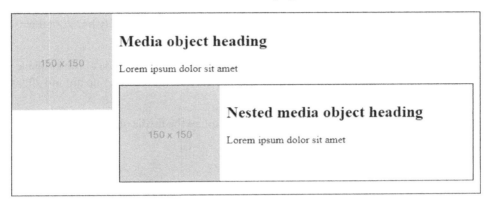

Figure 5.3 – The media object aligned with CSS Grid

Marvellous! Apart from the bottom margin of the nested media object, it looks fantastic. Even though the use case is not a prime example of a grid, CSS Grid can solve the challenge ahead with minimal code.

Let's now try Flexbox:

```
.media-object {
  display: flex;
  align-items: flex-start; /* Otherwise the image stretches */
}
```

To stretch the nested element to the parent width, we also need to add the following CSS code:

```
.media-object-content {
  flex-grow: 1;
}
```

Arguably, it is even more understandable than the CSS Grid example because it does not rely on the `auto`/`1fr` definitions, which might be more obscure to a junior with no experience with CSS Grid. The Flexbox solution *talks* to us. The Flexbox solution is equally short, meaning we don't need to go to extra lengths to achieve the same result.

Performance-wise, there likely won't be much of a difference since the performance of CSS Grid and Flexbox is similar.

In summary, the difference between Flexbox and CSS Grid is minuscule for media objects, although we can keep in mind that the Flexbox version might be more legible for some.

Arranging teasers and card elements

A broad use case for CSS Grid and Flexbox is to style teasers and card elements on our pages. They usually consist of some image, a headline, perhaps a bit of text, and a link or **call-to-action**, **CTA** for short. Card elements can be considered vertical teasers, whereas purely horizontal teasers are extended media objects.

A typical horizontal teaser design has an image that takes up to around 20% of the available width, and the entire height, a card element's image is usually 100% wide and takes up around 20% to 30% of the height.

Let's assume the following HTML code. It strongly resembles the media object with a few differences, namely adding a button and different class names:

```
<!-- chapter5/02_teaser_element.html -->
<article class="teaser">
  <img
    class="teaser-image"
    src="https://via.placeholder.com/240x180"
    alt="Placeholder"
  >

  <div class="teaser-content">
    <h2>
      Awesome content
    </h2>
    <p>
      Click here for awesome content that will likely
        interest you.
    </p>
    <button type="button">
      Go to awesome content
    </button>
  </div>
</article>
```

Let's also assume the following default styling:

```
h2 {
  margin: 0;
```

```
}
.teaser {
  max-width: 700px;
  margin-bottom: 10px;
  border: 1px solid #aaa;
  border-radius: 4px;
}
.teaser .teaser-content {
  padding: 10px;
}
.teaser-content button {
  background-color: #aaa;
  padding: 10px;
  border: 0 none;
  border-radius: 4px;
}
```

This code yields the following design, shown in the following figure:

Figure 5.4 – The unarranged teaser/card element

The design already resembles a card element, as CSS applies the standard top-to-bottom flow of block elements. We'd first like to transform this into a media object-like element using CSS Grid. We want the content side to be vertically centered against the image and the image not to lose the aspect ratio:

```
.teaser {
  display: grid;
  grid-template-columns: auto 1fr;
  align-items: center;
}
```

This code is, again, relatively straightforward. The code is almost the same as for the media object. When we want to build the same thing using Flexbox, we will use the following code instead:

```
.teaser {
  display: flex;
}
.teaser-content {
  display: flex;
  justify-content: center;
  flex-direction: column;
  align-items: flex-start;
}
```

The result, in both cases, looks like the one shown in the following figure.

Figure 5.5 – The arranged teaser/card element

Using Flexbox for this example code seems a little more complex than the media object example using Flexbox, but for a reason: this structure gives us a lot more flexibility. By creating a second Flexbox container, we can vertically center all elements without losing flexibility when transforming everything into a card element, which we're doing next.

Assume we'd want to add a class to the outermost element of the `teaser` element called `.teaser-vertical`. This class would adapt the flow of the element to be vertical:

```
<article class="teaser teaser-vertical">
  <img
    class="teaser-image"
    src="https://via.placeholder.com/240x180"
    alt="Placeholder"
  >

  <div class="teaser-content">
    <h2>
      Awesome content
    </h2>
```

```
    <p>
      Click here for awesome content that will likely
         interest you.
    </p>
    <button type="button">
      Go to awesome content
    </button>
  </div>
</article>
```

Let's try to achieve the reflow with CSS Grid first. First, we'd need to change the grid template to use rows instead of columns. The first idea could be to use `grid-auto-flow`, which won't do anything since we have previously defined the column template.

We, therefore, need to adapt the template columns and add rows for this to work. The next issue is the image: it won't automatically resize to fit the container, so we need to add an extra `justify-items: stretch;` for it to behave the way we'd like:

```
.teaser {
  display: grid;
  grid-template-columns: auto 1fr;
  align-items: center;
}
.teaser-vertical {
  grid-template-columns: 1fr;
  grid-template-rows: auto 1fr;
  justify-items: stretch;
}
```

This code isn't ideal for several reasons: first, we need to overwrite things. Although the *C* in *CSS* stands for *Cascading*, we rarely want that, as it adds complexity to our application. If the definition for `.teaser-vertical` is buried deep in another file, the necessity to reset the columns might not be evident at first glance. Second, we're not reusing a lot of the original teaser definition.

The solution Flexbox offers for this issue feels a lot handier:

```
.teaser-vertical {
  flex-direction: column;
  max-width: 240px; }
```

We tell Flexbox to rearrange the entire thing in a column. Then, it'll take over the rest. Again, the result is the same in both cases, shown in the following figure:

Figure 5.6 – The fully styled card element

To summarize, we would likely use Flexbox in this specific example. Even though the initial setup is a tad larger, the flexibility is the game-changer, especially for responsive websites.

Arranging forms and form elements

Another more nuanced use case for both CSS Grid and Flexbox is building forms. Although they work with similar patterns, forms rarely look alike. They can consist of standalone elements, compound elements (e.g., parts of address fields such as street name and number), and elements placed inline, such as radio buttons; they can have extensions, such as icons indicating the type; and often need to be fully responsive.

Arranging a form to be understandable to the user is essential for a good user experience and can tremendously impact the conversion rate. However, we're not focusing on UX but on DX, the developer experience. So, let's see how we can use Flexbox and CSS Grid to solve different form-related challenges.

Input groups

The first element we'll look at is a so-called input group. Bootstrap defines input groups as an extension to any form control with text, icons, or buttons. These are especially useful to indicate the kind of data (not the data type, though) the user should enter, such as their social media handle or a currency amount.

The examples in the Bootstrap documentation show exactly these, as shown in the following figure:

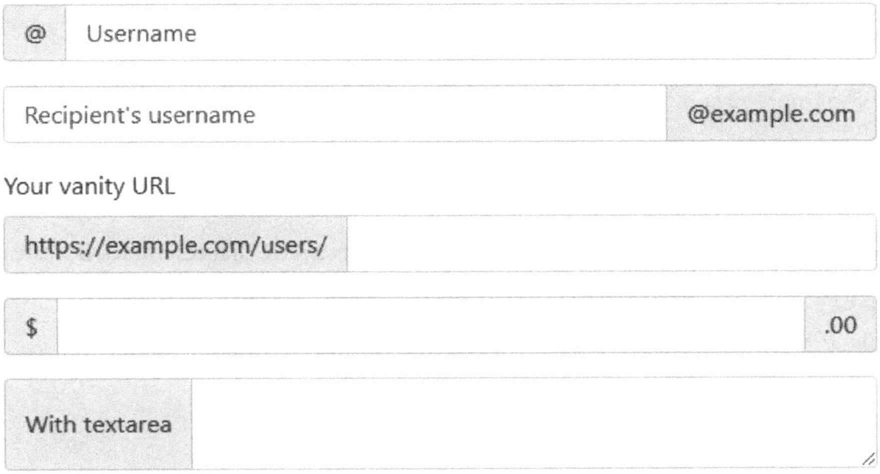

Figure 5.7 – The input group examples, as shown in the Bootstrap documentation

The elements themselves are relatively straightforward, but their extensions make them extremely useful for the user: they provide additional context by prepending an @ to the username, adding @ example.com to the end to indicate part of an email address, adding a URL to indicate a path or add a dollar sign and .00 around a field to indicate an integer amount of currency.

Generally, these elements behave similarly to media objects: they have one element with a fixed width tailored to its content (the extension) and an element that fills out the remaining space (the input field). However, we can add an extension to the left, right, or both sides.

Let's consider the following HTML for the three different cases:

```
<!-- chapter5/03_form_elements.html -->
<div class="input-group">
  <div class="input-extension">
    @
  </div>
  <input placeholder="Username">
</div>

<div class="input-group">
  <input placeholder="Your subdomain">
  <div class="input-extension">
    .example.com
  </div>
</div>
```

```html
<div class="input-group">
  <div class="input-extension">
    $
  </div>
  <input placeholder="Transaction amount">
  <div class="input-extension">
    .00
  </div>
</div>
```

We'll also consider the following CSS to give these elements a style that resembles Bootstrap:

```css
/* chapter5/03_form_elements.html */
input, input:hover, input:focus {
  border: 0 none;
  outline: none;
  padding: 8px;
}

.input-group {
  border: 1px solid #999;
  border-radius: 4px;
  overflow: hidden;

  margin-bottom: 16px; /* For visual separation */
}

.input-extension {
  background-color: #ddd;
  font-weight: bold;
  padding: 8px;
}
```

This code will be rendered as shown in the following figure:

Figure 5.8 – Three input groups, one with a single input extension before the input field, one with an input extension after the input field, and one with two input extensions before and after the field

We can see that the div elements with the .input-extension class are rendered above and below the actual input field. What we can't see in the screenshot, though, is that the actual input fields will likely have some length that does not fill the entire parent container.

We must differentiate the three cases to style this example with CSS Grid. Since we explicitly need to specify the columns of the grid, we need to have three different versions of the columns:

- To put the input extension on the left, we'd use grid-template-columns: auto 1fr;

- To put the input extension on the right, we'd use grid-template-columns: 1fr auto;

- To align input extensions to both sides, we'd even need an extra column, resulting in grid-template-columns: auto 1fr auto;

Since we can't style the parent based on its children, we'd need three classes to cover all three cases:

```
.input-group {
  display: grid;
}

.input-group-extension-left {
  grid-template-columns: auto 1fr;
}

.input-group-extension-right {
  grid-template-columns: 1fr auto;
}
```

```css
.input-group-extension-both {
  grid-template-columns: auto 1fr auto;
}
```

Lastly, we need to apply the classes to each element:

```html
<div class="input-group input-group-extension-left">
  <div class="input-extension">
    @
  </div>
  <input placeholder="Username">
</div>

<div class="input-group input-group-extension-right">
  <input placeholder="Your subdomain">
  <div class="input-extension">
    .example.com
  </div>
</div>

<div class="input-group input-group-extension-both">
  <div class="input-extension">
    $
  </div>
  <input placeholder="Transaction amount">
  <div class="input-extension">
    .00
  </div>
</div>
```

Even though this solution works perfectly, we lose a lot of flexibility. Think of automatically generated forms: we'd need to know in advance whether there will be an extension at all, where it is, and whether there are potentially even two of them.

In addition, the developers need to keep in mind that they need to add the respective classes because the form element won't render correctly if they are omitted. Flexbox, on the other hand, offers us a much more convenient solution:

```css
.input-group {
  display: flex;
}
.input-group input {
  flex: 1;
}
```

This solution yields the same result without needing extra classes, giving the developers all the flexibility they need with less code overall. The result for both solutions can be seen in the following figure.

Figure 5.9 – Form fields with form extensions neatly aligned

We can see that the form extensions only take up as much space as necessary while allowing the input field to grow to all the remaining width.

Compound form elements

A compound form element can be understood as a group of form elements that act as one and should rarely be separated. They often have a specific visual order and arrangement so the user recognizes the pattern. For example, think of address fields where a smaller field follows a street name field for the street number. The street name may be required, whereas not every address has a street number (believe me, I've dealt with international address formats, and they can get pretty specific at times).

Another famous example is credit card forms. They often follow the pattern of *full-width input for the card number, followed by two half-width fields for the expiration date and CVC*. People who use credit card forms regularly might not even read the labels anymore and type their card number, expiration date, and CVC in one fluid motion.

Let's consider the following HTML structure for a compound form element for credit cards:

```
<!-- chapter5/04_compound_form_elements.html -->
<div class="input-credit-card">
  <input class="input-card-number" placeholder="Credit card number">
  <input class="input-expiration-date" placeholder="Expires">
  <input class="input-cvc" placeholder="CVC">
</div>
```

Our goal is to align these fields in a pattern, as shown in the following figure.

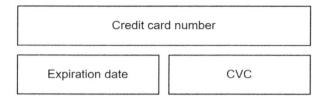

Figure 5.10 – A credit card form as might appear on an e-commerce website

We can see that the form field for the number takes up an entire row, while the expiration date and CVC fields share the second row. This layout won't change much, as even on smaller mobile devices, the entered content is only five characters for the expiration date field and three for the CVC field.

If we were to style this compound field with Flexbox, we'd need the following code to align it according to the schematic:

```
.input-credit-card {
  display: flex;
  flex-wrap: wrap;
  gap: 10px;
}
.input-card-number {
  width: 100%;
  margin-bottom: 10px;
}
.input-expiration-date {
  flex: 1;
}
.input-cvc {
  flex: 1;
}
```

We can see that the placement of the elements relies solely on their size. Due to `flex-wrap: wrap;` and the card number field having a width of 100%, the other two fields end up on the second row. This approach makes us apply CSS to all fields, bloating the CSS.

A possible solution using CSS Grid would rely on a two-column layout. We can then tell the `.input-card-number` element to span two columns:

```
.input-credit-card {
  display: grid;
  grid-template-columns: 1fr 1fr;
  gap: 10px;
}
```

```
.input-card-number {
  grid-column: span 2;
}
```

This code does not rely on any sizing of the child elements, is very specific, and requires less code and fewer CSS selectors to be written.

The result for both approaches is, again, the same, as shown in the following figure.

Figure 5.11 – The aligned credit card form

The credit card number field spans the entire width, whereas the expiration date and CVC fields share a row.

Form layouts

At the beginning of the section, we mentioned that the layout of a form is essential for good form UX. Large forms must be grouped and arranged logically, so the user feels guided and is not overwhelmed by many form fields.

A good practice that is straightforward is to stick to the standard top-down approach. One form field takes up a single row in the form, visually separated by grouping related fields in boxes or with portions of whitespace. For this approach, we need neither Flexbox nor CSS Grid. If we use block-level elements, CSS automatically stacks the fields on top of each other. We only need to take care of the fields themselves (think: compound fields); the rest works already.

The top-down approach is, however, not the only one, but certainly a popular one because it is more accessible than multi-column layouts. For example, when we put fields next to each other in two- or even three-column layouts, we can use either Flexbox or CSS Grid – both work perfectly. A grid layout might fit our needs better because it gives us more flexibility for placing singular form elements, but Flexbox can be used if no such flexibility is necessary.

We've seen that both CSS Grid and Flexbox have their use cases, especially for form elements. Form extensions can best be built with Flexbox, as it requires less code and gives us more flexibility, whereas CSS Grid works better for compound form elements, such as credit card forms. Depending on the use case, we can use either when it comes to aligning form elements. When deciding on one tool or the other, we can try both and see which one fits our needs better.

As for most things in software development, this platitude holds for this decision as well: if we feel it could be done more simply, it most likely can.

The following section covers complex header, navigation, and footer elements. It also provides tips for creating entire page layouts.

Building page layouts and partials

With the release of CSS Grid, page layouts started to use actual grid layouts instead of pseudo-grids built with Flexbox. As we've seen in the examples of Awesome Analytics, CSS Grid is made for the job: we can build entire pages with CSS Grid only, even having collapsible sidebars. However, behind the scenes, even these examples have used Flexbox to arrange some elements, namely the header and navigation elements.

As with form layouts, we must choose the right tool for the job. Depending on the design, a header or a footer can be built with Flexbox or CSS Grid. Let's look at a few page partials and build an entire page layout with a mix of Flexbox and CSS Grid.

Headers and navigation

There are several different approaches to building navigations and header bars. For example, some pages hide the menus entirely behind hamburger icons. Even on the desktop, other pages show partial navigation that enlarges once the user hovers over or clicks it. Yet other pages show the full navigation from the very start.

An often-used pattern for large websites is using mega menus. A mega menu can be compared to a drop-down navigation that accommodates many links to sub-pages that may interest users. Usually, a mega menu groups link visually, so they fall into subcategories of a main category. A page can have one or multiple mega menus hidden behind one or more top-level navigation items, which are always visible.

To illustrate what a mega menu could look like, let's look at the navigation of the Chicago Transit Authority website in the following figure.

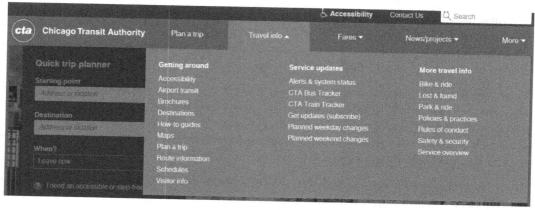

Figure 5.12 – A mega menu as used by the Chicago Transit Authority

In the top header bar, we can see multiple top-level navigation items, such as **Plan a trip**, **Travel info**, **Fares**, **News/projects**, and **More**. These items, except **Plan a trip**, offer a mega menu, indicated by the chevron icon next to them.

Inside the mega menu opened by clicking on **Travel info**, we can see three categories with up to 10 additional navigational items.

A reiteration of the lessons about design choices from *Chapter 4*

The Chicago Transit Authority wants to solve its users' problems, namely getting from *A* to *B* and receiving info about their travel, as efficiently as possible. By showing many relevant items at once, the user can find what they're looking for relatively quickly without having to traverse several pages.

The user doesn't need to be convinced to use public transport services. If they're on the website, they likely already decided to do so but have specific questions about their trip. Therefore, in this case, solving the user's problems is much more important than selling or convincing.

Let's build such a mega menu. We start with a header bar. For the time being, we don't care about its placement or whether it sticks to the top of the viewport; we only want to build a mega menu with both CSS Grid and Flexbox.

Consider the following HTML structure:

```
<!-- chapter5/05_header_and_nav.html -->
<header>
  <div class="container">
    <img
      src="https://via.placeholder.com/300x75?text=Logo"
      alt="Logo"
    >
    <nav>
      <ul>
        <li>
          <span class="top-level">Services</span>
          <ul>
            <li>
              Building examples
              <ul>
                <li><a href="/websites">Websites</a></li>
                <li><a href="/designs">Designs</a></li>
                <li><a href="/software">Software</a></li>
              </ul>
            </li>
            <li>
```

```
                Expert consulting
                <ul>
                    <li><a href="/faq">Consulting FAQ</a></li>
                    <li><a href="/calendar">
                        Book an appointment</a></li>
                    <li><a href="/team">
                        Meet our experts</a></li>
                </ul>
            </li>
            <li>
                Sales
                <ul>
                    <li><a href="/how-to-sell">
                        How to sell</a></li>
                    <li><a href="/marketing">Marketing</a></li>
                    <li><a href="/strategies">
                        Strategies</a></li>
                </ul>
            </li>
        </ul>
    </li>
    <li>
        <span class="top-level">Products</span>
        <!-- More sub menus -->
    </li>
    <li>
        <span class="top-level">About the company</span>
        <!-- More sub menus -->
    </li>
    <li>
        <span class="top-level">Contact us</span>
        <!-- More sub menus -->
    </li>
    </ul>
  </nav>
 </div>
</header>
```

The header element contains a .container element, which we'll use to restrict the maximum width of the entire header content. The container contains a logo image and navigation filled with nested unordered lists. We use the top-level list items as navigation items in line with the logo. The first nested list will be our mega menu container, with its list items being categories. This structure lets us focus entirely on styling while offering an accessible way to navigate the page. We also start with the following CSS:

```
header {
  background-color: #ffffd1;
  height: 75px;
}

.container {
  margin: 0 auto; /* No Flexbox or CSS Grid required! */
  max-width: 1024px;
  width: 100%;
}
```

This code gives us the result shown in the following figure on screens larger than 1024px.

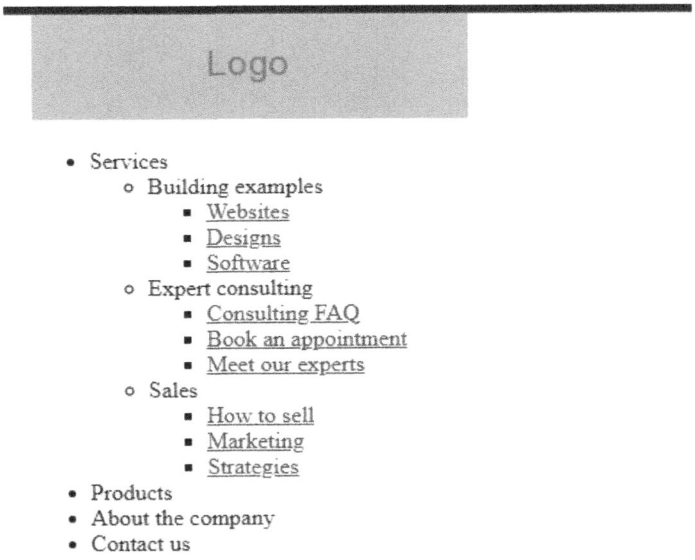

Figure 5.13 – The unstyled mega menu

We can see how the nested lists give us a structure of links we can style to visually represent categories, just like the Chicago Transit Authority does.

Let's first take care of positioning the top-level elements. We can use Flexbox and CSS Grid to align them in the header bar. However, since the entire navigation is nested in a `<nav>` element, Flexbox would be a more straightforward solution.

We also adjust the height of the `.top-level` items and center them on both axes. Also, we add `position: relative;` to the nav element, so the sub-menu can later be positioned absolutely and fill the width of the entire nav:

```css
.container {
  display: flex;
  align-items: flex-start;
}

nav {
  flex: 1;
  position: relative;
}

.top-level {
  height: 75px;
  display: flex;
  justify-content: center;
  align-items: center;
}
```

Next, we align the top-level navigation elements. We reset the list styles to remove the enumeration points and any additional padding and margins we don't need. We then apply the following CSS Grid code to align the top-level elements:

```css
nav ul {
  list-style-type: none;
  padding: 0;
  margin: 0;
}

nav > ul {
  display: grid;
  grid-template-columns: repeat(auto-fit,
    minmax(100px, 1fr));
}
```

Last but not least, we need to style the submenus. We add `position: absolute;` and `width: 100%;` to them so they fill the entire width of the navigation. We align the categories with CSS Grid, too:

```css
nav > ul > li > ul {
  width: 100%;
```

```
    position: absolute;
    background-color: #fff5ba;
    display: grid;
    grid-template-columns: repeat(auto-fill,
        minmax(200px, 1fr));
}

nav > ul > li > ul > li {
    padding: 8px;
}
```

We can see the result in the following figure:

Figure 5.14 – The (almost) finished mega menu

We can see that the mega menu now spans the entire navigation width and has three category columns.

The last thing missing is the open-on-hover functionality. We can achieve that by initially hiding the submenu with `display: none;` and only applying the styles for `nav > ul > li > ul` if the `li` element in the selector is hovered over by the user. However, the practice of revealing this content on hover is not accessible and is therefore not recommended in practice. In our case, it only serves as an example:

```
nav > ul > li > ul {
    display: none;
}

nav > ul > li:hover {
    background-color: #fff5ba;
}

nav > ul > li:hover > ul {
    width: 100%;
    position: absolute;
    background-color: #fff5ba;
    display: grid;
    grid-template-columns: repeat(auto-fill,
        minmax(200px, 1fr));
}
```

With that, our mega menu is complete.

We've seen that Flexbox and CSS Grid are necessary for a complex task like the mega menu to achieve the design and interaction we'd like. By applying Flexbox to the header bar and using CSS Grid to align child elements, we have created a neatly aligned mega menu for our users to find what they're looking for quickly.

Footers

A staple of most corporate websites is the footer. It contains links that may be useful but not as essential as those in the main navigation, or even sometimes information mandatory by law. Germany, for example, has the so-called **Impressumspflicht gemäss § 5 Telemediengesetz**, Article 5 of the German Telemedia Act, which stipulates the mandatory existence of contact data on any website. So that's something you know now!

For example, look at the page footer from the DeepL website in the following figure.

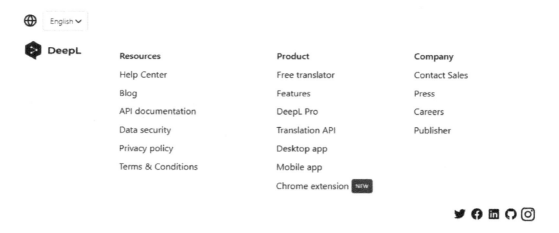

Figure 5.15 – The footer of DeepL

We can see several different elements. First, there is a language switcher with an icon in the top left of the footer. It looks like it occupies an entire row. Second, we have a four-column layout with a logo and three columns containing links, similarly structured to the mega menu we discussed in the previous section. Lastly, social media icons are in the bottom right, occupying an entire row.

The developers at DeepL have decided to use Flexbox for the entire footer layout. This approach has several advantages: first, on smaller devices, the logo is not in a column anymore but occupies an entire row itself. Second, `flex-wrap` can make the link columns somewhat responsive: on smaller devices, the columns wrap around.

Let's try to rebuild this structure with CSS Grid instead and consider the following HTML structure, which is a rebuild of the DeepL footer:

```
<!-- chapter5/06_footer.html -->
<footer>
  <div class="language-switch">
    <img
      src="https://via.placeholder.com/30x30"
      alt="Lang switch icon"
    >
    <select name="lang" id="lang">
      <option value="EN">English</option>
      <option value="FR">French</option>
      <!-- ... -->
    </select>
  </div>

  <img
    src="https://via.placeholder.com/100x45"
    alt="Logo"
    class="logo"
  >

  <nav class="links">
    <ul>
      <li>
        Resources
        <ul>
          <li><a href="...">Help Center</a></li>
          <li><a href="...">Blog</a></li>
          <li><a href=»...»>API documentation</a></li>
          <li><a href="...">Data security</a></li>
          <li><a href="...">Privacy policy</a></li>
          <li><a href="...">Terms & Conditions</a></li>
        </ul>
      </li>
      <!-- More links omitted for brevity -->
    </ul>
  </nav>
  <nav class="social-media">
    <ul>
      <li>
        <a href="...">
          <img
            src="https://via.placeholder.com/30x30"
```

```
                alt="Social media icon"
          >
        </a>
      </li>
      <!-- More icons omitted for brevity -->
    </ul>
  </nav>
</footer>
```

For the styling part, we will omit responsiveness.

By wrapping the language switch in its own `<div>` element, we already met the first challenge: having the language switch occupy a single line. However, our structure might pose a challenge: the navigation and logo should be placed in a four-column layout.

Still, the navigation is a single element, so we need to ensure that the `<nav>` element is a single grid element spanning 75% of the available width. We then apply a three-column layout inside the `<nav>` element instead. Again, we can do so with Flexbox. The social media icons are their own container, putting them on a single line.

Expressed as a grid template, we could apply the following style:

```
footer {
  display: grid;
  grid-template:
    "langswitch . . ." 75px
    "logo nav nav nav" auto
    ". . . socialMedia" 75px
  ;
}

.language-switch {
  grid-area: langswitch;
}

.logo {
  grid-area: logo;
}

.links {
  grid-area: nav;
}

.social-media {
  grid-area: socialMedia;
}
```

The advantage of using CSS Grid for these tasks is the lack of extra elements (we use entirely semantic HTML with no extra containers) and the verbosity of the grid template code.

To then style the links, we apply the following CSS code:

```
footer ul {
  list-style-type: none;
  padding: 0;
  margin: 0;
}

.links > ul,
.social-media ul {
  display: flex;
  flex-direction: row;
}

.links > ul > li,
.social-media li {
  flex: 1;
}
```

The rest is aligning the elements vertically and applying some paddings and margins to better space the elements. The result, however, is pretty close to the initial example of DeepL, as shown in the following figure.

Figure 5.16 – The rebuilt footer layout, resembling the footer layout from Figure 5.15

We can see the language switch on a separate line, the four columns containing the logo and links, and an extra line for social media icons. To add responsiveness to the footer, Grid allows us to rearrange the elements by changing the grid areas. The parts using Flexbox work best when we add `flex-wrap: wrap;`. We could switch to a two-column layout for tablet-sized screens and a single-column layout for mobile devices.

This endeavor is yet another example of a mixture of Flexbox and CSS Grid: the overall structure is best solved with CSS Grid, while Flexbox can take over the details.

Building entire pages

At the beginning of the chapter, we mentioned that people used Flexbox for everything and are now advocating using CSS Grid for all layouts. While this applies to complex layouts, they can also be built with Flexbox. Sometimes, we need neither, for example, when building one-column layouts or apps for very narrow devices. Features such as keeping the footer always at the page bottom can be solved with either.

The quintessence of this section and the entire chapter is that these tools best work in conjunction.

We've now covered a wide variety of use cases: we've arranged card elements, teaser boxes, form elements, a navigation bar, and a footer. To put the theory into practice, the next section introduces a new change request for Awesome Analytics.

Practicing with Awesome Analytics

Not only have we learned more about CSS Grid and Flexbox but so has the lead developer of Awesome Analytics, who happens not to know any CSS since they're a backend developer and have never touched any frontend code. They read many age-old articles on Flexbox and how it solves every possible problem. They call us in an urgent meeting and tell us their plans: they want us to replace CSS Grid with Flexbox on the dashboard!

Naturally, we're a bit baffled. We've been hired explicitly as a CSS Grid experts and are now expected to rebuild the entire Awesome Analytics dashboard in Flexbox. After thinking about it for a bit, the lead developer recognizes our job title and description and tells us to replace any Flexbox used so far with CSS Grid.

So, to summarize, the lead developer wants us to replace CSS Grid with Flexbox and Flexbox with CSS Grid. For some reason, they also managed to convince management of this idea.

We leave the meeting room, slowly start asking ourselves how we ended up in this company, and sit down at our desk. Time to get our hands dirty.

Analyzing the code base

In the chapter5 folder of the repository, we find a folder called Awesome Analytics. There is essentially the same code we used in *Chapter 2, Project Introduction: What We'll Work on and First Tasks*, with the difference that the grid is now already implemented.

Scanning through the code base, we find occurrences of Flexbox in the following files:

- `page-header.css`: This contains the header bar
- `chart-boxes.css`: The styling for the chart boxes
- `typography.css`: Styling the links, which we won't touch since the lead developer would never expect Flexbox to be used for typography

We find CSS Grid only in `grid.css`, the solution we implemented in *Chapter 2* for the layout and the chart box arrangement.

We go through each file and adjust it to use Flexbox instead of CSS Grid and CSS Grid instead of Flexbox respectively.

Adjusting the header

We start with the page header. It consists of two child elements: the logo and a login icon. The logo text is centered on the brand icon. The login icon is aligned to the right. Replacing Flexbox with CSS Grid is relatively straightforward in this case. We change the code according to the following code snippet:

```
.page-header {
  padding: var(--spacing-1);
  display: grid;
  grid-template-columns: 1fr auto;
  border-bottom: var(--border-standard);
}

.page-title {
  display: grid;
  grid-template-columns: auto 1fr;
  align-items: center;
}
```

Generally speaking, Flexbox works better for single-column layouts and CSS Grid works better for two-dimensional layouts. The page header and title adjustment serve to demonstrate this: while the grid approach technically work, the Flexbox solution is more readable and thus more maintainable.

Adjusting the chart boxes

The chart boxes make heavy use of Flexbox to make the charts, which are entirely controlled by `chart.js`, resize correctly. By using a 100%-width single column and two rows, we can emulate the behavior of Flexbox. In addition, the title of a chart box can be aligned similarly to the page header:

```
.chart-box {
  background-color: var(--color-gray-0);
```

```
  border: var(--border-standard);
  border-radius: 4px;
  padding: var(--spacing-1);

  min-width: 0;
  min-height: 0;

  display: grid;
  grid-template-columns: 100%;
  grid-template-rows: auto 1fr;
}

.chart-box header {
  display: grid;
  grid-template-columns: 1fr auto;

  text-transform: capitalize;
}
```

Again, perhaps Flexbox felt like a better fit here because it would've fit better for the page header: Flexbox is usually used for single-row and single-column layouts, our very use case.

While we could have implemented the chart boxes as a single grid, we would've needed to adjust the HTML for that, which we usually want to avoid for simple layout changes.

Adjusting the page layout

The page layout has used CSS Grid so far, but replacing it with Flexbox is relatively straightforward. First, we use Flexbox on the entire body and tell it to wrap. We then make the `.page-header` element span the entire available width with `width: 100%;` and use the `flex` shortcut to tell the sidebar and chart box container how much available space they may occupy:

```
.body {
  display: flex;
  flex-wrap: wrap;
}

.page-header {
  width: 100%;
}

.sidebar {
  flex: 0 1 auto;
}
```

```
.main-page-content {
  flex: 1;
}
```

This code feels a bit simpler than a pure CSS Grid implementation, but it may break the layout more easily. Using Flexbox for such a layout is feasible, although making it responsive is more complex in the long run, as we need to add explicit widths and use `flex-wrap` to achieve responsiveness.

Additionally, implementing the layout with a mobile-first approach would mean we have to reset the properties on larger viewports, for example, by using `width: auto;`, to return to our original setup.

Adjusting the chart box container

The most complex task is to adjust the chart box container. The boxes should, ideally, fill empty holes and align themselves in a grid. The chart box container is the perfect use case for CSS Grid. However, rebuilding this behavior with Flexbox is very complex.

First, Flexbox doesn't recognize empty spaces the way CSS Grid does since it doesn't work with any discrete unit, which would be the grid cell for CSS Grid. Second, we need to use either margin on the chart boxes and sacrifice the simplicity that `row-gap` and `column-gap` offer, or live with the fact that making a box "twice as large" requires more effort.

One attempt to rebuild the grid layout is shown here:

```
/* chapter5/Awesome Analytics/assets/grid.css */
.main-page-content {
  display: flex;
  flex-wrap: wrap;
  column-gap: var(--spacing-1);
  row-gap: var(--spacing-1);
}

.chart-box {
  height: 400px;
  flex: 0 1 25%;
  width: 25%;
}

.chart-box-wide {
  flex: 0 1 50%;
  width: 50%;
}

.chart-box-tall {
  height: 800px;
}
```

The result of this rather dubious task is shown in the following figure.

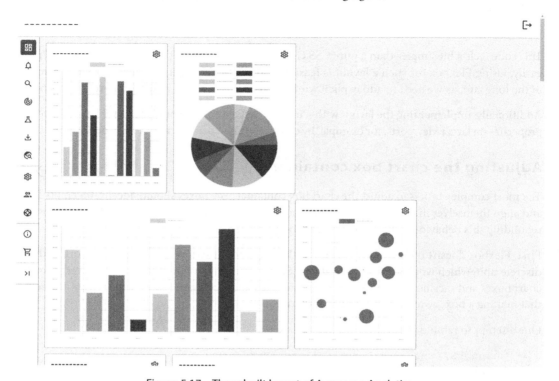

Figure 5.17 – The rebuilt layout of Awesome Analytics

While the header, sidebar, and overall layout are still intact, the chart box container looks broken. There are ways to achieve the CSS Grid layout perfectly with Flexbox, but they are rather complex and require more effort. We won't do that. Theoretically, we should stop here and talk with the lead developer.

Unfortunately, we haven't added any value for the end user besides breaking the entire chart box layout. Instead, we've made simple things more complex using tools we probably shouldn't have, and deteriorated the DX.

Conclusion

We saw that we could rebuild some things with CSS Grid that previously used Flexbox and vice versa. Some things become simpler when we use Flexbox, and others get tremendously more complex. The task at hand illustrated this with multiple elements.

Please note that this Flexbox/CSS Grid comparison was meant as an exercise. By now, we should know that we probably shouldn't fulfill our manager's every wish and instead should convince them to allow us to choose the right tools for the job. As mentioned previously, both tools have specific use cases, and there is no one-size-fits-all solution.

There is also no definitive guide on what we should build with CSS Grid and what we should build with Flexbox – the web is too complex for that.

Summary

We've now analyzed some example use cases for CSS Grid and Flexbox. It is essential to remember that both tools have advantages and disadvantages when aligning elements. The development community has jumped onto CSS Grid just like it did with Flexbox once it appeared on the scene. There is an old saying: *if the only tool you know is a hammer, every problem starts to look like a nail.* However, we must remember that we can use any tool in our toolbox as long as it fits our needs.

We'll look at the design and UX perspective in the next chapter again. We'll learn about the general benefits of using grid layouts and where not to use them. Sometimes, it is best to abandon the known tools and take a different route.

6

Benefits of Grid Layouts and When Not to Use Them

This chapter title might spark controversy. Generally, grids are an established feature of web design and have been around since the early table-based layouts we once used to structure downright everything. However, grids are not always the answer. In the summary of the last chapter, we quoted an old saying: *if the only tool you know is a hammer, every problem starts to look like a nail*. This saying is true in design, too.

When confronted with a design task, we might jump to grids immediately because our muscle memory tells us to do so. We know grids. We have a set of ideal grid layouts that we can apply to virtually any design problem. However, perhaps there would be better, more fitting solutions – but we might not see them.

In this chapter, we want to open our tunnel vision toward grids and see how they can benefit and hinder us. We want to think about alternatives and use our creativity to understand that even though we know a tool, such as CSS Grid, we don't always have to use it and need to know when to say *let's not use CSS Grid for this problem*.

In detail, we'll look at the following topics:

- The benefits of grid layouts
- The drawbacks of grid layouts
- The alternatives for grid layouts
- A list to help us decide

Technical requirements

Since this chapter is mainly about design, we don't need coding tools. However, a simple web browser to look at the examples in detail might be helpful.

Cherishing the benefits of grid layouts

The entire book has so far been about grids – how we can use CSS Grid to create them, configure their finest details, design them, and use them to our advantage. We know that grids work. We've seen them countless times. We take this as a fact. But why? What are the reasons for this unreasonable effectiveness of grids on the web?

Let's look at some of the main advantages of grid layouts to understand why they've become a staple of web design.

The ease of design and development

A grid can be simple or complex, but it can always be described with a few variables. Usually, we see a certain number of columns with a given total width. Sometimes, we also see descriptions of rows, usually with a given height. Elements can span one or more columns and one or more rows.

For example, imagine that we want to implement a grid, with a maximum total width of 960px and with six possible columns. The main content should span four columns and be surrounded by two one-column sidebars. There are rows of 50px height each, the header spans two rows, the main content all the rest, and the footer spans another two rows. The header and footer both span six columns.

From this description alone, we immediately know what the grid looks like. We don't even need visuals to implement this. Some frameworks even offer this exact solution out of the box. Alternatively, we can deduce the grid area template directly, as shown in the following code snippet:

```
.grid {
  grid-template:
    "header    header   header" 100px
    "sidebar1 content sidebar2" 1fr
    "footer    footer   footer" 100px
    / 160px 640px 160px
  ;
}
```

We've calculated that a single column has a width of 160px. So, the content spans four times that, resulting in 640px. Two rows of header and footer result in a single rows of 100px.

Many design tools and toolboxes offer ready-made grid templates with standard gutters and widths. Often, these tools also offer vertical grids (that is, grid rows) so that we can align texts, images, buttons, and other components to them. The following figure shows an example of such a design system.

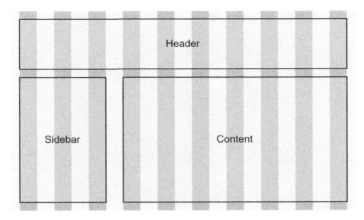

Figure 6.1 – An example of a design system using a grid template

We can see that a grid is beneath the elements. It helps to align things according to the columns and ensures that a developer can understand how many columns each element spans.

How we then implement these grids with CSS Grid is a different question, but at least in the design process, grids take away a lot of the overhead. However, CSS Grid even allows us to build these layouts faster, as the syntax is very legible and made to be understood.

Many CSS frameworks offer grid solutions by offering utility classes, such as Tailwind, or complete grid implementations, such as Bootstrap.

You might see a chicken and egg problem here – is the ease of design and development a reason for grids being famous, or has their popularity made them more accessible to be designed and developed? It could go either way.

Visual appeal

A carefully crafted grid can make the difference of a website feeling like something a true expert has made versus something a junior or person unfamiliar with any design has come up with. It's a well-known fact that humans love symmetry and well-structured things. We tend to process things quicker that are in a clear structure because of our exceptional skills in pattern recognition.

For example, have a look at the following figure. It shows a right angle.

Figure 6.2 – A right angle

Except, it doesn't. The angle is slightly less than 90 degrees. We might either immediately notice that it isn't exactly 90 degrees or feel that something is odd about it. Pattern recognition in our brains kicks in immediately.

We like things that repeat, have similar ratios (think 16:9 or 3:2), and behave like things we already know. We do because our brain tends to be *lazy*. Carlos E. Perez has excellently formulated this in his *The Lazy Brain Hypothesis* post on Medium: "*One way to reduce energy is to not do any work at all! A brain does what it does because it avoids doing any work if it can.*" Grid layouts build on that.

Using ratios for column widths or row heights, we can create things that are nice to look at and don't need much attention from our brain to process. Grids help direct focus by giving more important elements more space. The brain recognizes these patterns and acts accordingly.

Simple to adapt and expand

Grids are inherently simple to adapt and expand. Do we need more vertical space? We add a few more rows. Do we need another element on the horizontal axis? We reduce the size of other elements by a few columns. Standard grid layouts, such as the already mentioned 12-column layouts in `960px` width (also called a **960 grid**), allow us to do precisely that. In addition, grid layouts are simpler to adapt because they offer a lot of structure.

The average CSS framework offers classes for column spans. For example, think of Bootstrap's `.col-3` or `.col-6` classes that work in a 12-column grid. So, adjusting an element's size is usually a matter of adjusting a single class name. On the other hand, if we've built our CSS grid ourselves, we can adjust an element's size with little effort by adjusting the grid template or the number of columns and rows it spans.

Let's look at the grid definition we've used before to describe grid design systems.

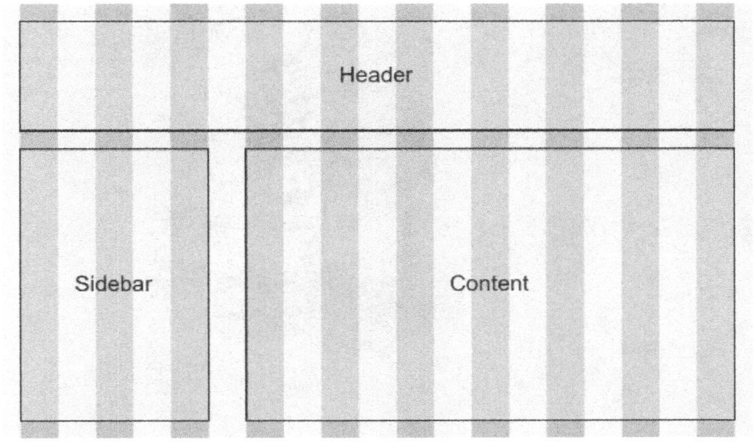

Figure 6.3 – An example of a design system using a grid template

We see a header bar. Underneath is a three-column wide sidebar and a seven-column wide content section next to it. If we wanted to expand the sidebar, we have two possibilities – add more columns to distribute the space a little more granularly or sacrifice a column of the content section and enlarge the sidebar by a single column.

We now know about some of the key benefits of grid layouts and how they support us when designing. They are simple to conceive and adapt and offer some visual appeal to the end users. Of course, these are all things we want, but sometimes, it is beneficial to go the extra mile and think outside the box – quite literally.

Understanding the drawbacks of grid layouts

When using a tool, it is imperative to know its drawbacks. No tool is perfect, and there are no one-size-fits-all solutions, especially for design tasks. Grids do help us and have advantages, and often, we don't even notice the drawbacks, but they do exist, and we can handle a tool better once we understand its limitations and the limits it applies to us as developers.

Compatibility with content

Sometimes, our content doesn't fit in a grid. Of course, there is content predestined for a grid, such as photo galleries or card teasers, but some content should best be kept without a grid and free-flowing. In addition, not all content we intend to publish fits in a grid. For example, in the following figure, let's look at a grid-based design.

Figure 6.4 – A grid-based layout with a stock image, title, and text

It shows a beach stock image with palm trees on the right side. There is a title and text to the right of the image. While drawing the focus to the stock image, the text loses its significance. In this case, we would want to fuse text and image to form a union.

The empty sky on the left side of the image would offer some whitespace to place the text. However, to place the text, we need to think without grids. A possible example is shown in the following figure.

Figure 6.5 – A beach stock image with a title and text positioned on the image

We've achieved a unison of image and text. The image now has a direct connection to the text and vice versa.

> **A source for stock images**
>
> The beach image in the last two figures was a picture I found on `https://www.pexels.com`. Pexels is a free stock image platform that does not require attribution and allows you to alter and reuse any image published there.
>
> However, the platform must alter images before printing and selling them on physical objects, such as posters. Since we've used it with text and in a different context, this specific use case is allowed, according to Pexels' license published at `https://www.pexels.com/license/`.
>
> Another great source for stock images is Unsplash: `https://unsplash.com/`.

Losing identity

In 2022, there is a trend away from largely opinionated CSS frameworks to utility frameworks. For example, Bootstrap, a highly opinionated framework, is losing popularity, whereas Tailwind and other such frameworks are becoming increasingly popular. One of the reasons is that all Bootstrap pages look alike unless developers invest a significant amount of effort into theming.

Grids, to some degree, are opinionated as well. Since they offer a lot of structure, many standard grids, such as the 12-column `960px` grid, can be recognized at first glance. However, although they were once the holy grail of layouts, they can harm our brand identity by not making our design stand out enough. Sebastian Scheerer has written an excellent article on Designmodo about why blindly following design trends can hurt a business. They explain how new trends can create a *"sea of sameness"* over several products and websites, essentially taking away their uniqueness. They argue that the overuse of a design trend or concept can diminish its impact. You can read the full article here: `https://designmodo.com/web-design-trends-problem/`.

For example, in the following figure, let's look at parts of the Drupal landing page (`https://www.drupal.org`) from 2023, which uses a 960-grid.

Figure 6.6 – The Drupal landing page

We see that a lot of available space isn't used on larger displays. To compare it, let's look at a part of the landing page of the Fedora project (`https://getfedora.org/`) in the following figure.

Want more Fedora options?

Fedora Spins

If you prefer an alternative desktop environment such as KDE Plasma Desktop or Xfce, you can download a Fedora Spin for your preferred desktop environment and use that to install Fedora, pre-configured for the desktop environment of your choice.

Learn more

Fedora Labs

Fedora Labs is a selection of curated bundles of purpose-driven software and content as curated and maintained by members of the Fedora Community. These may be installed as standalone full versions of Fedora or as add-ons to existing Fedora installations.

Learn more

Fedora ALT Downloads

The Fedora Alternative Downloads are either special-purpose - for testing, for specific architectures - or are more standard versions of Fedora in alternative formats such as network installer format or formatted for BitTorrent download.

Learn more

Support Resources

Documentation

Extensive documentation is available at the Fedora documentation page.

Fedora Docs

Support

Get support from our the community on the Fedora Discussion Forum.

Fedora Discussion

Chat

Users and developers are available in the #fedora channel on Fedora Chat.

Fedora Chat

Figure 6.7 – The Fedora project landing page

Although different (especially in the number of columns used), the pages look alike. Part of that is the container width of 960px. In addition, since both pages use a 12-column layout behind the scenes, they are likely to use element widths that divide 12 evenly, such as 3 or 4 columns. As a result, both pages deliver a similar feeling.

The restrictions a grid applies reduce the number of possible designs and, thus, make them look more alike.

The temptation of packing things too tight

A grid-based layout can help us compact our content for maximum efficiency. There are techniques, such as borders and drop shadows, to distinguish different content entities, so we may as well pack things tight.

Sometimes, however, we don't want that. More white space can give a website a more relaxed feeling and ease pressure. A user might feel stressed and overwhelmed if the information density is too high, potentially working against our brand identity and vision. Grid structures can lead us to pack things tight.

Let's look at the Chicago Transit Authority site (https://www.transitchicago.com), which we already analyzed in a previous chapter. The following figure shows their landing page.

Figure 6.8 – The entire landing page of the Chicago Transit Authority

We can see a hero image with an overlay to search for connections and a **call-to-action** (CTA for short). The CTA is slightly wider than the grid, but the rest is perfectly aligned. Underneath, we see many teasers and a box with delays and service interruptions. All these teasers are perfectly aligned to the grid, packing all the information very tight. The Chicago Transit Authority has achieved very high information density, which benefits its clients. They can find what they're looking for in seconds without much scrolling.

In the following figure, let's compare the Chicago Transit Authority to the Swiss Federal Railways website's landing page (`https://www.sbb.ch`).

Figure 6.9 – The landing page of the Swiss Federal Railways website

The page has a much lower information density. It seems calmer and more relaxed, although it offers similar features, such as an interface for finding connections. They use two different grids, with elements occasionally escaping both.

Using a grid can create higher information density, almost to the point of feeling natural to do so. If we decide on a grid with boxes that spans the entire page, we already decide on the density, perhaps without knowing what information we want to place.

Depending on the use case, this is perfectly fine, but we need to keep in mind that high information density can impact conversion rate, readability, and focus.

Being restricted

In the previous section, we discussed the ease of development and design with grids. However, their structure takes away some of the possibilities we have. We are inherently limited by the number of columns and rows and their sizes. To over-dramatize it, no element may escape the grid.

Although a grid's symmetry and structure benefit the overall user experience, sometimes, we want to break symmetry to achieve specific effects. For example, brutalist web design values effectiveness over attractiveness. A grid might hinder us depending on the values, messages, and contents we want to bring across.

It can be beneficial to think first without grids. However, we can still use grids if we can see that we need a lot of structure and symmetry.

Learning about some alternatives for grid layouts

Let's discuss how we can escape grids or alter them so that their disadvantages don't matter anymore. What could some alternatives to grid-based layouts be? Is it even possible to work without grids entirely?

Breaking out of the grid

We can ensure that elements don't fill entire grid cells or purposefully make them overflow grid cells. Although technically still using a grid, we give the illusion of breaking out of it. This way, we can still have all the benefits of grids.

The Texas-based nail studio Cure Nails (`https://curenails.co`) uses this technique to create more dynamic layouts. It makes elements overlap each other, as shown in the following figure.

Figure 6.10 – Part of the website of Cure Nails

We can see several elements, with a central image showing a pair of hands. The title to the right overlaps with the image, fusing it with the content. A second image to the left adds contrast.

Building such a layout is possible with CSS Grid and a few adjustments to element positioning. Cure Nails themselves use Flexbox for this layout, however.

Using animations

We can physically escape the grid by animating elements. Popular approaches are parallax effects, where an element scrolls either slower or faster than the rest of a page, giving the illusion of depth. Such an effect can make an element escape a grid temporarily.

Another approach could be animations to let elements enter the screen. For example, they could fly in from outside the viewport and zoom in or out to give the page a more dynamic approach when loading.

The previous example, Cure Nails, also uses animations and a parallax effect to further break out of the grid.

Using different shapes

We may even want to ditch rectangles altogether. Instead, we can create interesting layouts that offer something new by using circles, hexagons, or triangles. For example, the Swiss Federal Railways website (`https://www.sbb.ch`) uses trapezoids on the landing page, as shown in the following figure.

Figure 6.11 – Trapezoids used as content boxes

We can see two trapezoids overlapping – one contains text only and acts as a CTA, whereas the larger one serves the purpose of a hero image. Another example is the concept of using diagonal lines to separate elements.

The digital agency KRYPTIS (`https://www.kryptis.com`) has even declared them an integral part of their visual language, up to the point of showing screenshots – an inherently rectangular thing – in a 3D perspective to create the illusion of diagonal lines, as shown in the following figure.

Figure 6.12 – The landing page of the website of digital agency KRYPTIS

All diagonal lines are parallel and go from the top right to the bottom left. The screenshots, however, are tilted the other way around to keep balance and give them special attention. Also, the white space offered by the significant element on the right relaxes things and makes them appear less busy.

Munich-based designer Andrei Gorokhov (`http://gorohov.name`) has based his entire website layout on hexagons, as shown in the following figure.

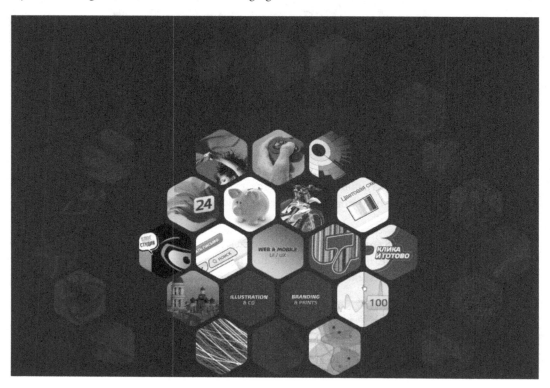

Figure 6.13 – The website of Munich-based designer Andrei Gorokhov

The hexagons are used as teasers to show different works. In addition, their arrangement allows for higher information density (as the famous YouTuber CGP Grey put it, *"Hexagons are the Bestagons!"*) and for a more visually exciting arrangement.

Vlog.it (`https://vlog.it/`) has even gone a step further and uses several nested circles as its main navigational element, as shown in the following figure.

Figure 6.14 – The landing page of vlog.it

Each circle opens a different modal with a vlog. The circles rotate, bringing motion into the primary control. Radial menus have been a staple of game design for ages already. They do work but need extra effort to be implemented on the web.

A list to help us decide

To decide whether we should use a grid or whether we should pursue an alternative, the following list can be helpful.

Grids work well for the following use cases:

- Websites or applications with a lot of content that needs structure and should be visually pleasing and straightforward to understand

- When we want to add consistency to our design in terms of sizes, hierarchies, and white space

- When designing for responsive layouts that need to work on many different screen sizes

- When creating data-heavy interfaces such as analytics dashboards or data management software, where a lot of information should be presented in a clear, consistent layout that is quick to scan

Grid alternatives work best for the following use cases:

- When the message of the website or application should be to convince or be creative or artistic

- When designing for projects with little content

- When working on projects whose brand or product identity work with grid alternatives already

Summary

We've seen the advantages and disadvantages of using grids. A grid is simple to design, implement, and adapt and has a visual appeal. However, grids can be restrictive, might not fit our content, and pose a loss of brand identity.

We've also learned that a website can use alternative layouts, even abandoning the rectangular shape ingrained into the web.

We now know what grids can and cannot do, and we've learned sometimes to take a step back and ask ourselves whether we even need a grid in the first place. We've seen unique alternatives to grid layouts that are inspiring and perhaps give us more ideas for our future projects.

From a purely design-based chapter, we will go into a purely code-based one. In the following chapter, we'll look at how we can polyfill and simulate some cutting-edge features related to CSS Grid.

Part 3 –
Exploring the Wider Ecosystem

This chapter examines the possibilities that JavaScript, PostCSS, and Browserify give us to implement features currently not released for CSS Grid. You will implement polyfills for additional features, such as new selectors, lay out alternatives, and animate grids. You will also learn about different CSS frameworks that use CSS Grid or emulate grids using Flexbox, or even float-based techniques.

Finally, you will implement the same layout in many different ways and understand the advantages and drawbacks of the frameworks discussed.

This part has the following chapters:

7

Polyfilling CSS Grid's Missing Features

Although CSS Grid Level 1 was released in 2020, at the time of writing, not all features are supported in every major browser. Currently, `subgrid` is only supported by Firefox and Safari, with a distinct lack of support in Chromium-based browsers, such as Google Chrome or Microsoft Edge. Unfortunately, `masonry` support is even worse – no major browser supports it by default. Firefox offers an implementation that needs to be enabled manually.

CSS, being a living standard with the release of CSS3, evolves. New features are defined in drafts first, then discussed, and afterward, redefined as standards. Sometimes, these discussions and redrafts can go on for literally decades. For example, the first draft of CSS Grid was released in 2007. The current *CSS Grid Level 1* definition was only released around 13 years later. So, naturally, developers read these standards and get excited about these new features. That's why there are polyfills.

A **polyfill** is a reimplementation in userland code of a non-supported feature, primarily JavaScript. There are still actively maintained polyfills for PHP and some polyfills for Python. Polyfills aim to make features available for developers to work with, but they usually impact performance, usability, or, in a worst-case scenario, both.

However, in this chapter, we'll look at polyfills. Polyfills are helpful to support older platforms while still using cutting-edge technology. They also let us peek behind the scenes of the polyfilled features – we get a sense of how they are meant to work code-wise. Since CSS Grid Level 1 enjoys widespread support and IE11 has been deprecated for ages, we'll fully focus on non-supported features and even some that are not fully defined yet.

In detail, we'll look at the following topics:

- Understanding the tools necessary to create CSS polyfills
- Creating a polyfill for `subgrid`
- Creating a polyfill for `masonry`
- Creating a polyfill for possible `nth-row` and `nth-col` pseudo-classes
- Animating grids
- Understanding why we should not use polyfills unless there are justifiable reasons

Technical requirements

This chapter will make heavy use of Node.js and npm. Therefore, we'll need the following tools:

- A browser, preferably Chromium-based, such as Google Chrome, Brave, Microsoft Edge, or Vivaldi, but Firefox or Apple Safari works too. However, for the `subgrid` polyfill, a Chromium-based browser is advised.
- An **integrated development environment** (**IDE**) or text editor, such as WebStorm, VS Code, or Vim, with HTML and CSS syntax highlighting.
- Internet access is necessary to access the code.
- Git (this is optional; we can also download the folder from GitHub).
- Node.js with at least version 14 and npm with at least version 6.

If Node.js is not currently installed on your system, or you've got the wrong version, the **node version manager** (**nvm**) is a fantastic tool to handle different Node.js versions on one system.

All the code for this chapter can be found on GitHub in this repository: `https://github.com/PacktPublishing/Mastering-CSS-Grid/tree/main/chapter7`.

Understanding the tools to write a CSS polyfill from scratch

To write CSS polyfills, we first need to understand our possibilities to even hook into CSS in the first place. We cannot hook into the rendering engine of every browser itself, at least not with browser plugins or a custom build, and we can't directly add code to the inner workings of the browser from a website. That would be a substantial security risk at best. Besides, CSS rendering engines are arguably some of the most optimized software in the world, and we don't want to mess with them.

So, what else can we do? We could use preprocessors, such as SASS or LESS. However, that would mean we potentially need to ship polyfill code to clients that do support the polyfilled feature, which is not ideal.

There are, however, a few tricks up our sleeves on how we can ship the CSS and only execute the polyfilling code once necessary. One such solution is to use PostCSS in the browser.

A note on writing polyfills with PostCSS

While possible, it is not recommended to use this approach in a production environment. There are alternative solutions for most of the polyfilled features, and it's best to usually wait for the features to be implemented with CSS.

The PostCSS approach was made famous in 2016 by Philip Walton on his blog. Philip Walton was the maintainer of a set of CSS polyfills and currently works at Google, specifically on Chrome. In his post, we learn about Houdini, a CSS extension API available in Chrome that lets us implement polyfills more directly by hooking into the rendering engine. Unfortunately, while Houdini is a fantastic alternative to PostCSS-based polyfills, it is currently only supported by Chromium-based browsers.

Their post was the main inspiration for the PostCSS approach used in this chapter. The post can be read here: `https://philipwalton.com/articles/the-dark-side-of-polyfilling-css/`.

To understand how we can use PostCSS to create polyfills, we first need to understand PostCSS itself.

Understanding PostCSS

PostCSS (`https://postcss.org/`) calls itself a *"tool for transforming CSS with JavaScript,"* which is precisely what it does. Out of the box, PostCSS does nothing. We can, however, add functionality to it with plugins. One such plugin is the autoprefixer mentioned on its landing page. It adds vendor prefixes to some browser-specific features, such as `:fullscreen`, transforming it into `:-webkit-full-screen`, `:-ms-fullscreen`, and `:fullscreen`.

There are plugins galore. A search on GitHub for `postcss` yields roughly 8,000 results, most of them being plugins. These plugins offer all kinds of functionality, from additional color spaces and transforming every `px` value to `rem` to nested selectors best known from SASS, URL transformers, and mixins support. For example, Tailwind heavily uses PostCSS by offering a plugin out of the box.

PostCSS works in Rollup, Webpack, Brunch, Broccoli, Parcel, Browserify, and many other build tools. To work with PostCSS, according to their documentation, we need to install it, create a `postcss.config.js` file, which is even optional in some cases, add it to our build tool, and install and use plugins.

Understanding how to write PostCSS plugins

We've now learned that most of the work PostCSS does lives in its plugins. To create polyfills, we can create plugins that transform our CSS.

PostCSS parses any given CSS string and transforms it using an **abstract syntax tree** (**AST**) (a graph representing the parsed code) and different functions called at specific events during the parsing process. The transformed CSS is then returned as a string.

A PostCSS plugin is a JavaScript object containing a name and one or more plugin functions. According to its docs, a PostCSS plugin might look like the following:

```
module.exports = (opts = {}) => {
  return {
    postcssPlugin: 'PLUGIN NAME',
    Once (root) {
      // Calls once per file since every file has a single
      Root
    },
    Declaration (decl) {
      // All declaration nodes
    }
  }
}
module.exports.postcss = true
```

While parsing CSS, PostCSS encounters different elements, for which it calls listeners in the used plugins. PostCSS knows the following elements of a CSS document:

- Root: Represents the entire CSS document
- AtRule: Statements that start with @, such as @media for media queries
- Rule: A CSS rule, such as .grid {} with all its declarations
- Declaration: A single declaration, such as display: block
- Comment: A CSS comment

We can specify the following listeners to target these elements inside our plugin. Note that they all start with a capital letter, except prepare, which is a function that returns an object of listeners:

- AtRule: Called for every AtRule encountered.
- AtRuleExit: When PostCSS starts to process all the child elements of AtRule.
- Comment: Called for every comment encountered.

- `CommentExit`: Called once after a `Comment` listener is done, and called for every Comment listener.

- `Declaration`: Called for every declaration.

- `DeclarationExit`: Called as soon as a `Declaration` listener is done, and called for every Declaration listener.

- `Document`: When encountering a `Document` node, this is useful when we parse an HTML input file and want to extract all of its CSS.

- `DocumentExit`: Called once a `Document` listener is done, and called for every Document listener.

- `Exit`: Called once all listeners of the given CSS are done processing.

- `Once`: Called once on the `Root` node.

- `OnceExit`: Called once when all elements of a `Root` node are processed.

- `Root`: Called once on the root node.

- `RootExit`: Called once when all elements of a root node are processed.

- `Rule`: Called when a `Rule` is encountered, and called for every `Rule` element.

- `RuleExit`: Called once a Rule is processed.

- `prepare`: Called before executing the plugin. We can use it to alter our plugin at runtime further and add more functionality. It typically returns an object containing some of the aforementioned listeners.

With these functions, PostCSS offers us complete control over our CSS. Every function receives an object that we can alter. We can, for example, replace values in declarations, add class names to rules, or remove comments entirely.

Understanding Browserify

Since many libraries only work when used in a Node.js environment, meaning when they are executed on the server, we may not be able to use them in the browser. Browserify helps with this specific problem – it transforms a given JavaScript file such that it is executable in a browser, with all its dependencies packed into it.

Browserify offers a simple CLI tool that takes any JavaScript file as an input and outputs the browsersified content on `stdout` (**standard output**, the destination of all command output, except for errors, which go in `stderr`; these two definitions come from POSIX-compatible operating systems, so any OSX or Linux distribution), from which it can be written into a file.

We can install it with npm and use its CLI tool in one of our commands, such as `npm run build`.

Tying loose ends

We now know about PostCSS and Browserify. To help us create CSS polyfills, we most likely want to execute them in the browser but deliver any CSS from the server. So, to create a framework for our polyfills, we need to use both PostCSS and Browserify.

> **Note**
>
> A possible starting pointWe can find a starter kit and an empty plugin in the `chapter8/01_polyfill_starter_kit` folder in the repository. It contains all the parts described in this section. To get started, we can either code the starter kit ourselves with the help of this section or use the provided starter kit instead.

We will install both of them using npm. When starting from scratch, our `package.json` file should look like the following:

```
{
  "scripts": {
    "build": "./node_modules/.bin/browserify src/main.js >
      dist/main.js"
  },
  "dependencies": {
    "postcss": "^8.4.21",
    "browserify": "^17.0.0"
  }
}
```

We can see that we've already added a build script that takes anything that lies in `src/main.js` and transforms it, using Browserify, into a file called `main.js` in the `dist/` folder. Since we want to polyfill CSS, we will create a `styles.css` file in the project root. We can use all these files in our HTML:

```
<!DOCTYPE html>
<html>
<head>
  <link rel="stylesheet" href="styles.css">
</head>
<body>

<script src="dist/main.js"></script>
</body>
</html>
```

Inspired by Philip Walton's blog post about polyfilling CSS, we will create two functions in separate files within `src/` called `getPageStyles.js` and `replacePageStyles.js`.

The getPageStyles function gathers all CSS from every linked CSS file and style tag (except inline styles) and returns their content as a single CSS string:

```
const getPageStyles = () => {
  // Query the document for any element that could have
    styles.
  const styleElements = [...document.querySelectorAll
    ('style, link[rel="stylesheet"]')]

  // Fetch all styles and ensure the results are in
    document order.
  // Resolve with a single string of CSS text.
  return Promise.all(styleElements.map((el) => {
    if (el.href) {
      return fetch(el.href).then((response) =>
        response.text());
    } else {
      return el.innerHTML;
    }
  })).then((stylesArray) => stylesArray.join('\n'))
}

module.exports = getPageStyles
```

The replacePageStyles function removes all of these elements and appends a single style tag with our transformed CSS, essentially replacing all pre-loaded styles:

```
const replacePageStyles = (css) => {
  // Get a reference to all existing style elements.
  const existingStyles = [...document.querySelectorAll
    ('style, link[rel="stylesheet"]')];

  // Create a new <style> tag with all the polyfilled
    styles.
  const polyfillStyles = document.createElement('style')
  polyfillStyles.innerHTML = css
    document.head.appendChild(polyfillStyles)

  // Remove the old styles once the new styles have been
    added.
  existingStyles.forEach((el) => el.parentElement.
    removeChild(el))
}

module.exports = replacePageStyles
```

Lastly, we create a file called `src/postcss-myplugin.js` that contains our plugin. The plugin doesn't do anything for the time being. It should look like this:

```
const plugin = () => ({
  postcssPlugin: 'myPlugin',
  prepare() {
    return {
      Rule(rule) {}
    }
  }
})
```

Now, we tie in the `getPageStyles` and `replacePageStyles` functions with PostCSS and our PostCSS plugin in `main.js`:

```
const postcss = require('postcss')
const getPageStyles = require('./getPageStyles.js')
const replacePageStyles = require('./replacePageStyles.js')
const myPlugin = require('./postcss-myplugin.js')

;(async () => {
  const pageCss = await getPageStyles()

  const processed = postcss([myPlugin]).process(pageCss,
    { from: undefined })

  replacePageStyles(processed.css)
})()
```

PostCSS, whenever it processes something, wants to know where the CSS originated. Since we, essentially, don't know once we have collected all the styles (the `getPageStyles` function collects them from the DOM and additional CSS files and concatenates them into a single string), we pass `undefined` as its `from` option.

With these files and Browserify, we've laid a foundation to create custom CSS polyfills. In addition, we learned about the listeners we can use and what PostCSS can do.

Creating a polyfill for subgrid

First, let's create a polyfill for `subgrid`. The `subgrid` keyword is a possible value for both `grid-template-rows` and `grid-template-columns`. Usually, it is used with nested grids when we want to reuse the grid rows and columns of a parent element. However, it does not simply copy the entire grid definition. The `subgrid` keyword is meant to *keep the grid intact* in this element.

Understanding how subgrid is meant to work

For subgrid to have any effect, the element should span multiple rows, columns, or both, depending on which declaration uses it. For example, consider the following grid:

```css
.grid-container {
  width: 800px;
  display: grid;
  grid-template-columns: 100px 1fr 100px 100px 100px;
  grid-template-rows: 100px 100px 100px 100px 100px;
  gap: 10px;
}
```

It consists of five columns, one occupying all remaining space, while the others have a fixed width of 100px. It also has five rows, each 100px in height.

We will also introduce the .grid-element class to give our grid elements some default styling for visibility, also allowing us to specify tall and wide elements that span two rows or columns:

```css
.grid-element {
  border: 3px solid #2146C7;
  display: flex;
  align-items: center;
  justify-content: center;
}

.wide {
  grid-column: span 2;
}

.tall {
  grid-row: span 2;
}
```

Now, let's introduce a class that uses subgrid:

```css
.subgrid {
  display: grid;
  grid-template-rows: subgrid;
  grid-template-columns: subgrid;
}
```

We will use the CSS with the following HTML:

```html
<div class="grid-container">
  <div class="grid-element">A</div>
  <div class="grid-element wide tall subgrid">
```

```
        <div>Sub grid el</div>
        <div>Sub grid el</div>
    </div>
    <div class="grid-element">C</div>
    <div class="grid-element">D</div>
    <div class="grid-element">E</div>
    <div class="grid-element">F</div>
    <div class="grid-element">G</div>
    <div class="grid-element">H</div>
    <div class="grid-element">I</div>
    <div class="grid-element">J</div>
    <div class="grid-element">K</div>
</div>
```

The result looks like the following figure:

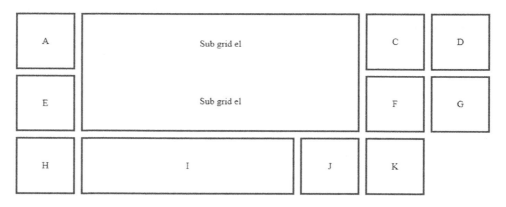

Figure 7.1 – The base grid definition we use to test our polyfill

We can see that the central element takes up two rows and two columns. Since the display: grid; rule defaults to a single column and an automatically generated number of rows, the Sub grid el strings show up somewhat aligned.

Since it is used for both rows and columns, subgrid should now create a grid inside the large element. This grid should have the same grid lines as the parent grid, essentially continuing the grid lines between the elements, with the **A**, **E**, **I** and **J** content.

Let's polyfill this behavior.

Why and when the polyfill may be useful

As we discussed in *Chapter 3*, *Building Advanced Grid Layouts*, subgrids are a powerful tool to keep layouts consistent when using nested grids. Complex layouts can greatly benefit from subgrids, and it helps us to create visual rhythm.

Once subgrid receives full support in all major browsers, many complex layouts that were built previously may benefit from refactoring. We can prevent this refactoring by polyfilling the feature now and removing the polyfill later.

Writing a polyfill

The plan is as follows:

1. Identify any grid element that uses `subgrid` in some form.

2. Determine its position within the grid (for example, row 1 and column 2) and its size (for example, two rows tall and two columns wide).

3. Extract the grid rows and columns from the parent, extracting the ones that are relevant to the grid element (for example, from the `100px 1fr 100px 100px 100px` grid column definition, we only need `1fr 100px`, as the element starts at the second column and is two columns wide).

4. Apply the extracted `grid-template-columns` and `grid-template-rows`, if applicable.

We first need a utility function to determine the element's position. We'll call it `determinePosition`, and pass the element itself, the row gap size, column gap size, grid row definitions, and grid column definitions. This function is placed within the `prepare` function of our PostCSS plugin, so we can use it in one of our hooks.

To determine the position, we first calculate the width and height of the element by using `clientWidth` and `clientHeight`. We then determine its exact pixel position using `offsetTop` and `offsetLeft`. Next, we subtract column and row sizes from these offset values one by one until no offset is left.

We can then continue subtracting columns and rows from the element's width and height until we reach 0, determining its width in the number of columns and height in the number of rows:

```
const determinePosition = (
  el, rowGap, columnGap,
  gridTemplateRows, gridTemplateColumns
) => {
  let offsetLeft = el.offsetLeft - el.parentNode.offsetLeft
  let offsetTop = el.offsetTop - el.parentNode.offsetTop

  let elWidth = el.clientWidth
  let elHeight = el.clientHeight
```

```
const rowGapInt = parseInt(rowGap)
const colGapInt = parseInt(columnGap)

// Float and rounding to deal with half-pixels
const rowDefinitions = gridTemplateRows.split(' ').map(
  r => Math.round(parseFloat(r))
)
const colDefinitions = gridTemplateColumns.
  split(' ').map(
  c => Math.round(parseFloat(c))
)

let currentRow = 0
while (offsetTop > 0) {
  offsetTop -= rowGapInt
  offsetTop -= rowDefinitions[currentRow]

  currentRow++
}

let height = 0
while (elHeight > 0) {
  elHeight -= rowGapInt
  elHeight -= rowDefinitions[currentRow + height]

  height++
}

let currentCol = 0
while (offsetLeft > 0) {
  offsetLeft -= colGapInt
  offsetLeft -= colDefinitions[currentCol]

  currentCol++
}

let width = 0
while (elWidth > 0) {
  elWidth -= colGapInt
  elWidth -= colDefinitions[currentCol + width]

  width++
}
```

```
  return {
    row: currentRow,
    col: currentCol,
    width: width,
    height: height,
  }
}
```

Now, we will start transforming our CSS. First, we need to determine every element that uses a subgrid. For that, we check in the `Rule` listener if the rule contains `display: grid;`. If so, we check for both `grid-template-rows: subgrid;` and `grid-template-columns: subgrid;`. We memorize these selectors in an array:

```
const plugin = () => ({
  postcssPlugin: 'subgrid',
  prepare() {
    const determinePosition = (
      el, rowGap, columnGap,
      gridTemplateRows, gridTemplateColumns
    ) => {
      // ...
    }

    const subgridElements = []

    return {
      Rule (rule) {
        if (rule.nodes.some(
          n => n.prop === 'display' && n.value === 'grid')
        ) {
          // We've got a candidate

          const hasRowsSubgrid = rule.nodes.some(
            n => {
              return n.prop === 'grid-template-rows'
                && n.value === 'subgrid'
            }
          )
          const hasColsSubgrid = rule.nodes.some(
            n => {
              return n.prop === 'grid-template-columns'
                && n.value === 'subgrid'
            }
          )
```

```
      if (hasRowsSubgrid || hasColsSubgrid) {
        subgridElements.push({
          selector: rule.selector,
          hasRowsSubgrid,
          hasColsSubgrid
        })
      }
    }
  },

  // ...
  }
 },
})
```

Since we can now determine the position of an element and know which elements we need to transform, we can apply *step 2* and *step 3* from our plan. In the `OnceExit` listener of our plugin, we loop through all of our selectors and determine its parent element. We get pixel-perfect sizes for the row gaps, column gaps, grid rows, and grid columns from its computed styles.

Next, we can calculate the element's position with these values and slice out the relevant row and column definitions. Finally, we combine these together in a single string and apply them as an inline style to the element:

```
OnceExit() {
  subgridElements.forEach(subgridEl => {
    Array.from(document.querySelectorAll(subgridEl.selector)).
  forEach(domEl => {
      const { rowGap, columnGap, gridTemplateRows,
        gridTemplateColumns } =
        getComputedStyle(domEl.parentNode)
      const { row, col, width, height } =
        determinePosition(
          domEl, rowGap, columnGap, gridTemplateRows,
          gridTemplateColumns
        )

      const gridRows = gridTemplateRows.split(' ')
      const gridCols = gridTemplateColumns.split(' ')

      let style = ''

      if (subgridEl.hasRowsSubgrid) {
        style += `
          row-gap: ${rowGap};
```

```
        grid-template-rows: ${gridRows.slice
          (row, row + height).join(' ')};


    }

    if (subgridEl.hasColsSubgrid) {
      style += `
        column-gap: ${columnGap};
        grid-template-columns: ${gridCols.slice(col,
          col + width).join(' ')};


    }

    domEl.setAttribute('style', style)
  })
 })
}
```

When we execute Browserify and load our polyfill, we get the following result:

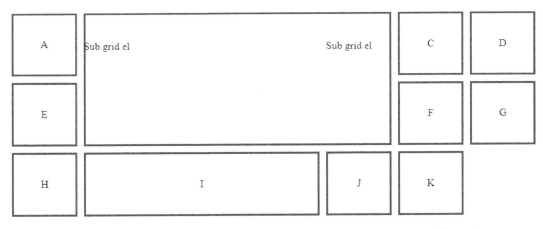

Figure 7.2 – The previous grid, now having the subgrid elements aligned differently

We can see the Sub grid el strings are now aligned along the **A** and **C** elements, indicating that there are now two grid rows. The second Sub grid el string is also aligned with the **J** grid element, indicating that the same grid line defines its grid column. The polyfill works!

We need to apply this behavior in the browser, since we can't tell the exact position of an element during build time. So, we need the HTML context to determine the relevant grid rows and columns.

We successfully created our first CSS Grid polyfill as a PostCSS plugin!

Why we shouldn't use this polyfill

Although this polyfill works, we shouldn't use it in production. Because of the extra JavaScript necessary to execute the polyfill, it impacts performance on weaker devices. Using inline styles also isn't recommended, since the polyfill might come into conflict with other libraries and cause unexpected behavior.

The next polyfill we will build is for a layout feature that has countless implementations for many frameworks, but it has not been shipped with CSS Grid itself at the time of writing – masonry layouts.

Creating a polyfill for masonry

Now that we've created our first polyfill, we can also use the same approach to create a polyfill for `masonry`. However, we won't be able to recreate the full functionality of the feature, since it involves reordering elements within the grid, especially when used for `grid-template-columns`.

Nevertheless, we'll create a polyfill that can be used with `grid-template-rows` that aligns all elements given in a masonry layout.

Understanding how masonry is meant to work

Masonry layouts work well with content of unknown sizes. As a famous example, Pinterest uses a masonry layout to align images of differing heights, as shown in the following figure.

Figure 7.3 – A masonry layout that can be found on Pinterest

We see various images on Pinterest's **Celebrating women in every era everywhere** page. They all have equal widths but differing heights, but the space between the images doesn't differ. There are no recognizable rows.

CSS Grid's `masonry` is meant to create such a layout. When used with `grid-template-rows`, it essentially removes the rows and aligns elements so that they all have the same gap. When used with `grid-template-columns`, the layout is applied not for rows but for columns. It would then remove any column constraints and keep the same gaps between elements.

Masonry offers many more features, such as `align-tracks`, `justify-tracks`, and `masonry-auto-flow`. However, we will not polyfill these features, as they would exceed the scope of this section. Instead, we will focus on the row-based masonry layout.

Why and when the polyfill may be useful

This polyfill is useful if we want a masonry layout without having to manually arrange elements in divs for columns or rows and rebuild the details with Flexbox. Therefore, it reduces the amount of HTML and CSS necessary to tightly arrange content of various sizes.

Writing the polyfill

To begin, we will use the same setup we used for the `subgrid` polyfill – we will start with PostCSS and Browserify and create the `getPageStyles` and `replacePageStyles` functions. We then create an empty PostCSS plugin and an HTML structure to test our polyfill, which can be found in the following code snippet:

```
<div class="grid-container">
  <div class="grid-element">
    <img src="https://via.placeholder.com/150x186"
      alt="...">
  </div>
  <div class="grid-element">
    <img src="https://via.placeholder.com/150x116"
      alt="...">
  </div>
  <div class="grid-element">
    <img src="https://via.placeholder.com/150x143"
      alt="...">
  </div>
  <div class="grid-element">
    <img src="https://via.placeholder.com/150x265"
      alt="...">
  </div>
  <div class="grid-element">
    <img src="https://via.placeholder.com/150x287"
```

```
        alt="...">
  </div>
  <div class="grid-element">
    <img src="https://via.placeholder.com/150x109"
      alt="...">
  </div>
  <div class="grid-element">
    <img src="https://via.placeholder.com/150x93"
      alt="...">
  </div>
  <div class="grid-element">
    <img src="https://via.placeholder.com/150x115"
      alt="...">
  </div>
  <div class="grid-element">
    <img src="https://via.placeholder.com/150x130"
      alt="...">
  </div>
  <div class="grid-element">
    <img src="https://via.placeholder.com/150x171"
      alt="...">
  </div>
  <div class="grid-element">
    <img src="https://via.placeholder.com/150x268"
      alt="...">
  </div>
  <div class="grid-element">
    <img src="https://via.placeholder.com/150x227"
      alt="...">
  </div>
  <div class="grid-element">
    <img src="https://via.placeholder.com/150x159"
      alt="...">
  </div>
  <div class="grid-element">
    <img src="https://via.placeholder.com/150x293"
      alt="...">
  </div>
</div>
```

We use the following CSS:

```
.grid-container {
  width: 400px;
  display: grid;
  grid-template-columns: 150px 150px 150px 150px 150px;
```

```
  grid-template-rows: masonry;
  gap: 10px;
}
```

Without our polyfill, the result of the HTML and CSS is what we see in the following figure:

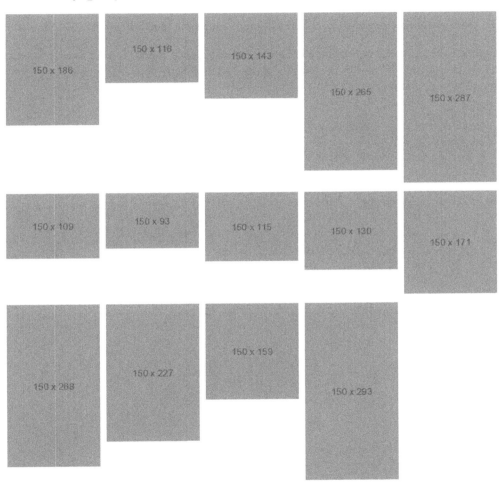

Figure 7.4 – The grid we apply masonry to

The plan for our polyfill is as follows:

1. Memorize all containers that use `grid-template-rows: masonry;`.

2. Loop through all the containers.

3. Loop through all of their children except the first row.

4. Determine the distance between the end of the preceding elements (not the grid cell but its content).

5. Shift the child element up so that the distance equals the specified gap.

We can use the `Rule` listener to find all selectors that use `grid-template-rows: masonry;`. First, we check whether the rule contains the `display: grid;` and `grid-template-rows: masonry;` declarations:

```
const plugin = () => ({
  postcssPlugin: 'masonry',
  prepare() {
    const masonrySelectors = []

    return {
      Rule (rule) {
        if (
          rule.nodes.some(n => n.prop === 'display' &&
            n.value === 'grid')
          && rule.nodes.some(n => n.prop ===
            'grid-template-rows' && n.value === 'masonry')
        ) {
          masonrySelectors.push(rule.selector)
        }
      },

      OnceExit() {
        // ...
      }
    }
  },
})

plugin.postcss = true

module.exports = plugin
```

The second step is a little trickier. Since we're using images, we must wait until they're loaded. For that, we use the `load` event on the window. Next, we loop through all selectors and remove the `grid-`

`template-row` definition. We also assign `grid-auto-rows: min-content;` to make the rows as small as possible:

```
OnceExit() {
  window.addEventListener('load', () => {
    masonrySelectors.forEach(selector => {
      Array.from(document.querySelectorAll
        (selector)).forEach(el => {
        el.style.gridTemplateRows = ''
        el.style.gridAutoRows = 'min-content'

        // ...
      })
    })
  })
}
```

Next, we get the gap and column definitions, from which we determine the number of columns:

```
OnceExit() {
  window.addEventListener('load', () => {
    masonrySelectors.forEach(selector => {
      Array.from(document.querySelectorAll
        (selector)).forEach(el => {
        el.style.gridTemplateRows = ''
        el.style.gridAutoRows = 'min-content'

        const { rowGap, gridTemplateColumns } =
          getComputedStyle(el)
        const numberOfColumns = gridTemplateColumns.
          split(' ').length

        // ...
      })
    })
  })
}
```

We then need to determine the height of every element. Since we don't know what the content exactly is, we can't use `offsetHeight` or `height` – these two properties would yield the grid row height. So instead, we hide every grid element and unhide every one of them individually, before asking for their height and hiding them again.

This technique takes advantage of `grid-auto-rows: min-content;` – it automatically resizes the row to fit the content height. We can then get this height.

After we've determined the height of every element, we can unhide all of them again:

```
OnceExit() {
  window.addEventListener('load', () => {
    masonrySelectors.forEach(selector => {
      Array.from(document.querySelectorAll
        (selector)).forEach(el => {
        el.style.gridTemplateRows = ''
        el.style.gridAutoRows = 'min-content'

        const { rowGap, gridTemplateColumns } =
          getComputedStyle(el)
        const numberOfColumns = gridTemplateColumns.
          split(' ').length

        Array.from(el.children).forEach(el =>
          el.style.display = 'none')
        Array.from(el.children).forEach(el => {
          el.style.display = 'block'
          el.setAttribute('data-height',
            getComputedStyle(el).height)
          el.style.display = 'none'
        })
        Array.from(el.children).forEach(el =>
          el.style.display = 'inline')

        // ...
      })
    })
  })
}
```

Last, we loop through all the children except those in the first row. Then, we calculate the distance between the current element and the element above and shift the current element up with a negative top margin:

```
OnceExit() {
  window.addEventListener('load', () => {
    masonrySelectors.forEach(selector => {
      Array.from(document.querySelectorAll
        (selector)).forEach(el => {
        el.style.gridTemplateRows = ''
```

```
        el.style.gridAutoRows = 'min-content'

        const { rowGap, gridTemplateColumns } =
          getComputedStyle(el)
        const numberOfColumns = gridTemplateColumns.
          split(' ').length

        Array.from(el.children).forEach(el =>
            el.style.display = 'none')
        Array.from(el.children).forEach(el => {
          el.style.display = 'block'
          el.setAttribute('data-height',
            getComputedStyle(el).height)
          el.style.display = 'none'
        })
        Array.from(el.children).forEach(el =>
          el.style.display = 'inline')

        for (let i = numberOfColumns;
          i < el.children.length; i++) {
          const currentEl = el.children[i]
          const aboveEl = el.children[i - numberOfColumns]
          const aboveElOffsetTop = aboveEl.offsetTop

          const shiftUp = currentEl.offsetTop
            - aboveElOffsetTop
            - parseInt(aboveEl.getAttribute('data-height'))
            - parseInt(rowGap)

          currentEl.style.marginTop = `-${shiftUp}px`
        }
      })
    })
  })
}
```

Once we build the polyfill and reload the browser, the elements are shifted up, as shown in the following figure.

Masonry polyfill

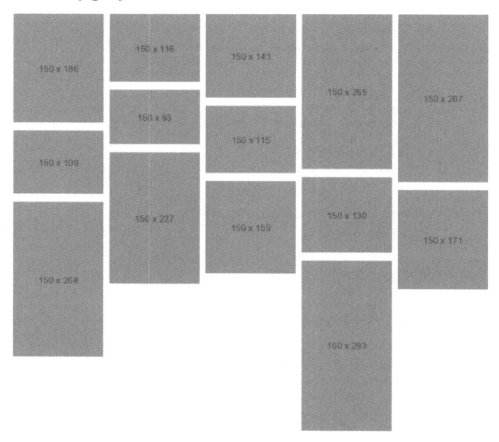

Figure 7.5 – The same grid, aligned in a masonry layout

We can see that the gap between all the elements is now the same. The polyfill seems to work.

Creating a polyfill for masonry is straightforward for the initial setup, but it gets more complex when we want to make features more complete.

Why we shouldn't use this polyfill

As we discussed in *Chapter 3, Building Advanced Grid Layouts*, masonry layouts have a negative impact on accessibility, because the visual and logical order diverge.

The polyfill does many calculations, which would be necessary every time the screen size changes. The number of necessary calculations would impact performance and could even cause visual glitches – for example, a flickering, delayed adaptation or large layout shifts.

Now that we've covered polyfills for already existing proposals, in the next section, we will create a polyfill for a feature request on GitHub that is still in active discussion and not part of the standard at the time of writing.

Creating a polyfill for additional pseudo-classes

A feature that has not yet (at the time of writing) left the issue state on the CSSWG Drafts GitHub repository of the W3C is additional selectors for auto-filled, implicit grids. The entire issue can be found here: `https://github.com/w3c/csswg-drafts/issues/1943`.

Understanding the idea behind nth-row and nth-col

The author of the original GitHub issue stated in 2017 that they'd like to see a `:nth-row()` selector. It would target all elements in a given row or pattern, similar to `:nth-child()`. Let's also consider a pseudo-class called `:nth-col()`. It would function the same way but target columns instead.

We could, for example, give differing background colors to all elements in every odd row, or target every fifth column to attach different borders.

Why and when the polyfill may be useful

This polyfill can be especially useful to implement galleries or table-like structures on dashboards, as it eases the styling of odd elements. Like the `nth-child` selector, it allows us to apply styling to specific elements based on their visual position. Styling based on position is not possible in grids without extra effort, especially when we take responsiveness and fluidity into account.

Writing the polyfill

The polyfill starts with the same setup as the previous polyfills. We use the following HTML structure:

```
<h1>Grids styled with nth-row and nth-col</h1>

<div class="grid-container">
  <div class="grid-element">A</div>
  <div class="grid-element wide">B</div>
  <div class="grid-element">C</div>
  <div class="grid-element">D</div>
  <div class="grid-element">E</div>
  <div class="grid-element">F</div>
  <div class="grid-element">G</div>
```

```
    <div class="grid-element tall">H</div>
    <div class="grid-element">I</div>
    <div class="grid-element">J</div>
    <div class="grid-element">K</div>
    <div class="grid-element">L</div>
    <div class="grid-element">M</div>
    <div class="grid-element">N</div>
</div>
```

We use the following CSS to apply default styles:

```
.grid-container {
  width: 400px;
  display: grid;
  grid-template-columns: 100px 1fr 100px 100px 100px;
  grid-template-rows: 100px 100px 100px 100px 100px;
  gap: 10px;
}

.grid-element {
  border: 3px solid #2146C7;
  display: flex;
  align-items: center;
  justify-content: center;
}

.wide {
  grid-column: span 2;
}

.tall {
  grid-row: span 2;
}

/* Every even col is yellow */
.grid-element:nth-col(2n) {
  background-color: #f7f380;
}

/* Every even row is blue */
.grid-element:nth-row(2n) {
  background-color: #74ddf2;
}

/* Every odd col is green */
.grid-element:nth-col(2n + 1) {
```

```
    background-color: #77dd77;
}
```

At the end of the CSS snippet, we've already included rules that use the `:nth-row()` and `:nth-col()` selectors.

The result without the polyfill can be seen in the following figure.

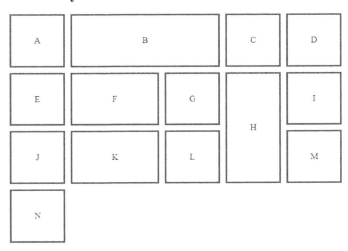

Figure 7.6 – A grid with some default styling

The plan for our polyfill is as follows:

1. Gather all the `:nth-row()` and `:nth-col()` rules.

2. Replace them with generated CSS class names, such as `.nth-row-2n-plus-1`, to replace `:nth-row(2n + 1)`.

3. Keep the classes and their regularity (`2n + 1`, `2n`, `1 + 5n`, and so on) in the same place.

4. Go through each child element of a grid and determine its position.

5. Check whether the position fits any of the regularities; if so, attach classes.

Since rows and columns can be handled the same way, we can abstract the functionality for both into a single function, which we will call `handleSelector`. We also install and import **slugify**, a library to create slugs out of any string, and **algebra.js**, a library that can help us determine whether a row or column satisfies the regularity:

```
const slugify = require('slugify')
const { Equation, parse } = require('algebra.js')
```

```
const plugin = () => ({
  postcssPlugin: 'nth-row-col',
  prepare() {
    const classNameToRegularity = {
      row: {},
      col: {},
    }
    const potentialGridSelectors = []
    slugify.extend({'+': 'plus'})

    const handleSelector = (rule, kind) => {
      const matches = [...rule.selector.matchAll(new
        RegExp(`:nth-${kind}\\(([0-9a-z+\\- ]+)\\)`, 'g'))]

      matches.forEach(match => {
        // Replace :nth-col selector with class name
        let regularity = match[1]
        if (regularity === 'even') {
          regularity = '2n'
        }
        if (regularity === 'odd') {
          regularity = '2n + 1'
        }

        const replacementSelector = `.nth-$
          {kind}-${slugify(regularity)}`
        rule.selector = rule.selector.replace(match[0],
          replacementSelector)

        // Store regularity and class name for future use
        if (!classNameToRegularity[kind]
          [replacementSelector]) {
          classNameToRegularity[kind][replacementSelector]
            = new parse(regularity)
        }
      })
    }
    // ...
  },
})
```

We can pass the entire rule and the kind (either `'row'` or `'col'`) to the `handleSelector` function – it then memorizes the selector and the regularity.

Next, we implement a function called determinePosition. Its functionality is similar to the one we've already implemented for the subgrid polyfill, but it does not determine an element's width and height:

```
const determinePosition = el => {
  const { rowGap, columnGap, gridTemplateRows,
    gridTemplateColumns } =
    getComputedStyle(el.parentNode)

  let offsetLeft = el.offsetLeft - el.parentNode.offsetLeft
  let offsetTop = el.offsetTop - el.parentNode.offsetTop

  const rowGapInt = parseInt(rowGap)
  const colGapInt = parseInt(columnGap)
  const rowDefinitions = gridTemplateRows.split(' ')
    .map(r => Math.round(parseFloat(r)))
  const colDefinitions = gridTemplateColumns.split
    (' ').map(c => Math.round(parseFloat(c)))

  let currentRow = 0
  while (offsetTop > 0) {
    offsetTop -= rowGapInt
    offsetTop -= rowDefinitions[currentRow]
    currentRow++
  }

  let currentCol = 0
  while (offsetLeft > 0) {
    offsetLeft -= colGapInt
    offsetLeft -= colDefinitions[currentCol]
    currentCol++
  }

  // Add 1 to have one-indexed rows and cols
  return {
    row: currentRow + 1,
    col: currentCol + 1,
  }
}
```

We then implement the actual plugin. In the Rule listener, we handle all relevant selectors:

```
return {
  Rule (rule) {
    if (rule.selector.includes(':nth-col')) {
```

```
      handleSelector(rule, 'col')
    }

    if (rule.selector.includes(':nth-row')) {
      handleSelector(rule, 'row')
    }

    // If the rule is display: grid, the selector of it is
       a candidate whose
    // child elements may be targeted by a nth-col()
       selector.
    if (rule.nodes.some(n => n.prop === 'display' &&
      n.value === 'grid')) {
      potentialGridSelectors.push(rule.selector)
    }
  },
  OnceExit() {
    // ...
  }
}
```

Finally, we implement the `OnceExit` listener:

```
OnceExit() {
  potentialGridSelectors.forEach(selector => {
    [...document.querySelectorAll(selector)]
      .filter(el => getComputedStyle(el).
        display === 'grid')
      .forEach(el => {
        [...el.children].forEach(child => {
          const { row, col } = determinePosition(child)

          child.setAttribute('data-row', row)
          child.setAttribute('data-col', col)

          for ([className, regularity] of
            Object.entries(classNameToRegularity['row'])) {
            if (!regularity.toString().includes('n')) {
              if (parseInt(regularity.toString()) === col) {
                child.classList.add(className.replace
                  ('.', ''))
              }
            } else {
              const eq = new Equation(regularity, row)
          // Here, we deal with equations like 2n+1 = 3
```

```
        // (2n+1 being the odd numbers)
        // By solving for n, with n being an element of the
        // integers, we can figure out if the
        // result (3) satisfies the expression 2n+1. Solving
        // for n: 2n+1 = 3 => 2n = 2 => n = 1.
        // Since the result is a whole number, it satisfies
        // the rule. However: 2n+1 = 4 =>
        // 2n = 3 => n = 1.5, which is not a whole number, so
        // not satisfied.
              if (eq.solveFor('n').denom === 1) {
                child.classList.add(className.replace
                  ('.', ''))
              }
            }
          }

        for ([className, regularity] of
          Object.entries(classNameToRegularity['col'])) {
          if (!regularity.toString().includes('n')) {
            if (parseInt(regularity.toString()) === col) {
              child.classList.add(className.replace
                ('.', ''))
            }
          } else {
            const eq = new Equation(regularity, col)

            if (eq.solveFor('n').denom === 1) {
              child.classList.add(className.replace
                ('.', ''))
            }
          }
        }
      })
    })
  })
}
```

Using `algebra.js`, we can create equations that we can solve for n. The column or row fits the regularity if the result is an integer (a denominator of 1). We then attach the class.

When built, we can see that the rows and columns are now differently colored, as shown in the following figure:

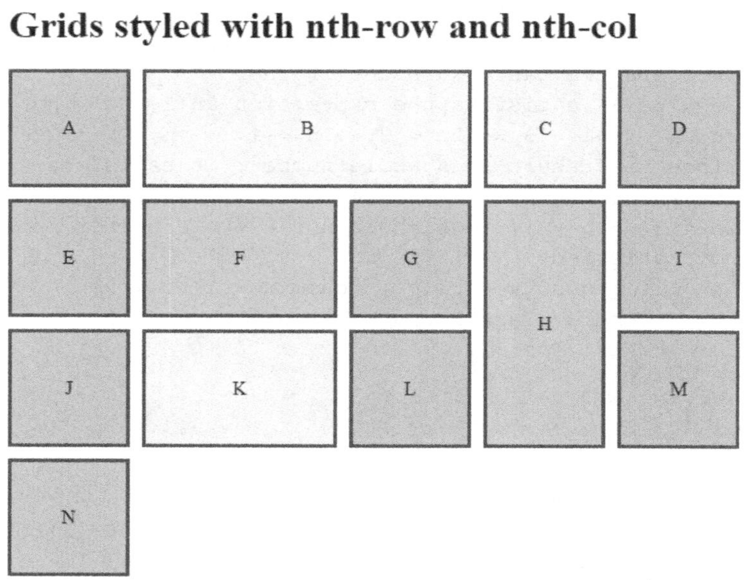

Grids styled with nth-row and nth-col

Figure 7.7 – A grid styled with the nth-col and nth-row selectors

Our third homemade polyfill shows that it works well – the element with the **B** content spans two columns, and the element with the **C** content, therefore, starts at an even column and is colored yellow. The same works for the **H** element, which spans two rows.

Why we shouldn't use this polyfill

This feature has, so far, only been discussed on GitHub. The CSS working group has not yet released any official document regarding these selectors. There are still many unanswered questions, such as their behavior if an element is visually hidden, or how row and column membership are determined.

The chances are good that we might not see this feature come to major browsers for quite some time. Therefore, what we implemented is, technically speaking, not a polyfill but an additional feature for CSS. We have to fully support it ourselves and cover every edge case.

With the third polyfill, we've explored many possibilities of CSS Grid that are not yet available, if they'll ever be.

The `:nth-col()` and `:nth-row()` selectors rely on calculations for which we need an extra library. We've shown that the selectors work as intended, although the calculations may be difficult to understand at first glance. The selectors are useful for some cases, such as galleries or data tables.

The next section covers a library for grid animations. This library introduces a strikingly simple way to animate grid rearrangements.

Animating grids

Another open issue in the CSSWG Draft repository is the ability to animate every grid aspect natively. So far, transitions have not covered many aspects, and animations can be complex.

The whole issue from 2021 can be found here: `https://github.com/w3c/csswg-drafts/issues/6736`.

Understanding the goal of grid animations

Smoothly animated grids can significantly enhance the user experience. For example, these animations can indicate new or removed elements within a grid, allow a user to smoothly resize the grid if there are power-user applications that let the user highly customize the UI, or make the grid reflow in case of content changes.

The CSSWG Draft issue mentions a library called `animate-css-grid`. We can use it to animate our CSS grids fully.

Using the animate-css-grid library

To begin, we will install the library with npm. We can then attach the animations using the following code snippet:

```
import './node_modules/animate-css-grid/dist/main.js'

const grid = document.querySelector('.grid-container')
animateCSSGrid.wrapGrid(grid)
```

Whenever the grid changes, it is now animated.

The library offers many options to tweak the animations further:

- `stagger`: Staggers animations with a given integer of milliseconds
- `duration`: The duration of each animation in milliseconds
- `easing`: The animation easing function as a string; the available functions are the following:
  - `'linear'`
  - `'easeIn'`, `'easeOut'`, and `'easeInOut'`

- `'circIn'`, `'circOut'`, and `'circInOut'`
- `'backIn'`, `'backOut'`, and `'backInOut'`

- `onStart`: A callback that receives all animated elements as a list, called right before animating
- `onEnd`: A callback that receives all animated elements, called right after an animation

The library also offers an additional function to force animations, called `forceGridAnimation()`, and an additional function to remove any grid animations, called `unwrapGrid()`.

Understanding why we should not use polyfills

In general, features that need to be polyfilled are either prone to change or will be implemented sooner or later. This is an actual fact not only for CSS but also JavaScript, PHP, Python, and other languages. Usually, we either need to support legacy systems or try to use things that are not entirely ready yet. In any case, we have alternative solutions to using polyfills – we can try to upgrade the legacy systems, drop support for them, or wait until we can use the feature with its full release.

Usually, polyfills are not mandatory. We can circumvent our issues with older language constructs or redesign our application (both code-wise and visually) to fit the available features. On the other hand, if we desperately need a polyfill, it might be the symptom of a more significant problem, such as unnecessarily supporting systems that are **end of life** (**EOL**) or lack upgrades.

We've seen what it takes to create a polyfill and that its complexity can explode quite quickly. Usually, the return on investment of polyfills is small, especially when homemade. Often, some polyfills will already exist, but they often introduce a lot of code that can impact performance.

Summary

This chapter served to show us what it takes to implement features on CSS Grid and what it takes to create polyfills for CSS on our own. We've talked about the need, or lack thereof, for polyfills and how they can cause more harm than help to us.

We can create CSS polyfills quickly with PostCSS and Browserify. Still, often we shouldn't, as the specifications of the polyfilled features are often either not complete or browser vendors are about to deliver an implementation themselves.

In the next chapter, we'll look at some popular CSS frameworks. We'll inspect their grid implementations and see how they might use CSS Grid if they're using it at all. Looking at CSS Grid in the wild helps us understand how some of the foremost CSS experts understand CSS Grid.

8

Grids in the Wild – How Frameworks Implement Grids

We've now learned the ins and outs of CSS Grid. We've learned most of the things to know and can build beautiful layouts with it. However, we won't encounter a Vanilla **Cascading Style Sheets (CSS)** setup in most projects but will use a framework instead. LogRocket published a blog post in 2018 about the history of frontend frameworks, and according to author Michael Wanyoike, the first CSS libraries and frameworks began showing up in the mid-2000s. We can read the full post here: `https://blog.logrocket.com/history-of-frontend-frameworks/`.

Funnily enough, these frameworks immediately introduced grid systems, showing how much developers longed for grids to be useable on the web without much effort and reinventing the wheel every single time. Of course, once we developed a working system, we would reuse it often, so there were likely a tremendous number of libraries very early on.

In the past, Blueprint, 960 Grids, YUI, and YAML were the de facto standards. And yes, the YAML CSS framework and the **YAML** markup language, which stands for **Yet Another Markup Language**, are two entirely different things. The **YAML** framework's name stands for **Yet Another Multicolumn Layout**. However, the markup language predates the framework by around four years, which I imagine must have caused a lot of confusion among engineers.

Nowadays, we use more sophisticated frameworks, which we can configure with the help of PostCSS, Sass, and Less and optimize with build tools, such as Rollup or Webpack. Some of these frameworks come with grid systems, just like in the old days. Some, however, don't. And some make use of CSS Grid, and some, well, don't do that either.

In this second to last chapter, we will look at how famous and lesser-known frameworks implement grid systems and whether they use CSS Grid. We will uncover how their grid systems work and how we can implement layouts with them.

We'll look at the following topics in detail in this chapter:

- How **Tailwind** implements grids
- How **Bootstrap** implements grids
- How **Foundation** implements grids
- How **Bulma.io** implements grids
- How **UIkit** implements grids
- How **Pure.css** implements grids
- How **Tachyons** implements grids
- How **Cutestrap** implements grids
- How other frameworks don't implement grids
- Practice a framework with AwesomeAnalytics

Technical requirements

This chapter makes heavy use of Node.js and npm. Therefore, we'll need the following tools:

- A browser, preferably Chromium-based, such as Google Chrome, Brave, or Vivaldi, but Firefox or Apple Safari also works
- An **integrated development environment** (IDE) or text editor, such as WebStorm, **Visual Studio Code** (**VS Code**), or Vim, with HTML and CSS syntax highlighting
- Internet access is necessary to access the code
- Git (optional, we can also download the folder from GitHub)
- At least version 18 of Node.js

If Node.js is not currently installed on your system, or you've got the wrong version, **Node Version Manager** () is a fantastic tool for handling different Node.js versions on one system.

All the code for this chapter can be found on GitHub in this repository: `https://github.com/PacktPublishing/Mastering-CSS-Grid/tree/main/chapter8`.

Learning how Tailwind implements grids

Tailwind is a somewhat polarising framework. On their website, the developers claim that Tailwind allows us to *rapidly build modern websites without ever leaving our HTML*. Tailwind uses utility classes and considers itself *utility-first*.

We can see the landing page of Tailwind's website in the following screenshot:

Figure 8.1 – Tailwind's landing page

Utility classes are a CSS paradigm that, unlike Atomic CSS, **object-oriented CSS (OOCSS)**, or **Block Element Modifier (BEM)**, does not directly give names to components. Instead, it introduces classes named after what they do. The philosophy behind utility frameworks is maximizing single CSS classes' reusability.

For example, consider a hammer: we don't have different hammers for hanging picture frames, building shelves, and fixing broken machines (well, some people do, but most people don't); we only have a hammer, which we can reuse for multiple tasks. A hammer does one thing well: it lets us exert force onto a singular point.

Utility classes are just like the hammer. For example, instead of applying `display: flex;` to every CSS class needing a Flexbox container, Tailwind offers a class called `.flex`, which only applies `display: flex;`. We apply this class to every **Document Object Model** (**DOM**) element that should be a Flexbox container.

A note about the popularity and polarization of Tailwind

As stated at the beginning of the section, opinions about the utility approach differ wildly. Some praise it as the only sensible way of writing CSS, while others accuse the users of Tailwind of *not knowing CSS*. However, it is not up to this book to discuss whether Tailwind is a sensible framework. Nevertheless, some people use it, and the fact that Twitter regularly explodes because of Tailwind discussions makes it important enough.

It's an interesting spin on the old *tabs versus spaces* discussion, but we shall not engage in framework wars and instead focus on learning about them. Of course, once we know how Tailwind works, we can still decide to leave it and forget everything again.

The exciting thing about Tailwind is that it did not directly offer a grid approach up until the introduction of CSS Grid on the framework with `v1.9.0`. Instead, it offered an example of how to build grids with Flexbox and width classes. In addition, Tailwind offers different classes for the widths of elements. Some of these classes have hardcoded **root em** (**REM**) values, such as `.w-48`, which applies `width: 12rem;` to every DOM element with that class.

Tailwind also offers width classes with ratios, such as `.w-1/3`, translated to percentage values, such as `width: 33.33333%;`. Combined with the `.flex` class and additional utility classes for flex wrapping, flex growing and shrinking, and justifying and aligning content, we can build full-blown grids without any specific grid-system-related classes, as is the case with Bootstrap.

For example, let's look at the following grid component from the `v0.7.4` docs:

```html
<!-- Full width column -->
<div class="flex mb-4">
  <div class="w-full bg-grey h-12"></div>
</div>


<!-- Two columns -->
<div class="flex mb-4">
  <div class="w-1/2 bg-grey-light h-12"></div>
  <div class="w-1/2 bg-grey h-12"></div>
</div>

<!-- Three columns -->
<div class="flex mb-4">
  <div class="w-1/3 bg-grey-light h-12"></div>
  <div class="w-1/3 bg-grey h-12"></div>
  <div class="w-1/3 bg-grey-light h-12"></div>
</div>

<!-- Four columns -->
<div class="flex mb-4">
  <div class="w-1/4 bg-grey h-12"></div>
```

```
  <div class="w-1/4 bg-grey-light h-12"></div>
  <div class="w-1/4 bg-grey h-12"></div>
  <div class="w-1/4 bg-grey-light h-12"></div>
</div>

<!-- Five columns -->
<div class="flex mb-4">
  <div class="w-1/5 bg-grey h-12"></div>
  <div class="w-1/5 bg-grey-light h-12"></div>
  <div class="w-1/5 bg-grey h-12"></div>
  <div class="w-1/5 bg-grey-light h-12"></div>
  <div class="w-1/5 bg-grey h-12"></div>
</div>

<!-- Six columns -->
<div class="flex">
  <div class="w-1/6 bg-grey-light h-12"></div>
  <div class="w-1/6 bg-grey h-12"></div>
  <div class="w-1/6 bg-grey-light h-12"></div>
  <div class="w-1/6 bg-grey h-12"></div>
  <div class="w-1/6 bg-grey-light h-12"></div>
  <div class="w-1/6 bg-grey h-12"></div>
</div>
```

This example shows us how to build different column layouts with the help of the mentioned utility classes. They also applied some height and background colors to distinguish the columns. The result of this code is shown in *Figure 8.2*:

Figure 8.2 – Tailwind's example of flexbox-based grid layouts

We can see all the examples working perfectly. As long as we know Flexbox, we can build grids with it.

However, with the introduction of CSS Grid in Tailwind, we received a new tool we could now use to build actual grids: utility classes for CSS Grid. But unfortunately, in the current version of the Tailwind documentation (v3.2.7), they no longer offer any compound grid examples in the documentation – all they have is documentation for each individual utility class but no explanation of how to use them together.

To create grids with Tailwind's implementation of CSS Grid, we use these utility classes:

- `grid`: This designates an element as a grid container using `display: grid;`

  For columns:

  - `grid-cols-1` to `grid-cols-12`: This applies the following CSS with n being the number of columns specified by the class: `grid-template-columns: repeat(n, minmax(0, 1fr));`

  - `grid-cols-none`: This applies `grid-template-columns: none;`, useful for resets when creating responsive pages

  - `col-span-1` to `col-span-12`: This applies `grid-column: span n / span n;` to the element, with n being the number of columns specified in the class name

  - `col-start-1` to `col-start-13`: This applies `grid-column-start: n;` to the element, with n being the start column specified in the class name

  - `col-end-1` to `col-end-13`: This applies `grid-column-end: n;` to the element, with n being the end column specified in the class name

  - `col-auto`, `col-start-auto`, `col-end-auto`: This applies the `auto` value to the respective attributes

  - `col-span-full`: This applies `grid-column: 1 / -1;` to the element, making it span the entire row

  For rows:

  - `grid-rows-1` to `grid-rows-6`: This applies `grid-template-rows: repeat(n, minmax(0, 1fr));` to the element, with n being the number of rows specified in the class name

  - `grid-rows-none`: This applies `grid-template-rows: none;`, useful for resets when creating responsive pages

  - `row-span-1` to `row-span-6`: This applies `grid-row: span n / span n;` to the element, with n being the number of rows specified in the class name

  - `row-start-1` to `row-start-7`: This applies `grid-row-start: n;` to the element, with n being the start row specified in the class name

- `row-end-1` to `row-end-7`: This applies `grid-row-end: n;` to the element, with n being the end row specified in the class name

- `row-auto`, `row-start-auto`, `row-end-auto`: These apply the `auto` value to the respective attributes

Autoflow:

- `grid-flow-row`: This applies `grid-auto-flow: row;`

- `grid-flow-col`: This applies `grid-auto-flow: col;`

- `grid-flow-dense`: This applies `grid-auto-flow: dense;`

- `grid-flow-row-dense`: This applies `grid-auto-flow: row dense;`

- `grid-flow-col-dense`: This applies `grid-auto-flow: column dense;`

Auto columns:

- `auto-cols-auto`: This applies `grid-auto-columns: auto;`

- `auto-cols-min`: This applies `grid-auto-columns: min-content;`

- `auto-cols-max`: This applies `grid-auto-columns: max-content;`

- `auto-cols-fr`: This applies `grid-auto-columns: minmax(0, 1fr);`

Auto rows:

- `auto-rows-auto`: This applies `grid-auto-rows: auto;`

- `auto-rows-min`: This applies `grid-auto-rows: min-content;`

- `auto-rows-max`: This applies `grid-auto-rows: max-content;`

- `auto-rows-fr`: This applies `grid-auto-rows: minmax(0, 1fr);`

There are also more utility classes for gaps, to `justify-content`, `justify-items`, and `justify-self`, to `align-content`, `align-items`, and `align-self`, and to `place-content`, `place-items`, and `place-self`.

Worth mentioning is the distinct lack of grid areas and named grid lines. Unfortunately, Tailwind does not offer them out of the box as of February 2023. However, there are plugins we can install that offer these.

We can also apply arbitrary values to the `grid-cols-*` and `grid-rows-*` classes and expand the range of classes by extending the theme via `tailwind.config.js`. To apply arbitrary values, we use the square bracket syntax. For example, to have three columns, each with `100px` of width, we can use the `grid-cols-[100px_100px_100px]` class, which is translated into `grid-template-columns: 100px 100px 100px;`. We've replaced the spaces with underscores since CSS class names can't contain spaces.

Let's create a basic grid with the built-in CSS classes. For that, we'll use the following HTML with a built version of Tailwind:

```
<div class="grid grid-cols-3 grid-rows-3 gap-6
  w-[600px] mb-6">
  <div class="border-2 border-blue-600 bg-blue-400">1</div>
  <div class="border-2 border-blue-600 bg-blue-400">2</div>
  <div class="border-2 border-blue-600 bg-blue-400">3</div>
  <div class="border-2 border-blue-600 bg-blue-400">4</div>
  <div class="border-2 border-blue-600 bg-blue-400">5</div>
  <div class="border-2 border-blue-600 bg-blue-400">6</div>
  <div class="border-2 border-blue-600 bg-blue-400">7</div>
  <div class="border-2 border-blue-600 bg-blue-400">8</div>
  <div class="border-2 border-blue-600 bg-blue-400">9</div>
</div>
```

We've added nine elements, all sharing the same styling to distinguish the grid cells. We've applied an arbitrary width value of 600px using the square bracket syntax to the container. The grid definition uses three columns and three rows. We've also applied a gap of 6, which means 1.5rem, which, with Tailwind's default theme config, results in 24px. The result can be seen in *Figure 8.3*:

Figure 8.3 – An essential grid built with Tailwind's grid utility classes

We can see the three rows and columns applied to the nine elements. Since the default row and column size definition is minmax(0, 1fr), the rows only take up as much space as necessary.

To create a grid with arbitrarily sized elements, we use the square bracket definition, which we can use for both rows and columns, as shown in the following code snippet:

```
<div class="grid grid-cols-[100px_100px_100px] grid-rows-
[100px_100px_100px] gap-6">
  <div class="border-2 border-blue-600 bg-blue-400">1</div>
  <div class="border-2 border-blue-600 bg-blue-400">2</div>
  <div class="border-2 border-blue-600 bg-blue-400">3</div>
  <div class="border-2 border-blue-600 bg-blue-400">4</div>
  <div class="border-2 border-blue-600 bg-blue-400">5</div>
  <div class="border-2 border-blue-600 bg-blue-400">6</div>
```

```
    <div class="border-2 border-blue-600 bg-blue-400">7</div>
    <div class="border-2 border-blue-600 bg-blue-400">8</div>
    <div class="border-2 border-blue-600 bg-blue-400">9</div>
</div>
```

The elements are styled the same way, we also have a gap value of 6, but this time we have rows and columns of 100px each. The result can be seen in *Figure 8.4*:

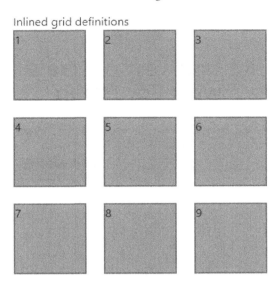

Figure 8.4 – A grid with grid elements sized 100px by 100px

Since we've adjusted the grid sizes, we can see how the grid elements have changed their sizes.

The square bracket syntax allows us to build any grid, just like when we use `grid-template-rows` and `grid-template-columns` directly. However, the lack of grid areas removes some of the verbosity that CSS Grid offers and might make it hard to re-adjust if we're used to working with them.

Tailwind polarizes, but its flexibility is loved by many. The way Tailwind offers CSS Grid with utility classes gives us most of the flexibility of using Vanilla CSS and allows us to create most, if not all, possible grid structures. Curiously, Tailwind is one of the few popular frameworks in 2023 that implements CSS Grid and doesn't rely on Flexbox to offer a grid system.

Learning how Bootstrap implements grids

Bootstrap is arguably one of the most popular CSS frameworks, if not the most. Twitter released Bootstrap in 2011 to streamline its frontend development efforts and reduce friction loss and maintenance.

We can see the landing page of Bootstrap's website in the following screenshot:

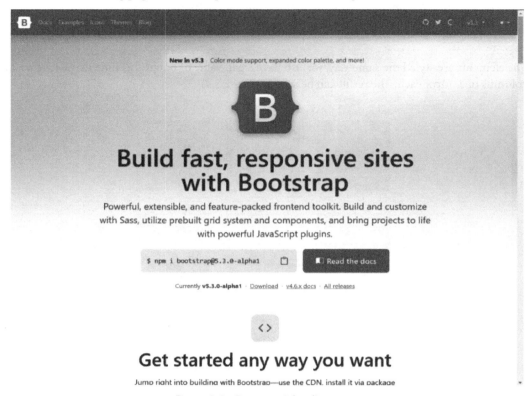

Figure 8.5 – Bootstrap's landing page

For this reason, Bootstrap has always been a highly opinionated framework with ready-made components, such as alert boxes, modals, and full-blown page navigations. Some components even offer **JavaScript** (**JS**) integrations with the Bootstrap libraries and with the help of jQuery. However, Bootstrap can be themed to some degree, allowing us to divert from the *Bootstrap look* that websites using standard Bootstrap usually have.

Apart from the **user interface** (**UI**) components, Bootstrap also offers layout options, namely a grid. When we open the Bootstrap documentation, the very first section informs us that Bootstrap does not use CSS Grid for its grid layout but Flexbox. Possible reasons for this decision may be backward compatibility or that larger projects tend to move slower.

A container `div` defines a grid with the `.container` class, rows, represented by `div` tags with a `.row` class (and optionally one of the `.row-cols-*` classes), and columns, defined with several `.col-*` classes. Bootstrap offers a 12-column grid out of the box. The number of columns can be configured using the `$grid-columns` and `$grid-row-columns` Sass variables, however.

Let's look at the following HTML structure from the docs to understand how grids are built:

```
<div class="container text-center">
  <div class="row">
    <div class="col">
      Column
    </div>
    <div class="col">
      Column
    </div>
    <div class="col">
      Column
    </div>
  </div>
</div>
```

We can see a single container with a single row and three columns. These columns are sized equally. Flexbox allows that. The result of this code can be seen in *Figure 8.6*, taken from the docs:

Figure 8.6 – A three-column layout implemented with Bootstrap

We may also explicitly set the columns' sizes by adding a dash to the class name followed by a number indicating how many columns the element should span, for example, `.col-6` or `.col-3`. Finally, we can create responsive layouts by adding one of the breakpoint names (`sm`, `md`, `lg`, `xl`, and `xxl` by default, but configurable). For example, to have a two-column wide element that spans three columns on larger screens, we use the `col-2 col-lg-3` class combination.

Let's recreate the classic *header-sidebar-content-footer* layout. For that, we need a container with three rows. The first row contains a single column for the header. The second row contains two columns, one for the sidebar and one for the content. We want them full-width but next to each other on larger viewports. Finally, the third row contains a single row with the footer. The following code snippet shows our HTML structure:

```
<div class="container">
  <div class="row">
    <header class="col">Header</header>
  </div>
  <div class="row">
    <aside class="col col-sm-4">Sidebar</aside>
    <main class="col col-sm-8">Content</main>
  </div>
```

```
  <div class="row">
    <footer class="col">Footer</footer>
  </div>
</div>
```

The result for larger screens can be seen in the following screenshot:

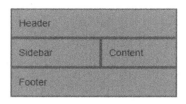

Figure 8.7 – The Holy grail layout created with Bootstrap's grid

We see the mobile layout on smaller screens, as shown in *Figure 8.8*:

Figure 8.8 – The previous layout on a smaller viewport with elements stacked on top of each other

Using the `row-cols-*` classes, we can explicitly set the number of columns per row. Besides the general structure classes, Bootstrap offers many classes to steer the Flexbox behavior, resembling utility classes, such as `align-items-center` or `justify-content-start`.

However, much like any Flexbox layout, we have no way of explicitly setting the height of a row in the grid definition and have to set the height with additional selectors. Also, the extra elements needed to add rows add complexity.

Bootstrap is a staple of modern web development. It has been around for what feels like eons and has strongly influenced how we build websites today. Although it doesn't use CSS Grid, it has a solid Flexbox-based grid implementation that allows us to build complex responsive layouts.

Learning how Foundation implements grids

Similar to Bootstrap, Foundation is a true veteran of CSS Frameworks. Its first release dates back to September 2011, putting its date of initial release near Bootstrap's.

We can see the landing page of Foundation's website in the following screenshot:

Figure 8.9 – Foundation's landing page

Foundation has received many updates over the years, with the current version being Foundation 6. Although many asked whether it was still maintained, the developers stated in December 2022 that they were working on a beta for Foundation 7.

Foundation has had three different grid systems, all still documented and available, although two are deactivated by default. We'll go through all of them next.

Float grid

The oldest grid implementation of Foundation, the float-based grid, is only necessary if we need to support **Internet Explorer 10 (IE10)**. Arguably, not many projects need to support this browser, but it's valuable that a framework still offers this support if needed. Suppose we actually ever need to support IE10, however. In that case, we should probably chat with our requirements engineers, as the lack of possibilities to implement grids is probably our most minor concern.

It's based on a row system with `1200px`-wide rows with 12 columns. We define a row by giving a container the `row` class. A row's columns need the `columns` class (or `column`, as a grammar-related alias). We can define a column element's size by adding classes that start with the breakpoint (`small`, `medium`, and `large`) and the desired size as a number, separated by a dash. For example, to have a three-column wide element, we apply the `small-3` class. If we want responsive columns, we add the `size` classes for the desired viewports.

If we do not apply a `size` class, it automatically takes up the available width. In a row containing only a single column, the column always takes up the entire space, two unsized columns share the available space, and an unsized column next to a sized one takes up the remaining space.

For example, to achieve a holy-grail layout (header, sidebar, content, footer) with the float-based grid, we would need the following structure:

```html
<header>
  Header, no grid necessary.
</header>

<div class="row">
  <aside class="columns small-12 medium-4">
    Sidebar
  </aside>

  <main class="columns">
    Content
  </main>
</div>

<footer>
  Footer, no grid necessary
</footer>
```

This system has many more facets we don't cover (alignment, automatic unstacking, collapsed rows, offsets, and block grids) because it is outdated.

Flex grid

Next in line, Foundation offers a Flexbox-based grid. It behaves as a drop-in replacement for the float-based grid. According to the documentation, though, the developers don't recommend the flex grid either unless support for IE10 is necessary. Since Foundation 6.4, the flex grid, like the float grid, is disabled.

The structure of the Flexbox-based grid is the same as the float-based grids. It uses row containers containing columns of sizes defined with the breakpoints. It has the exact alignment and unstacking, collapsed rows, offsets, and block grid classes.

XY grid

The current and recommended version is the XY grid. Although it is also based on Flexbox, its general structure is different. Instead of rows, we define grids with the `grid-x` class and don't define columns but cells of various sizes with the `cell` class. The sizing classes are the same, for example, `medium-6` or `small-8`.

Unlike the float-based and Flexbox-based grids, the XY grid automatically stretches the entire width. However, an element with the `grid-container` class can surround the grid, giving it a size of `1200px` and applying some padding. In addition, unlike the float-based and the flex grid, we can add padding-based or margin-based gutters by applying `grid-padding-x` (for padding within all grid cells) or `grid-margin-x` (for margin on all grid cells). Finally, offsets are achieved with the `offset-*` classes, for example, `offset-3` for a column that starts after three-twelfths of the grid, again the same syntax used for the float and flex grid.

Flexbox-related features are also available:

- `shrink`: This makes cells shrink to only the size necessary for their content
- `align-right`, `align-center`, `align-justify`, and `align-spaced`: These are utilities for `justify-content`
- `align-top`, `align-middle`, `align-bottom`, and `align-stretch`: These are utilities for `align-items`
- `align-center-middle`: This is a shortcut for the `align-center align-middle` class list
- `flex-dir-row`, `flex-dir-row-reverse`, `flex-dir-column`, and `flex-dir-column-reverse`: These are utility classes for `flex-direction`
- `flex-child-auto`, `flex-child-grow`, and `flex-child-shrink`: These are utilities for `flex-grow` and `flex-shrink`, used on cells
- `order-*`: The utilities for the flexbox attribute order can be `order-1` to `order-12`

These helpers make the XY grid a very versatile Flexbox utility.

The main difference between the grid systems of other frameworks is the ability to define vertical grids. We define a vertical grid by using the `grid-y` class instead of `grid-x`. However, not all grid features are available for vertical grids. For example, offsets, block grids, and collapsed margins and paddings (which they call collapsed cells) are not available for vertical grids.

Also, a vertical grid needs a defined height. If we need a grid spanning the entire viewport (`100vh`), we can use the `grid-frame` class, which is applied to a container surrounding our grid containers.

Let's rebuild the holy-grail layout with the XY grid:

```
<div class="grid-frame">
  <div class="grid-y">
    <header class="cell small-2">
      Header, 2/12 tall
    </header>

    <div class="grid-x">
      <aside class="cell medium-4">
        Sidebar
      </aside>

      <main class="cell">
        Content
      </main>
    </div>

    <footer class="cell small-2">
      Footer, 2/12 tall
    </footer>
  </div>
</div>
```

This code snippet shows that we can achieve a full-page layout with little effort.

Unlike other CSS frameworks, Foundation has kept legacy grid systems in its code base to allow for backward compatibility and to support older browsers where necessary. Although very much built like Bootstrap, the grids also offer vertical grids, which we rarely see in frameworks.

Learning how Bulma.io implements grids

Bulma.io (**Bulma**) is an opinionated, customizable CSS framework with ready-to-use components. It is Sass-based and offers dozens of variables to adjust to our liking. Some components include delete buttons with cross icons, colored tag lists, card components, menus, modals, and form fields.

We can see the landing page of Bulma's website in the following screenshot:

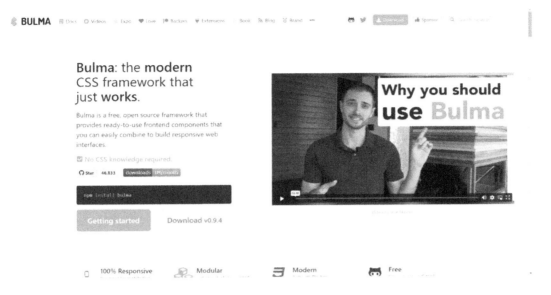

Figure 8.10 – Bulma's landing page

Bulma's grid system is called `columns` and consists of two building blocks: a column container with the `columns` class and single column elements with the `column` class. The columns are auto-sized by default. For example, a four-column layout can be achieved with the following code snippet:

```
<div class="columns">
  <div class="column">
    First column
  </div>
  <div class="column">
    Second column
  </div>
  <div class="column">
    Third column
  </div>
  <div class="column">
    Fourth column
  </div>
</div>
```

We may also set sizes explicitly by using a set of rather verbose classes:

- `is-three-quarters`
- `is-two-thirds`
- `is-half`
- `is-one-third`
- `is-one-quarter`
- `is-full`
- `is-four-fifths`
- `is-three-fifths`
- `is-two-fifths`
- `is-one-fifth`

We apply these classes to any column element. All non-sized columns share the remaining space equally.

If we'd like to use a 12-column grid instead, we can use classes from `is-1` to `is-12` (so, `is-3` for 3 columns wide within the 12-column grid) to set an element's size. For example, to achieve a one-quarter-wide sidebar, we would use one of the two variants found in the following HTML structure:

```html
<!-- Relative version -->
<div class="columns">
  <div class="column is-one-quarter">
    Sidebar
  </div>
  <div class="column is-9">
    Main content
  </div>
</div>

<!-- 12-column grid version -->
<div class="columns">
  <div class="column is-3">
    Sidebar
  </div>
  <div class="column">
    Main content
  </div>
</div>
```

Since Bulma offers us both, we may also mix and match. Bulma also offers ways to offset elements within the grid, so we can avoid adding extra empty elements. We use the same classes but add the `offset` word to them for that. So, if we want an element offset by one-third, we add the `is-offset-one-third` class.

But there's even more. The `is-narrow` class makes an element only take up as much space as necessary for its content. The `is-multiline` class on the column container element makes the grid break rows when there's not enough space for all elements. Finally, the `is-centered` and `is-vcentered` classes let us center elements horizontally and vertically within the grid.

By default, all grids have gaps. However, we can specify a gapless grid by adding the `is-gapless` modifying class on the column container. We may also specify different gap sizes by applying classes from `is-0` (gapless) to `is-8` (with default settings: `2rem`), with `is-3` being the default size.

Bulma allows us to have responsive grids with the following min-width breakpoints:

- `mobile`: Everything until `tablet`
- `tablet`: `769px`
- `desktop`: `960px + (2 * $gap)`
- `widescreen`: `1152px + (2 * $gap)`
- `fullhd`: `1334 + (2 * $gap)`
- `touch`: Until the end of `tablet`

(The default value of `$gap` is `32px`, which we can adjust with config.)

Bulma's columns are only activated from `tablet` onward, which means they stack on top of each other on smaller viewports. We can change this, however, by adding the `is-mobile` class to the column container.

Similarly, if we only want columns from `desktop` onward, we can apply the `is-desktop` class. Activating the grid only on larger viewports works the same way. We can see an example in the following code snippet:

```
<div class="columns is-desktop">
  <div class="column">...</div>
  <!-- ... -->
</div>
```

We add the breakpoint to the class to adjust column sizes for different viewports. For example, to have a three-quarter wide column on a desktop that is full-width on mobile and tablet, we add the `is-full is-three-quarters-desktop` class list to the column element. We can apply this technique to gap classes and the classes used to center elements.

Let's rebuild the holy-grail layout (header, sidebar, content, and footer) with Bulma:

```
<div class="columns is-desktop is-multiline">
  <header class="column is-full">
    Header
  </header>
  <aside class="column is-one-quarter">
    Sidebar
  </aside>
  <main class="column is-three-quarters">
    Content
  </main>
  <footer class="column is-full">
    Footer
  </footer>
</div>
```

We may also nest grids. Since the grid is based on a 12-column layout, nested grids keep visual consistency.

Compared to the Bootstrap approach with multiple row elements, the `is-multiline` class gives Bulma's grid system the flare of using CSS Grid. Moreover, since Bulma relies on spelled words for numbers and verbs, junior developers and people unfamiliar with the code base can read it and understand the layout from the HTML and its classes alone.

Unfortunately, the grid system does have some drawbacks compared to using CSS Grid. For example, we can't specify different values for vertical and horizontal gaps, use grid area, or use names to describe the position of elements.

In summary, Bulma, being an opinionated framework, allows for ease of development and, through its verbose class names, allows us to understand better the intent of a given HTML structure. Moreover, its grid system feels much like CSS Grid, without advanced features, such as grid areas.

Learning how UIkit implements grids

UIkit describes itself as a lightweight and modular CSS framework for developing fast and powerful web interfaces. UIkit is developed by the people at YOOtheme, a Hamburg-based company that specializes in developing themes for WordPress and Joomla. Since the initial release of UIkit 3 in January 2017, it has received regular updates and is currently on version 3.16, as of February 2023.

We can see the landing page of UIkit's website in the following screenshot:

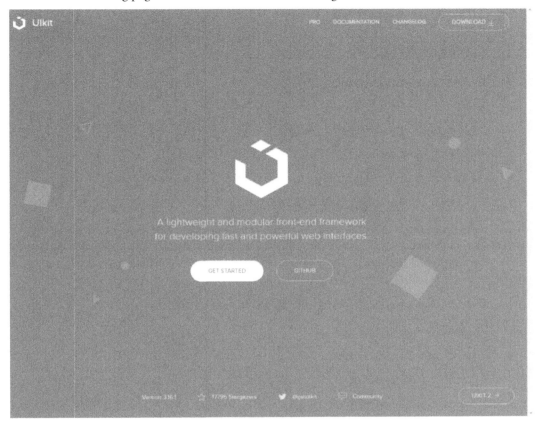

Figure 8.11 – UIkit's landing page

UIkit takes a drastically different approach to defining grids. Its usage of JS and attribute selectors allow us to build a grid with attributes defined on the container. To mark an element as a grid container, we apply the `uk-grid` attribute to the element:

```
<div uk-grid>
   <div>A</div>
   <div>B</div>
   <div>C</div>
   <div>D</div>
   <div>E</div>
</div>
```

The JS library we need to include transforms this attribute into a CSS class. All elements are equally sized by default but can be sized individually using classes from the `width` component of the framework.

The `width` component offers several possibilities to assign widths to either specific or all grid elements. We can use the following classes to set the widths of any grid cell:

- `uk-width-1-1` (full-width)
- `uk-width-1-2`
- `uk-width-1-3` and `uk-width-2-3`
- `uk-width-1-4` and `uk-width-3-4`
- `uk-width-1-5`, `uk-width-2-5`, `uk-width-3-5`, and `uk-width-4-5`
- `uk-width-1-6` and `uk-width-5-6`

We can use the same ratios to set the width for all elements. For example, the `uk-child-width-1-3` class sets the width of each grid element to one-third. Since the grid system is Flexbox-based, all elements overflowing a row break to the next. Other classes to set the width of elements are `uk-width-expand` and `uk-width-auto`; both are also available as the `uk-child-*` variants.

Unlike other CSS frameworks, UIkit also offers CSS classes for fixed-width cells:

- `uk-width-small`: 150px
- `uk-width-medium`: 300px
- `uk-width-large`: 450px
- `uk-width-xlarge`: 600px
- `uk-width-2xlarge`: 750px

It is worth noting that the `uk-child-*` variants are directly overwritten by classes set on the grid elements.

UIkit also offers five different breakpoints to create responsive grids:

- Using no breakpoint at all: Defaults to all viewport widths and those smaller than `s`
- `s`: Small, 640px and larger

- m: Medium, 960px and larger

- l: Large, 1200px and larger

- xl: Extra-large, 1600px and larger

We can steer widths in different breakpoints by applying the @breakpointName syntax to any width class. For example, uk-width-xlarge@m.

To set gaps on the grid, UIkit offers four different sizes by providing the uk-grid-small, uk-grid-medium, uk-grid-large, and uk-grid-collapse classes. We may also apply different gaps for rows and columns using the uk-grid-row-* and uk-grid-column-* classes with one of the four size keywords.

UIkit has some more tricks up its sleeve, however. Much like the uk-grid attribute that gets transformed into a CSS class, we can add the uk-height-match attribute with either a selector or the value row selector to the grid container to let UIkit's JS align the element heights for us. An example from the docs reads as follows:

```
<div uk-grid uk-height-match="target: > div > .uk-card">
  <div>
    <div class="uk-card uk-card-default"></div>
  </div>
  <div>
    <div class="uk-card uk-card-default"></div>
  </div>
</div>
```

The attribute's value tells us that all elements matching this selector have the same height.

But there's even more magic. The uk-grid attribute can take values as well. By specifying the attribute as uk-grid="masonry: true", we get behavior similar to CSS Grid's masonry layouts. The parallax: value, followed by a pixel value, such as 150, lets us move grid columns with a parallax effect, making them scroll differently from their neighboring columns.

UIkit is taking a new stance on grids and their **development experience**. The JS-enhanced features that come out of the box can benefit a UI and allow us to create more engaging and exciting layouts. On their website, they showcase different layouts. We can see such a layout in the following screenshot:

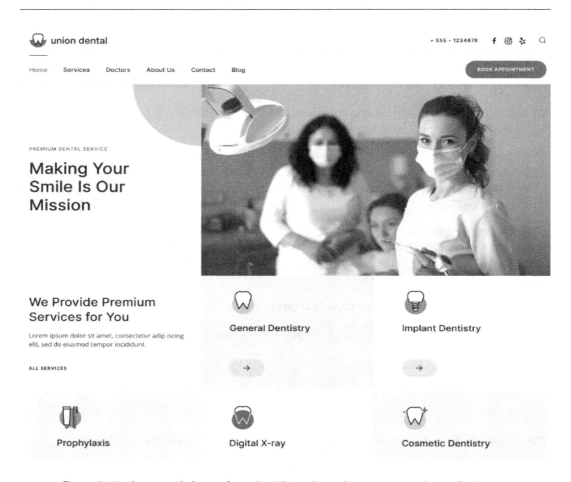

Figure 8.12 – An example layout from the UIkit website showcasing a website of a dentist

The close-to-full-width three-column layout gives the content a clear structure while still allowing the content to *breathe*. Although UIkit has been customized here, elements such as the navigation are still close to the unmodified UIkit.

We can find more such examples in their **Pro** gallery of ready-made designs.

Learning how Pure.css implements grids

Pure.css has been in development since 2013. It also describes itself as modular and tiny and claims to be usable in every web project. With 3.7 kb minified and gzipped (*gzip* being a compression algorithm used in HTTP compression to speed up the delivery of HTML, CSS, and JS files), it has a minimal bundle size while offering many features, such as form fields, buttons, tables, menus, and a grid. It is not as opinionated as other frameworks and aims to be a foundation to work with components from other frameworks, such as Bootstrap.

We can see the landing page of the Pure.css website in the following screenshot:

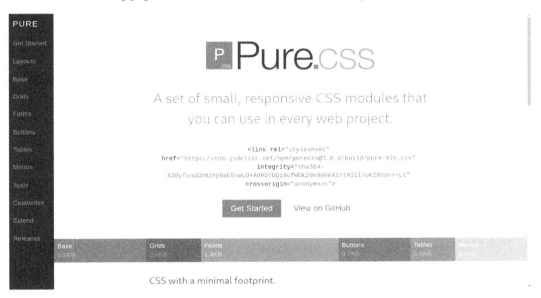

Figure 8.13 – Pure.css landing page

In Bootstrap, for example, modal windows are implemented with accessibility and maximum usability in mind – a feat that isn't simple to repeat. However, by introducing Pure.css as a basis and including the JS and styling necessary for modals from Bootstrap, we can use the advantage of Bootstrap's sophistication while keeping the simplicity of Pure.css.

The Pure.css grid is simple but powerful and comes in two forms: 5 columns and 25 columns. The Pure.css grid is also based on Flexbox. It knows two different concepts: grids and units. A unit is part of a grid. The CSS classes directly reflect this; pure-g is the class used to define an element as a grid container, while pure-u-* is used to style grid elements. The * character stands for one of the many possible sizes, all represented by fractions that are represented using a dash. For example, 1-5 would stand for one-fifth.

The available sizes are as follows:

- `1-5`
- `2-5`
- `3-5`
- `4-5`
- `1, 1-1, 5-5, and 24-24`
- `1-24`
- `1-12, 2-24`
- `3-24, 1-8`
- `4-24, 1-6`
- `5-24`
- `1-4, 6-24`
- `7-24`
- `1-3, 8-24`
- `3-8, 9-24`
- `5-12, 10-24`
- `11-24`
- `1-2, 12-24`
- `13-24`
- `7-12, 14-24`
- `5-8, 15-24`
- `2-3, 16-24`
- `17-24`
- `3-4, 18-24`
- `19-24`
- `5-6, 20-24`
- `7-8, 21-24`
- `11-12, 22-24`
- `23-24`

This list contains a total of 28 different sizes. Arguably, the amount of freedom is close to not needing to offer any sizes, but Pure.css currently does not offer any customized sizes without custom CSS.

A simple example of a grid using Pure.css can be found in the following code snippet:

```
<div class="pure-g">
  <div class="pure-u-1-3">
    Sidebar
  </div>
  <div class="pure-u-2-3">
    Sidebar
  </div>
</div>
```

Although the class names differ, the fraction syntax resembles Tailwind's width-related classes.

Pure.css also offers responsive grids with a total of seven viewports:

- sm: This is a screen size above 568px width

- md: Screen sizes above 768px width

- lg: Screen sizes above 1024px width

- xl: Screen sizes above 1280px width

- xxl: Screen sizes above 1920px width

- xxxl: Screen sizes above 2560px width

- x4k: Screen sizes above 3840px width

To apply different sizes for different breakpoints, we add the breakpoint to the size class name, for example, pure-u-md-4-5.

Pure.css, as a small, lightweight, unopinionated framework, delivers a minimal grid with maximum size choices and no extra gimmicks. Its simplicity reflects the name of the framework well.

Learning how Tachyons implements grids

Although Tachyons has not been actively maintained for a few years, it remains a popular framework that is loved by many. Its *functional* (as the developers used to call it) approach feels very much like a predecessor of Tailwind's core principle of utility-first.

We can see the landing page of the Tachyons website in the following screenshot:

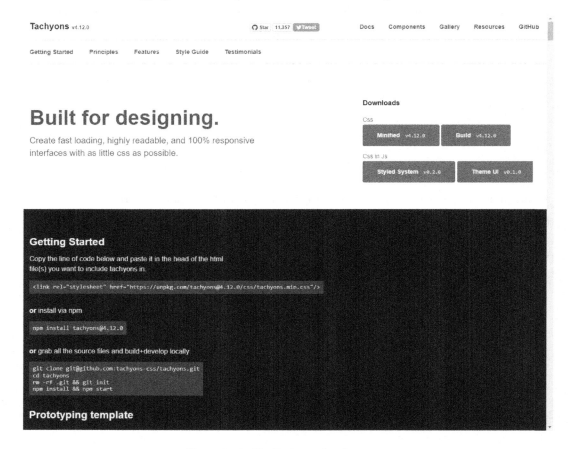

Figure 8.14 – The Tachyons landing page

A still-open pull request on GitHub from August 2022 implements support for CSS Grid but was never officially released. However, the latest stable version supports Flexbox, and the documentation offers examples of float-based grids built with utility classes.

Funnily enough, the Flexbox syntax is almost identical to that of Tailwind, and, according to the pull request, parts of the CSS Grid implementation would have followed suit.

Generally, Tachyons grids combine the `fl` class, which stands for `float: left;`, and a class that determines the width. Widths can be described as percentages of the full width, for example, `w-60` or `w-40`, or the `w-third` and `w-two-thirds` combinations.

Although outdated, the approach is minimal and elegant. Moreover, we can even build responsive float-based layouts since Tachyons offers support for breakpoints and responsive widths. Flexbox and CSS Grid, however, offer much more control and stability to the layout, as float-based layouts tend to behave differently based on their content.

Since Tachyons was discontinued, we may not hear much further from it, and it may well be a relic of the past.

Learning how Cutestrap implements grids

Cutestrap was developed roughly between 2016 and 2019. The original developer, Tyler Childs, stated that he primarily developed the framework for himself before making it open source. Somehow, it got traction on Hacker News, and people seemed to love it. With 2.7 kb minified and gzipped, it is smaller than Pure.css and offers even fewer features. However, it is one of the few frameworks to implement a grid system using CSS Grid.

We can see the landing page of the Cutestrap website in the following screenshot:

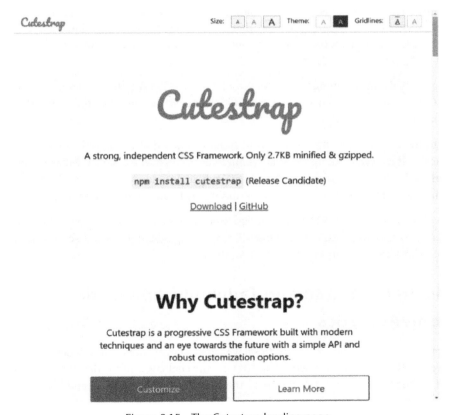

Figure 8.15 – The Cutestrap landing page

The grid system works with three CSS classes and a single custom property, which can be set with inline styles on the grid container. To define a grid, we use the `grid` class. It automatically applies `grid-template-columns: repeat(var(--columns), minmax(0, 1fr));`, the `--columns` custom property defaults to `auto-fit`, meaning that all elements are spaced out equally. The two `-medium` and `-large` classes only apply the grid once the viewport is larger than `45rem` or `80rem`. Setting `--columns` to any numerical value lets us steer the number of columns.

All in all, the grid system of Cutestrap is minimal. However, it offers a somewhat responsive approach and lets us arbitrarily choose the number of columns. Frankly, it saves us some keystrokes while writing, in any case.

Learning how other frameworks don't implement grids

With all the grid systems of various (but also often quite similar) syntax variations, there is also a diametrically opposed movement: not having grid systems at all.

For example, Spruce is a lesser-known CSS framework developed by Adam Laki and Szépe. It has 83 stars on GitHub but has been actively maintained since February 2022. Its philosophy is to be a modern Sass-based low-level framework that gives projects a solid foundation. More significant components use the BEM approach, and smaller components, such as buttons and form input fields, are styled with opinionated defaults.

According to the documentation, they think pre-implemented grid systems can be eliminated because of native CSS layout tools, such as CSS Grid and Flexbox. Therefore, they think that Bootstrap-like grids are not necessary anymore.

Tailwind technically doesn't offer a classic grid system, either. It offers sensible defaults for CSS Grid, but we may well overwrite them (or remove them entirely) and use CSS Grid as we see fit. Other frameworks left out a grid system, too: Bonsai.css only includes helpers for CSS Grid, Water.css only delivers the bare minimum without even mentioning grids, and so does sanitize.css.

Perhaps with the end of life of IE11 and fewer legacy devices over time, we may once think of Bootstrap's grid system as something of the past. After all, why reimplement grids and serve several kilobytes more when CSS Grid is the more convenient solution?

Practising Bootstrap and Tailwind frameworks with AwesomeAnalytics

Some board members of AwesomeAnalytics have taken a crash course on web development over the last few weeks. They thought they would understand the challenges of the development team better if they tried coding themselves. So they learned the basics of HTML and CSS and learned about some CSS frameworks, such as Bootstrap and Tailwind. And now they've called a meeting with the rest of the company.

A board member connects their laptop to the projector and shows what they've implemented over the last few weeks: a clone of AwesomeAnalytics. They used a CSS framework, but they can't recall which. However, they are sure that the code quality of what they've implemented is, as they say, *average at best* and that their development team would do a much better job. However, they snooped through the code base and noticed that we're not using a CSS framework at all!

Since they now know how to code themselves, they make the classic management mistake of telling people how to do their job: they want us to reimplement the dashboard with a CSS framework. Since they can't recall which one they've worked with, they let us decide which framework to use. Then, they tell us to start right away.

For simplicity reasons, we discuss Bootstrap and Tailwind in this section. However, nothing stops us from trying other frameworks, too.

Implementing Tailwind's grid

We can find a basic setup in the `chapter8/AwesomeAnalytics/TailwindBased/` folder.

Once we open a terminal, we must ensure we're using Node.js version 18 and install all dependencies by running `npm install`. Once all the dependencies are installed, we can run the `npm run build-tailwind` command, a wrapper for `npx tailwind` with default parameters, to create a usable Tailwind CSS file.

When we open the `assets/css/tailwind_output.css` file, we notice that it is empty, apart from some custom properties and reset code, because we did not yet use any Tailwind classes in our setup. Tailwind purges the built CSS file of unused utility classes, keeping the built file as small as possible.

In a second terminal, we run the `npm run serve` command to create a web server that serves AwesomeAnalytics. When we open the `index.html` file, we can see that the grid from *Chapter 2, Project Introduction: What We'll Work on and First Tasks*, is already in place. This is because we're using the same HTML structure for the dashboard as in that chapter.

As a first step, we remove the link to `assets/css/grid.css` and replace it with a link to `assets/css/tailwind_output.css`, as shown in the following code snippet:

```
<!DOCTYPE html>
<html>
<head>
  <title>AwesomeAnalytics - An example app for CSS
    Grid</title>

  <!-- More stylesheets -->

  <link rel="stylesheet" href=
    "assets/css/tailwind_output.css">
```

```
</head>
<!-- The rest of the HTML structure -->
```

This code now loads the built Tailwind file.

Next, we add the `grid` class to the body element, making it a CSS Grid container. We then apply the `grid-rows-[min-content_auto] grid-cols-[auto_1fr]` classes to the body element to replicate the grid behavior already in place in `assets/css/grid.css`. Our body tag should then look like the following:

```
<body class="body grid grid-rows-[min-content_auto]
  grid-cols-[auto_1fr]">
```

Next, we add the `col-span-2` class to the `header` element to make it span both columns (`auto` and `1fr`) we've defined on the body. Since the `header` element is already placed in the first row, its height is determined by the minimum height necessary for the content:

```
<header class="page-header col-span-2">
```

The sidebar element doesn't need any additional class since it's positioned in the first column of the second row already, putting it where it should be. The main element is another grid container. We add the `grid auto-rows-[400px] grid-cols-4 grid-flow-row-dense gap-[16px]` class list to define the grid for the chart boxes.

The `auto-rows-[400px]` class automatically creates rows using `grid-auto-rows` of `400px` of height each. The `grid-cols-4` class defines four columns, and the `grid-flow-row-dense` class defines `grid-flow` as row-dense. The `gap-[16px]` class sets the grid gaps to `16px` horizontally and vertically.

Finally, we can search and replace the `chart-box-wide` class with the `col-span-2` class and the `chart-box-tall` class with the `row-span-2` class. These classes ensure that the boxes are twice as wide or tall as the standard chart boxes.

The result can be seen in the following screenshot:

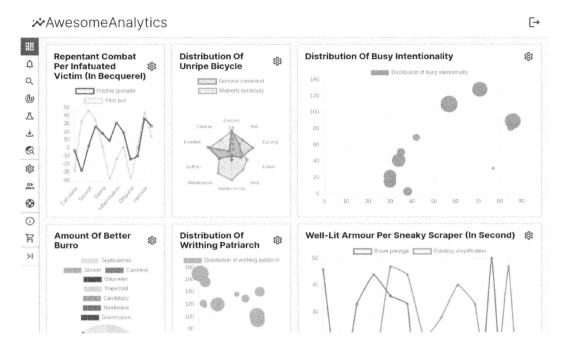

Figure 8.16 – The AwesomeAnalytics dashboard styled with the Tailwind grid utility classes

The grid behaves the same way as we saw in *Chapter 2, Project Introduction: What We'll Work on and First Tasks*. Tailwind's utility classes let us rebuild everything with little effort. The grid definition lives entirely in the DOM.

Implementing Bootstrap's grid

We can find a basic setup in the `chapter8/AwesomeAnalytics/BootstrapBased/` folder.

To get started, we open a terminal and navigate to the folder. Then, we run `npm install` to install all the dependencies. Bootstrap already comes with pre-built files we can use right away. The `npm run serve` command serves the website on `http://localhost:3000`.

In index.html, we replace the link to assets/css/grid.css with a link to node_modules/bootstrap/dist/css/bootstrap-grid.css. This link loads only the grid part of Bootstrap and allows us to use its classes:

```
<link rel="stylesheet" href="node_modules/bootstrap/dist/css/
bootstrap-grid.css">
```

We then add the container-fluid class to the body element. The standard container adds a maximum width and margin-left: auto; as well as margin-right: auto; to the container. However, we want the body to be full-width, which we achieve using the container-fluid class.

Next, we mark the header element as a row by adding the row class. This allows us to take advantage of the grid immediately by adding the col class to the logo and the col-auto class to the anchor tag containing the logout icon, and we can align these elements. The complete structure of the header can be found in the following code snippet:

```
<header class="page-header row">
  <h1 class="h1 page-title col">
    <span class="material-icons-outlined h1"
      aria-hidden="true">insights</span>
    AwesomeAnalytics
  </h1>

  <a href="/" class="col-auto">
    <span class="material-icons-outlined h1">logout</span>
  </a>
</header>
```

Next, we add a <div> element around the sidebar and main content. Since Bootstrap needs an element acting as a row, we'll give it the row class. We can then add the col-auto class to the sidebar element and the col class to the main element, resulting in the following HTML structure:

```
<div class="row">
  <!-- Side bar -->
  <aside class="sidebar collapsed col-md-auto">
    <!-- ... -->
  </aside>

  <!-- Main page content with charts -->
  <main class="main-page-content col">
    <!-- ... -->
  </main>
</div>
```

We now focus on the chart boxes. Since Bootstrap's grid is based on Flexbox, unfortunately, we can only implement multi-row or multi-column chart boxes. So, we implement multi-column chart boxes since it's closer to the implementation of Bootstrap's grid. Next, we attach the `container-fluid` class to the main element, making it a grid container.

Here, we're nesting Bootstrap grids, which wouldn't be necessary if we had multi-row and multi-column grids. We then add `div` elements around every chart box element to apply gutters later. To these container `div` tags, we add the `col-*` classes to the chart box elements, `col-3` for standard ones, and `col-6` for wide ones.

Once all chart boxes have column classes, we can add row elements around them. For that, we count the occupied columns and group chart boxes whose column width adds up to 12. So, for example, three chart boxes, two of them with the `col-3` class and one with the `col-6` class, become a single row because 3 + 3 + 6 = 12.

To add gutters, we use Bootstrap's spacing utilities. First, we apply the `g-4` class to each row, indicating that we want a grid gutter of size 4, which is `1.5rem`. We then add `p-3` (padding of size 3, which is `1rem`) to the columns.

Next, since the chart boxes are technically not sized by Flexbox anymore and don't stretch their available width, we need to add the `d-flex` and `align-items-stretch` classes from Bootstrap's Flexbox utilities to the containing `div` tags. Finally, by adding `flex-grow-1` to the chart box elements themselves, we tell them to fill all available widths and heights.

The resulting HTML structure is similar to the following code snippet:

```
<main class="main-page-content col container-fluid px-4">
  <div class="row g-4">
    <div class="col-3 p-3 d-flex align-items-stretch">
      <div class="chart-box flex-grow-1">
        <header>
          <h2 class="h3 bold">Title</h2>
          <a href=""><span class="material-icons-outlined"
            aria-hidden="true">settings</span></a>
        </header>
        <div class="chart-container">
          <canvas></canvas>
        </div>
      </div>
    </div>

    <div class="col-3 p-3 d-flex align-items-stretch">
      <div class="chart-box flex-grow-1">
        <header>
          <h2 class="h3 bold">Title</h2>
          <a href=""><span class="material-icons-outlined"
```

```
              aria-hidden="true">settings</span></a>
        </header>
        <div class="chart-container">
          <canvas></canvas>
        </div>
      </div>
    </div>

    <div class="col-6 p-3 d-flex align-items-stretch">
      <div class="chart-box flex-grow-1 chart-box
      flex-grow-1-wide">
        <header>
          <h2 class="h3 bold">Title</h2>
          <a href=""><span class="material-icons-outlined"
            aria-hidden="true">settings</span></a>
        </header>
        <div class="chart-container">
          <canvas></canvas>
        </div>
      </div>
    </div>
  </div>

  <div class="row gx-4">
    <div class="col-6 p-3 d-flex align-items-stretch">
      <div class="chart-box flex-grow-1 chart-box
      flex-grow-1-tall chart-box flex-grow-1-wide">
        <header>
          <h2 class="h3 bold">Title</h2>
          <a href=""><span class="material-icons-outlined"
            aria-hidden="true">settings</span></a>
        </header>
        <div class="chart-container">
          <canvas></canvas>
        </div>
      </div>
    </div>

    <div class="col-3 p-3 d-flex align-items-stretch">
      <div class="chart-box flex-grow-1">
        <header>
          <h2 class="h3 bold">Title</h2>
          <a href=""><span class="material-icons-outlined"
            aria-hidden="true">settings</span></a>
        </header>
        <div class="chart-container">
```

```
        <canvas></canvas>
      </div>
    </div>
  </div>

  <div class="col-3 p-3 d-flex align-items-stretch">
    <div class="chart-box flex-grow-1 chart-box
      flex-grow-1-tall">
      <header>
        <h2 class="h3 bold">Title</h2>
        <a href=""><span class="material-icons-outlined"
          aria-hidden="true">settings</span></a>
      </header>
      <div class="chart-container">
        <canvas></canvas>
      </div>
    </div>
  </div>
  </div>
  <!-- ... -->
</main>
```

We can see the result in the following screenshot:

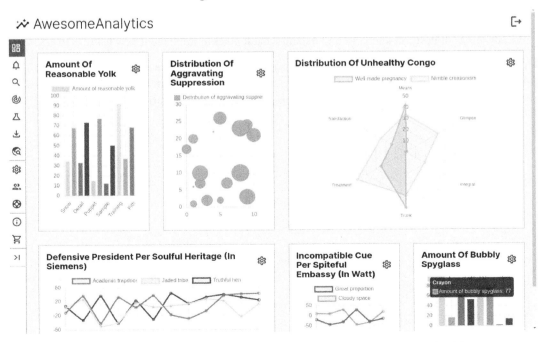

Figure 8.17 – The AwesomeAnalytics dashboard rebuilt with Bootstrap's grid

We can see the lack of multi-row chart boxes, but the rest works flawlessly. However, we may need to adjust the gutters or add custom gutter sizes to fit in with the rest of the design system.

Compared to Tailwind or even native CSS Grid implementations, this solution requires more HTML and CSS classes. In addition, it obfuscates the actual structure by having us add more div tags to steer Flexbox behavior we wouldn't need to steer if we had used CSS Grid.

The board of AwesomeAnalytics is finally happy! They encourage us to try more frameworks and continue learning about design and development trends, so the tool can always be considered *cutting edge*. They see that using a CSS framework has brought the layout forward, and they finally deem the product ready for launch.

Let's hope there is a market to which they can sell AwesomeAnalytics.

Summary

We've seen a few frameworks that use CSS Grid to implement grid systems, but most frameworks we discussed still use Flexbox. These grid systems offer structure and ease of development, but there is a trend to ditch them in favor of using the now widespread CSS Grid.

This chapter concludes our in-depth study of CSS Grid and its various use cases. We've discussed the basics, taking our first steps with the rather whacky example of AwesomeAnalytics, as well as design challenges, responsiveness, and several alternatives to grids.

We've discussed the pros and cons, how CSS Grid and Flexbox can work together, and how we can take advantage of PostCSS and JS to understand what it takes to implement new features in CSS Grid.

In the following chapter, we will have a brief overview of all topics once again and get a handy list of all features of CSS Grid, how to use it to achieve specific often-used patterns, understand the dos and don'ts of designing with grids, and receive a compact cheat sheet for various frameworks.

Part 4 –
A Quick Reference

After learning a lot about CSS Grid, its ecosystem, alternatives, design challenges, best practices, frameworks, and more, this chapter condenses this knowledge for you to look things up quickly. It will make this book a valuable companion in all your grid-based endeavors and help you absorb the ins and outs of CSS Grid.

This part has the following chapter:

- *Chapter 9, Quick Reference and Cheat Sheet*

9
Quick Reference and Cheat Sheet

A wise man once told me that *knowledge means knowing where it is written*. People say this sentence was a quote by famous scientist Albert Einstein, but as we all know, not everything written on the internet is necessarily true. Moreover, quotes attributed to Einstein are often not by Einstein at all.

Nevertheless, the quote holds. Nobody expects a developer to know every little detail of every tool they use by heart. There is way too much to know, and knowledge is generated through research and innovation daily. We see lists of the *100 best JavaScript frameworks of 2020* – nobody expects us to know them all by heart. Instead, we should know where to find information and knowledge if necessary.

This chapter aims to be a short, precise, and helpful collection of knowledge. Whenever we need to know something, we can quickly grab these pages and read up on them, aiming to make our lives easier. Ultimately, we will know where the knowledge is written down.

This quick reference contains the following categories:

- Important terms and their definitions
- CSS Grid – attributes, values, functions, and units
- CSS Grid recipes for everyday use cases
- Grid design best practices and do's and don'ts
- Framework cheat sheets for the Holy grail layout

Technical requirements

Since we won't be coding in this chapter and it serves primarily as a reference and cheat sheet, there are no technical requirements. The code snippets can be found at `https://github.com/PacktPublishing/Mastering-CSS-Grid/tree/main/chapter9`.

Important terms and their definitions

This section includes grid-related terms and definitions we regularly use when working with grids. These terms are common knowledge and will help us discuss grids and grid-related code with fellow developers.

The following figure gives us a condensed overview of all grid parts.

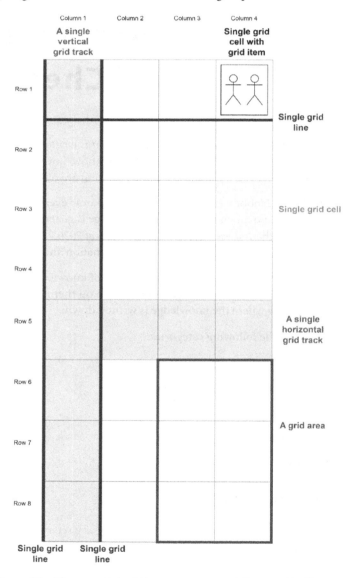

Figure 9.1 – The essential grid terms, as seen and discussed in Chapter 1

The grid parts are defined as follows:

- **Layout**: The visual arrangement of elements on a page. It can be, but doesn't have to be, a grid.

- **Grid**: The whole structure. This consists of all the arranged elements, layout, and attributes.

- **Grid cell**: A single cell of the grid, the smallest unit within a grid.

- **Grid lines**: Horizontal and vertical lines between grid cells.

- **Grid track**: An entire row or column of a grid.

- **Grid area**: A rectangle spanning one or more cells in both X and Y directions.

- **Grid item**: An item that is placed in grid cells. Depending on its row and column span, it can be placed in one or more grid cells.

- **Gutters or gaps**: The space between tracks. CSS Grid lets us control these with two different attributes individually.

- **Holy grail layout**: The heading, sidebar, content, and footer are arranged as shown in the following figure.

The following figure shows the structure of a Holy grail layout.

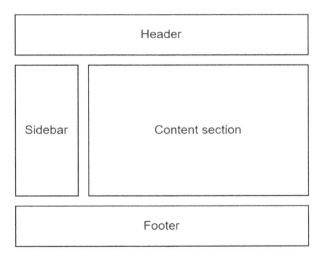

Figure 9.2 – A schematic of the Holy grail layout

The `header` spans the entire width, and the sidebar usually spans a small part of the width, whereas the content section fills the rest of the available width. The `footer` spans the entire width.

CSS Grid attributes, values, functions, and units

This section makes use of MDN Web Doc's value definition syntax. The entire definition of this syntax can be found here: `https://developer.mozilla.org/en-US/docs/Web/CSS/Value_definition_syntax`.

This section contains all grid attributes, their values, additional functions, and units.

Display property values

The following table contains all the values for `display` that we can use to introduce a grid to an element:

Attribute/expression	Description
`display: grid;`	This creates a block-level grid.
`display: inline-grid;`	This creates an inline grid.

Once we've defined an element to be a grid, we use grid templating to define the grid structure. The following section contains all tools we have to create grid templates.

Grid templating

Attribute/expression	Description
`grid-template-columns: <size>…;`	This defines grid columns by size, separated by spaces – for example, `grid-template-columns: 100px 150px 50% 1fr;`, with `<size>` being any valid sizing value. We can also name grid lines by adding one or more names in square brackets between sizes – for example, `grid-template-columns: [col-1-start] 100px [col-1-end col-2-start] 100px [col-2-end];`.
`grid-template-rows: <size>…;`	This defines grid rows by size, separated by spaces – for example, `grid-template-rows: 100px 150px 50% 1fr;`, with `<size>` being any valid sizing value. We can also name grid lines by adding one or more names in square brackets between sizes – for example, `grid-template-rows: [row-1-start] 100px [row-1-end row-2-start] 100px [row-2-end];`.

| `grid-template-areas = none \| <string>+` | This defines grid areas with rows surrounded by double quotes and columns inside rows separated by spaces – for example, `grid-template-areas: "header header" "sidebar content" "footer footer";`.

We can also add empty grid cells by replacing them with dots – for example, `grid-template-areas: "header header header" "sidebar . content";`.

We can assign elements to grid areas using `grid-area: <name>;`. |
|---|---|
| `grid-template = none \| [ <'grid-template-rows'> / <'grid-template-columns'> ] \| [ <line-names>? <string> <track-size>? <line-names>? ]+ [ / <explicit-track-list> ]?` | This is a combination of all `grid-template-rows`, `grid-template-columns`, and `grid-template-areas`. Consider the following `grid-template` definition:

```
grid-template:
  [header-row-start] "header header header"
100px [header-row-end]
  [content-row-start] "sidebar . content"
1fr [content-row-end]
  / 100px 100px 1fr;
```

It is equivalent to using this:

```
grid-template-columns: 100px 100px 1fr;
grid-template-rows: [header-row-start]
100px [header-row-end content-row-start]
1fr [content-row-end];
grid-template-areas: "header header header"
"sidebar . content";
``` |

Gaps

Value	Description
`column-gap: <size>;`	This defines a gap between all columns, with `<size>` being a valid sizing value.
`row-gap: <size>;`	This defines a gap between all rows, with `<size>` being a valid sizing value.
`gap: <row-gap> <column-size> | <size>;`	This serves as a shortcut for `row-gap` and `column-gap`. When a singular sizing value is used, it applies to rows and columns.

Aligning/justifying items

To further control the arrangement of an individual item or all items within a grid, we can align and justify them. To do that, we can use `align-items` and `justify-items`. The following two subsections cover all possible values for both.

Aligning items

Value	Description
start	 Aligns items at the start of their containing grid cells on the block/column axis.
end	 Aligns all items at the end of their containing grid cells on the block/column axis.
center	 Aligns all items at the center of their containing grid cells on the block/column axis.

Value	Description
stretch	Stretches all items to fill their containing grid cell on the block/column axis. This is the default behavior.

Justifying items

Value	Description
start	Aligns items at the start of their containing grid cells on the inline/row-axis, with respect to the direction.
end	Aligns all items at the end of their containing grid cells on the inline/row-axis, with respect to the direction.

Value	Description
center	Aligns all items at the center of their containing grid cells on the inline/row-axis.
stretch	Stretches all items to fill their containing grid cell on the inline/row axis. This is the default behavior.

Placing items

Value	Description
\<align-items\> \<justify-items\> | \<position\>	A shortcut to use align-items and justify-items. If a single value is used, it applies to align-items and justify-items – for example, place-items: center start; or place-items: stretch;.

Aligning/justifying content

Sometimes, we don't want a grid to fill its entire grid container – for example, imagine a 100vw wide container with a single column spanning 200px. The column does not fill the whole container for any screen wider than 200px. We use align-content and justify-content to arrange the entire grid content within the grid container.

Aligning content

Attribute/expression	Description
align-content: start;	Aligns the entire grid content to the start of the grid container on the block/column axis, with respect to the direction.

Attribute/expression	Description
`align-content: end;`	Aligns the entire grid content to the end of the grid container on the block/column axis, with respect to the direction.
`align-content: center;`	Aligns the entire grid content to the center of the grid container on the block/column axis.
`align-content: stretch;`	Stretches the grid content to fill the grid container on the block/column axis.
`align-content: space-around;`	Adds even spacing between rows, with half of that space at the start and the end of the grid container.
`align-content: space-between;`	Adds even spacing between rows, with no space at the start and the end of the grid container.
`align-content: space-evenly;`	Adds equal amounts of space between rows and at the start and the end of the grid container.

Justifying content

Value	Description
`justify-content: start;`	Aligns the entire grid content to the start of the grid container on the inline/row-axis, with respect to the direction.
`justify-content: end;`	Aligns the entire grid content to the end of the grid container on the inline/row-axis, with respect to the direction.
`justify-content: center;`	Aligns the entire grid content to the center of the grid container on the inline/row-axis.
`justify-content: stretch;`	Stretches the grid content to fill the grid container on the inline/row-axis.
`justify-content: space-around;`	Adds even spacing between columns, with half of that space at the start and the end of the grid container.
`justify-content: space-between;`	Adds even spacing between columns, with no space at the start and the end of the grid container.
`justify-content: space-evenly;`	Adds equal amounts of space between columns and at the start and the end of the grid container.

Placing content

Value	Description
`place-content: <align-content> <justify-content>` | `<position>`	A shortcut to use `align-content` and `justify-content`. If a single value is used, it applies to `align-content` and `justify-content`. For example: `place-content: center start;` or `place-content: space-around;`.

Automatic rows and columns

Automatic rows and columns are necessary for grids where we do not know the number of elements in advance. With `grid-auto-columns` and `grid-auto-rows`, we can control the sizes of additional columns and rows that may be added to a grid with extra elements. A potential use case is an image gallery with an infinite scroll.

Attribute/expression	Description
`grid-auto-columns:` `<size> …;`	For each element that would overflow a row, a column of width `<size>` is automatically added.
`grid-auto-rows:` `<size> …;`	For each element that would overflow a column, a row of height `<size>` is automatically added. This only works with `grid-auto-flow: columns;`.

Controlling the size of automatically added rows and columns gives us some control over how a grid behaves for an unknown number of elements. If these elements span multiple rows or columns, the automatic placement can cause empty cells in the grid. We can tell the grid in which order and how empty cells should be filled using `grid-auto-flow`.

Grid auto flow

Value	Description
`row`	Each element fills up the current row and adds new rows as necessary.
`column`	Each element fills up the current column and adds new columns as necessary.
`row dense`	Each element first tries to fill gaps in the already filled grid before placing it, according to `grid-auto-flow: row;`.
`column dense`	Each element first tries to fill gaps in the already filled grid before placing it, according to `grid-auto-flow: column;`.

Grid definition shortcut

CSS offers many shortcut definitions – for example, `flex:` for `flex-grow:`, `flex-shrink:`, and `flex-basis:`. Since CSS Grid is a rather complex tool and many aspects of a grid can be controlled, there is a shortcut for defining grids, called `grid:`

The `grid` property is a shortcut for `grid-template-columns`, `grid-template-rows`, `grid-auto-columns`, `grid-auto-rows`, and `grid-auto-flow`.

It may take one of the following values:

- A grid template as defined by `grid-template: ...;`

- A valid `grid-template-rows` value, followed by a slash, the `auto-flow` value, `dense` (this is optional; it indicates that `grid-auto-flow` is either `column` or `column dense`), and a valid `grid-auto-columns` value – for example, `grid: 150px 1fr / auto-flow dense 100px;`

- `auto-flow`, optionally followed by `dense` (indicating that `grid-auto-flow` is either `row` or `row dense`), a valid `grid-auto-rows` value, a slash, and a valid `grid-template-columns` value – for example, `grid: auto-flow dense 100px 100px / 150px 1fr;`

Individual grid item placement

CSS Grid allows us to place items within a grid precisely using the following properties:

Attribute/expression	Description
`grid-column-start: ...;`	This defines on which grid line an element starts on the X axis. It can either be the name or number of a grid line, `span <n>`, indicating that it should span n columns from its end, or `span <name>`, indicating that it should span columns from its end until it encounters the grid line named <name>.
`grid-column-end: ...;`	This defines on which grid line an element ends on the X axis. It can either be the name or number of a grid line, `span <n>`, indicating that it should span n columns from its start, or `span <name>`, indicating that it should span columns from its start until it encounters the grid line named <name>.
`grid-column: <grid-column-start> / <grid-column-end>;`	A shortcut to use both `grid-column-start` and `grid-column-end`. Using the `span` keyword twice has no effect here.
`grid-row-start: ...;`	This defines on which grid line an element starts on the Y axis. It can either be the name or number of a grid line, `span <n>`, indicating that it should span n rows from its end, or `span <name>`, indicating that it should span columns from its end until it encounters the grid line named <name>.
`grid-row-end: ...;`	This defines on which grid line an element ends on the Y axis. It can either be the name or number of a grid line, `span <n>`, indicating that it should span n rows from its start, or `span <name>`, indicating that it should span columns from its start until it encounters the grid line named <name>.

Attribute/expression	Description
`grid-row: ...;`	A shortcut to use both `grid-row-start` and `grid-row-end`.
`grid-area: ...;`	This defines in which grid area an element is placed. Grid areas can be defined using `grid-template-areas`.
`align-self: start;`	This behaves like `align-items: start;` but for a single grid item only.
`align-self: end;`	This behaves like `align-items: end;` but for a single grid item only.
`align-self: center;`	This behaves like `align-items: center;` but for a single grid item only.
`align-self: stretch;`	This behaves like `align-items: stretch;` but for a single grid item only.
`justify-self: start`	This behaves like `justify-items: start;` but for a single grid item only.
`justify-self: end`	This behaves like `justify-items: end;` but for a single grid item only.
`justify-self: center;`	This behaves like `justify-items: center;` but for a single grid item only.
`justify-self: stretch;`	This behaves like `justify-items: stretch;` but for a single grid item only.
`place-self: <justify-self> <align-self>	<position>;`	This behaves like `place-items: ...;` but for a single grid item only.

Sizing units, values, and functions

In many circumstances, we want CSS Grid to calculate the sizes of rows and columns for us. The list contains the following:

Attribute/expression	Description
`1fr`	This is one fraction (hence, FRaction) of free space – for example, a grid column definition of `1fr 2fr` would create two columns, the first taking up one-third of the free space and the second two-thirds. How much free space each unit gets depends on the number of free space units used.
`auto`	Behaves like the `1fr` unit when used exclusively but shrinks to `min-content` when used together with `fr`.

`min-content`	A valid value for any `<size>` value used in a grid. Defines the minimum content size, usually a single line or the widest character of a text.
`max-content`	A valid value for any `<size>` value used in a grid. Defines the maximum size of the content, usually when a text only has the minimum number of line breaks to fit the container's maximum width.
`fit-content(<size>)`	Calculates the size according to the `min(max-content, max(min-size, <size>)` formula.
`minmax(<min>, <max>)`	Defines a range of sizes between `<min>` and `<max>`, with `<min>` and `<max>` being either lengths, percentages, an `fr` unit, the `min-content` and `max-content` keywords, or `auto`.
`repeat(<n>, <size>)`	A valid `<size>` value, which repeats the `<size>` definition `<n>` times. It cannot be nested but can take multiple size values, which are repeated – for example, `repeat(2, 100px 200px)` results in `100px 200px 100px 200px`.
`repeat(auto-fit, <size>)`	A valid `<size>` value, which repeats the `<size>` definition as often as there are grid items. Any empty grid cells on the track are collapsed.
`repeat(auto-fill, <size>)`	A valid `<size>` value, which repeats the `<size>` definition as often as possible without the grid overflowing. Empty grid cells are left in place.

This past section represents (almost) everything there is to know about CSS Grid in 2023. We intentionally left out subgrid and masonry, as their final implementations are not yet supported in every major browser.

The following section provides code snippets for everyday use cases, which we can copy and adapt to our needs when creating grids.

CSS Grid recipes for everyday use cases

Sometimes, creating the same thing over and over can be tedious. This section contains some code snippets for everyday use cases of CSS Grid. They're meant as boilerplate code for further development and can ease the process of getting started.

Holy grail layouts

We can use the HTML structure in the following code snippet to create the layout:

```
<div class="layout">
  <header>
    Header
  </header>
  <aside>
    Sidebar
  </aside>
  <main>
    Content
  </main>
  <footer>
    Footer
  </footer>
</div>
```

We've added a single CSS class called `layout` to the `div` container. To apply the layout, we can use the following CSS:

```
:root {
  --sidebar-width: 1fr;
  --content-width: 3fr;
  --header-height: auto;
  --footer-height: auto;
  --gap-size: 16px;
}

.layout {
  display: grid;
  grid-template-columns: var(--sidebar-width)
    var(--content-width);
  grid-template-rows: var(--header-height) 1fr
    var(--footer-height);
  gap: var(--gap-size);
}

.layout header, .layout footer {
  grid-column: span 2;
}
```

Using CSS custom properties allows us to control the grid proportions in a central place. We can also use the values directly without CSS custom properties, as shown in the following code snippet:

```css
.layout {
  display: grid;
  grid-template-columns: 1fr 3fr;
  grid-template-rows: auto 1fr auto;
  gap: 16px;
}

.layout header, .layout footer {
  grid-column: span 2;
}
```

Responsive Holy grail layouts using grid areas

An alternative to using `grid-template-columns` and `grid-template-rows` is to use `grid-template` instead – for example, a possible way to implement the Holy grail layout responsively can be found in the following code snippet:

```css
:root {
  --sidebar-width: 1fr;
  --sidebar-height-mobile: auto;
  --content-width: 3fr;
  --header-height: auto;
  --footer-height: auto;
  --gap-size: 16px;
}

.layout {
  display: grid;
  gap: var(--gap-size);
  grid-template:
    "header" var(--header-height)
    "sidebar" var(--sidebar-height-mobile)
    "content" 1fr
    "footer" var(--footer-height)
    / 1fr
  ;
}

@media screen and (min-width: 1024px) {
  .layout {
    grid-template:
      "header header" var(--header-height)
```

```
      "sidebar content" 1fr
      "footer footer" var(--footer-height)
      / var(--sidebar-width) var(--content-width);
  }
}

.layout header {
  grid-area: header;
}
.layout aside {
  grid-area: sidebar;
}
.layout main {
  grid-area: content;
}
.layout footer {
  grid-area: footer;
}
```

This approach, too, uses CSS custom attributes to centralize the grid details. By adjusting the grid template with a media query, smaller screens receive a one-column layout, whereas screens with a width above 1,024 pixels receive a classic Holy grail layout.

Dashboard box arrangement

Another use case we saw when working with Awesome Analytics is boxes arranged in a grid. Usually, we use these on dashboards or to display news articles or images. We can see an example of such a layout from the second chapter in the following figure.

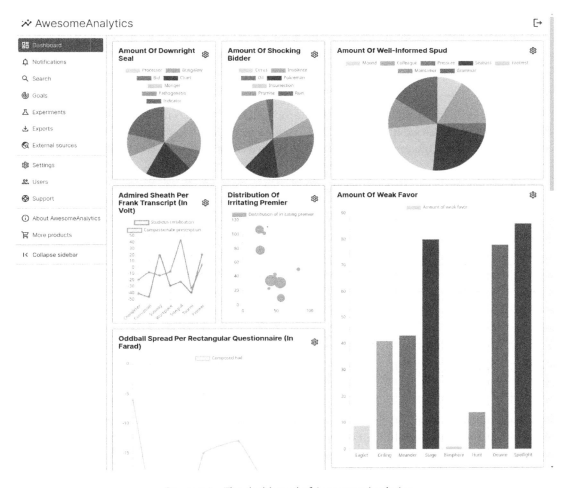

Figure 9.3 – The dashboard of Awesome Analytics

We see several boxes in the main content section, some larger than others. We can use the following CSS code to create the tools necessary for us to build such a layout:

```
.dashboard-grid {
  display: grid;
  grid-template-columns: 1fr 1fr 1fr 1fr;
  grid-auto-rows: 300px;
  grid-auto-flow: row dense;
}

.dashboard-grid .tall {
  grid-row: span 2;
```

```
}

.dashboard-grid .wide {
  grid-column: span 2;
}
```

This code creates a four-column layout with `300px-tall` rows. We may need to adjust these numbers for small devices. When we apply the `tall` class, an element spans two rows. The `wide` class tells the element to span two columns. A combination of the two creates a two-by-two large element.

We can add classes, such as `extra-wide` or `extra-tall`, to span more columns and rows. In the following code snippet, we can see how we would use these tools:

```
<div class="dashboard-grid">
  <div><!-- Standard-sized box --></div>
  <div class="wide"><!-- Wide box --></div>
  <div class="tall"><!-- Tall box --></div>
  <div class="wide tall"><!-- Two-by-two box --></div>
  <!-- More elements -->
</div>
```

The application of `grid-auto-flow` ensures that the grid has the fewest empty grid cells.

A fluid image gallery with a fixed aspect ratio and minimum element width

An image gallery is an alternative to the dashboard layout discussed in the previous section. Since images usually need to retain their aspect ratio (or at least not be skewed), fixed-height columns are rarely a good idea. Instead, we can use `aspect-ratio` and `auto-fit` in combination with `object-fit` to achieve a fully fluid image gallery layout.

We can see a possible HTML structure in the following code snippet:

```
<div class="gallery">
  <div>
    <img src="https://via.placeholder.com/300x120" alt=
      "...">
  </div>
  <div>
    <img src="https://via.placeholder.com/300x120" alt=
      "...">
  </div>
  <div>
    <img src="https://via.placeholder.com/300x120" alt=
      "...">
  </div>
```

```
  <div>
    <img src="https://via.placeholder.com/300x120" alt=
      „...">
  </div>
  <!-- More images -->
</div>
```

Note that we've used landscape images that are relatively wide in relation to their height. The following CSS code produces a fully fluid image gallery layout, with images of a minimum size of 150px by 150px:

```
.gallery {
  display: grid;
  grid-template-columns: repeat(auto-fit, minmax
    (150px, 1fr));
  gap: 16px;
}

.gallery > div {
  aspect-ratio: 1 / 1;
}

.gallery > div > img {
  width: 100%;
  height: 100%;
  object-fit: cover;
}
```

The use of minmax enlarges columns to fit the full width if the total width is not a multiple of 150px plus gaps.

Media objects

We discussed media objects in *Chapter 5, Implementing Layouts with Flexbox and CSS Grid*. To summarize, a media object is a media element (primarily an image) with some content next to it that doesn't flow around it – for example, we can see a standard media object in the following figure.

Figure 9.4 – A media object

To build the preceding media object, we use the following HTML structure:

```html
<article class="media-object">
  <img
    src="https://via.placeholder.com/240x180"
    alt="Placeholder"
  >

  <div>
    <h2>
      Awesome content
    </h2>
    <p>
      Click here for awesome content that will likely interest you.
    </p>
    <button type="button">
      Go to awesome content
    </button>
  </div>
</article>
```

To apply the overall layout, we can use the following CSS code:

```css
.media-object {
  display: grid;
  grid-template-columns: auto 1fr;
  align-items: center;
  border: 1px solid lightgray;
  border-radius: 4px;
  gap: 8px;
}
```

The `auto`-sized column ensures that the image does not take up more space than necessary.

Full-height pages with a sticky header

Many modern websites contain a sticky header. Also, we often have to create layouts for pages whose content does not fill an entire page, such as an error or login page, but needs to fill the entire viewport height. To create a `minimum-full-page` layout with a sticky header, we can use the following HTML structure:

```html
<div class="layout">
  <header>
    Header
  </header>
  <main>
```

```
    Content
  </main>
</div>
```

We also use the following CSS:

```css
.layout {
  display: grid;
  grid-template-rows: auto 1fr;
}
.layout > header {
  position: sticky;
  top: 0;
}
```

Even though the header is arranged in the grid, `position: sticky;` ensures the header always stays at the top of the viewport. Since the second row takes up all the free space, we don't need to give the layout a minimum height explicitly.

Screen-filling sections for landing pages

Landing pages often use sections the size of the entire viewport to manage and guide a user's attention – for example, full-page sections can showcase products, show many images at once, or convey critical messages.

To create such a layout, we use the following HTML structure:

```html
<div class="layout">
  <section>Section A</section>
  <section>Section B</section>
  <section>Section C</section>
  <!-- More sections -->
</div>
```

To arrange the sections, we use the following CSS code:

```css
.layout {
  display: grid;
  grid-auto-rows: 100vh;
}
```

Using `grid-auto-rows` ensures that there are only as many rows as necessary. By applying `100vh` as the row size, each row is as tall as the viewport.

Gantt charts

Gantt charts are a useful tool to show the phases of projects. Horizontal bars in different rows show when phases start and when they end. The following figure shows an example of a basic Gantt chart.

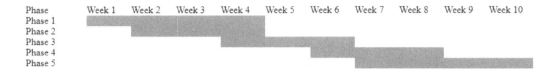

Figure 9.5 – A basic Gantt chart

To create this chart, we can use the following HTML structure:

```
<div class="gantt-chart">
  <div>Phase</div>
  <div>Week 1</div>
  <div>Week 2</div>
  <div>Week 3</div>
  <div>Week 4</div>
  <div>Week 5</div>
  <div>Week 6</div>
  <div>Week 7</div>
  <div>Week 8</div>
  <div>Week 9</div>
  <div>Week 10</div>

  <div class="phase-title">Phase 1</div>
  <div class="phase" style="grid-row: 2; grid-column: 2 /
    span 4;">
    From week 1 to week 4
  </div>

  <div class="phase-title">Phase 2</div>
  <div class="phase" style="grid-row: 3; grid-column: 3 /
    span 3">
    From week 2 to week 4
  </div>

  <div class="phase-title">Phase 3</div>
  <div class="phase" style="grid-row: 4; grid-column: 5 /
    span 3;">
    From week 4 to week 6
  </div>
```

```
<!--More phases... -->
</div>
```

To apply the layout and overall styling, we use the following CSS code:

```
.gantt-chart {
  display: grid;
  grid-template-columns: 100px repeat(10, 1fr);
}
.gantt-chart .phase-title {
  grid-column: 1;
}
.gantt-chart .phase {
  background-color: #aaf;
}
```

By applying inline styles, we keep the information in the DOM. Adding text to the bars allows screen readers to transport visual information. Since people with visual impairments often don't benefit from visual layouts, we also need to have a structure that is simple to understand and interpret. Adding labels and not solely relying on visual information improves accessibility.

Grid design best practices and do's and don'ts

When we design grids, it is essential to know the following things:

- **Do's**:

  - **Design with the target group in mind**: Is it a website to solve problems or to sell something? Should the site seem busy, or should it feel relaxed?

  - **Keep the content in mind**: What content should be placed on the site and in which form? What message should the content convey?

  - **Keep the stakeholders in mind**: What problems do they want to be solved? How can they influence the design?

  - Follow the design principles of **contrast**, **balance**, **repetition**, **rhythm**, **hierarchy**, and **proximity**.

- **Don'ts**:

  - Do not design for the best case only. Instead, work with edge-case content, such as extended text passages and less-than-ideal images.

  - Do not cramp things together too tightly. Leave some white space for elements to breathe and for the user not to lose focus.

- Do not design for a single screen. If possible, create a design that's fluid and responsive.

- Do not create adaptive designs only. They are much harder to implement.

- Do not work with grids because they're used on most websites. Instead, be creative and try to break out of the grid, or abandon it entirely for other geometric shapes.

The following section covers some popular frameworks. When working on large projects, we often use frameworks to ease development, offer better browser compatibility, and create a better developer and user experience. The code snippets in the following section help us get started on new projects.

A framework cheat sheet for the Holy grail layout

The Holy grail layout consists of a header, a sidebar, a content section, and a footer. We discussed this layout approach in the *Important terms and their definitions* section.

The general layout can be achieved with any framework that offers a grid system. However, the layout size, the overall width, the ratio of sidebar width to content width, the header height, and the footer height differ from website to website.

This section provides code snippets with sensible defaults for all the frameworks discussed in *Chapter 8, Grids in the Wild – How Frameworks Implement Grids*. We use the `<header>` tag to denote the header, the `<aside>` tag to denote the sidebar, the `<main>` tag to denote the content section, and the `<footer>` tag to denote the footer.

Tailwind

We can achieve the Holy grail layout with this HTML structure and the following CSS classes:

```
<div class="grid grid-cols-3">
  <header class="col-span-3 bg-slate-500 p-2 text-white">
    Header
  </header>

  <aside class="bg-slate-300 p-2">
    Aside
  </aside>

  <main class="col-span-2 bg-slate-200 p-2">
    Main
  </main>

  <footer class="col-span-3 bg-slate-400 p-2">
    Footer
  </footer>
</div>
```

Note that no arbitrary-value classes are necessary to achieve a basic Holy grail layout. Also, the layout is full-width, meaning it spans the entire page. Finally, the ratio of the sidebar to content is 1:2.

Bootstrap

One option to create a Holy grail layout is to wrap the entire layout in a container and use rows, in which the header and footer span the entire width. Such an example can be seen in the following code snippet:

```
<div class="container">
  <div class="row">
    <header class="col">
      Header
    </header>
  </div>
  <div class="row">
    <aside class="col-3">
      Sidebar
    </aside>
    <main class="col-9">
      Content
    </main>
  </div>
  <div class="row">
    <footer class="col">
      Footer
    </footer>
  </div>
</div>
```

The ratio of the sidebar to the <main> content element is 1:3.

Foundation (XY Grid only)

Foundation's XY Grid lets us mix grid-x and grid-y to achieve a Holy grail layout. We use grid-y to arrange header and footer in a column and grid-x to break up the center cell into a sidebar and content section:

```
<div class="grid-frame">
  <div class="grid-y">
    <header class="cell small-2">
      Header
    </header>
    <div class="grid-x">
      <aside class="cell medium-3">
```

```
      Aside
     </aside>
     <main class="cell medium-9">
       Main
     </main>
    </div>
    <footer class="cell small-2">
      Footer
    </footer>
   </div>
 </div>
```

Note that this allows us to size header and footer explicitly. If this isn't necessary, we can use grid-x only and keep header and footer as separate DOM elements. The ratio of the sidebar to the <main> content element is 1:3.

Bulma.io

Bulma.io's is-multiline modifier is the key to keeping the DOM minimal when implementing the Holy grail layout. We can use full-width columns for the header, footer, sidebar, and content sections individually. We can see an example in the following code snippet:

```
<div class="columns is-desktop is-multiline">
  <header class="column is-full">
    Header
  </header>
  <aside class="column is-one-quarter">
    Sidebar
  </aside>
  <main class="column is-three-quarters">
    Content
  </main>
  <footer class="column is-full">
    Footer
  </footer>
</div>
```

We must remember that the number of columns should always add up to either 12 (when using explicit 12-column-based units) or 1 (when using ratios, such as one-quarter). Otherwise, the content section breaks into separate lines. The ratio of the sidebar to the <main> content element is 1:3.

UIKit

UIKit's attribute-driven grid implementation allows us to reduce the necessary DOM to a minimum, using a single container for the sidebar and content section. We can see an example in the following code snippet:

```
<header>
  Header
</header>
<div uk-grid class="uk-grid-match">
  <aside class="uk-width-1-4">
    Sidebar
  </aside>
  <main class="uk-width-3-4">
    Content
  </main>
</div>
<footer>
  Footer
</footer>
```

Note that we added the `uk-grid-match` class to match the sidebar height and footer. The ratio of the sidebar to the `<main>` content element is 1:3.

Pure.css

Pure.css has an approach similar to that of Bulma.io, which means we can use the same DOM structure. The CSS classes differ but also allow us to define ratios for the sidebar and content:

```
<div class="pure-g">
  <header class="pure-u-1">
    Header
  </header>
  <aside class="pure-u-1-4">
    Sidebar
  </aside>
  <main class="pure-u-3-4">
    Content
  </main>
  <footer class="pure-u-1">
    Footer
  </footer>
</div>
```

Since Pure.css's grid is multiline by default, we can specify the header and footer elements' widths as 100% or 1. The ratio of the sidebar to the <main> content element is 1:3.

Tachyons

Tachyons uses a float-based grid, meaning we don't need extra container classes. However, we need to ensure not to add any other DOM elements to the container, as they might rip the layout apart and cause unexpected float behavior. We can see an example in the following code snippet:

```
<div>
  <header class="fl w-100">
    Header
  </header>
  <aside class="fl w-25">
    Sidebar
  </aside>
  <main class="fl w-75">
    Content
  </main>
  <footer class="fl w-100">
    Footer
  </footer>
</div>
```

Note that we use the fl class to specify float: left; on every element and use the w-100, w-25, and w-75 classes to specify the widths. The ratio of the sidebar to the <main> content element is 1:3.

Cutestrap

Cutestrap's minimalistic implementation of grids automatically generates grid columns of equal width, with no built-in way to specify the width of individual columns. Therefore, we must add CSS on top or use inline styles with some vanilla CSS Grid to mitigate this.

Since Cutestrap suggests using inline styles to specify the number of columns, using inline styles can be considered a convention. An example can be found in the following code snippet:

```
<header>
  Header
</header>
<div class="grid" style="--columns: 4;">
  <aside>
    Sidebar
  </aside>
  <main style="grid-column: span 3;">
    Content
  </main>
</div>
<footer>
  Footer
</footer>
```

Note that we cannot specify full-width elements with built-in classes, so we excluded the `header` and `footer` elements from the grid to minimize the use of inline styles. The ratio of the sidebar to the `<main>` content element is 1:3.

Summary

We've now revisited all the basics and advanced features of CSS Grid and some related topics, such as frameworks and design best practices. This chapter concludes our journey through the depths of CSS Grid. Thank you, dear reader, for taking the time to learn all the details about this fantastic tool that the development community has waited for for so long.

I hope this book has helped you to become a better developer, and I ask you to share your knowledge further. If you want to continue learning, Packt offers over 100 books related to CSS and dozens of books related to CSS Grid.

Index

www.packtpub.com

Subscribe to our online digital library for full access to over 7,000 books and videos, as well as industry leading tools to help you plan your personal development and advance your career. For more information, please visit our website.

Why subscribe?

- Spend less time learning and more time coding with practical eBooks and Videos from over 4,000 industry professionals

- Improve your learning with Skill Plans built especially for you

- Get a free eBook or video every month

- Fully searchable for easy access to vital information

- Copy and paste, print, and bookmark content

Did you know that Packt offers eBook versions of every book published, with PDF and ePub files available? You can upgrade to the eBook version at www.packtpub.com and as a print book customer, you are entitled to a discount on the eBook copy. Get in touch with us at customercare@ packtpub.com for more details.

At www.packtpub.com, you can also read a collection of free technical articles, sign up for a range of free newsletters, and receive exclusive discounts and offers on Packt books and eBooks.

Other Books You May Enjoy

If you enjoyed this book, you may be interested in these other books by Packt:

Responsive Web Design with HTML5 and CSS

Benjamin Frain

ISBN: 9781803242712

- Use media queries, including detection for touch/mouse and color preference.
- Learn HTML semantics and author accessible markup.
- Facilitate different images depending on screen size or resolution.
- Write the latest color functions, mix colors, and choose the most accessible ones.
- Use SVGs in designs to provide resolution-independent images.
- Add validation and interface elements to HTML forms.

The HTML and CSS Workshop

Lewis Coulson | Brett Jephson | Rob Larsen | Marian Zburlea | Matt Park

ISBN: 9781838824532

- Understand how websites are built, structured, and styled.

- Master the syntax and structure of HTML and CSS.

- Know how to build websites from scratch using HTML5 and CSS3.

- Create intuitive forms that allow users to input data.

- Style your website by integrating videos, animations, and themes.

- Design robust websites that work on all modern devices seamlessly.

Packt is searching for authors like you

If you're interested in becoming an author for Packt, please visit `authors.packtpub.com` and apply today. We have worked with thousands of developers and tech professionals, just like you, to help them share their insight with the global tech community. You can make a general application, apply for a specific hot topic that we are recruiting an author for, or submit your own idea.

Share your thoughts

Now you've finished *Mastering CSS Grid*, we'd love to hear your thoughts! Scan the QR code below to go straight to the Amazon review page for this book and share your feedback or leave a review on the site that you purchased it from.

https://www.amazon.in/review/create-review/error?asin=180461484X

Your review is important to us and the tech community and will help us make sure we're delivering excellent quality content.

Download a free PDF copy of this book

Thanks for purchasing this book!

Do you like to read on the go but are unable to carry your print books everywhere?

Is your eBook purchase not compatible with the device of your choice?

Don't worry, now with every Packt book you get a DRM-free PDF version of that book at no cost.

Read anywhere, any place, on any device. Search, copy, and paste code from your favorite technical books directly into your application.

The perks don't stop there, you can get exclusive access to discounts, newsletters, and great free content in your inbox daily

Follow these simple steps to get the benefits:

1. Scan the QR code or visit the link below

https://packt.link/free-ebook/9781804614846

2. Submit your proof of purchase
3. That's it! We'll send your free PDF and other benefits to your email directly

Made in the USA
Monee, IL
03 June 2024

59361910R00181